The Lost-Found Nation of Islam in America

Clifton E. Marsh

The Scarecrow Press, Inc.
Lanham, Maryland, and London
2000

SCARECROW PRESS, INC.

Published in the United States of America
by Scarecrow Press, Inc.
4720 Boston Way, Lanham, Maryland 20706
http://www.scarecrowpress.com

4 Pleydell Gardens, Folkestone
Kent CT20 2DN, England

This book was previously published as *From Black Muslims to Muslims: The Resurrection, Transformation, and Change of the Lost-Found Nation of Islam in America, 1930–1995, Second Edition.* Copyright © 1996 by Clifton E. Marsh. Reprint 2000.

Excerpts in Chapter V from *The Autobiography of Malcolm X*, by Malcolm X with the assistance of Alex Haley (New York: Grove Press, Ballantine Books, 1973, 1977) are printed by permission of Random House, Inc.

The interview with Imam Wallace D. Muhammed on July 25, 1979, is printed with his permission.

The interview with Dr. Abdul Alim Muhammed on September 9, 1994, is printed with his permission.

British Library Cataloguing in Publication Information Available

Library of Congress Cataloging-in-Publication Data

Marsh, Clifton E., 1946–
   The lost-found Nation of Islam in America / Clifton E. Marsh.
      p. cm.
   Includes bibliographical references and index.
   ISBN 1-57886-008-3 (alk. paper)
      1. Black Muslims—History. 2. Nation of Islam (Chicago, Ill.) I. Title: Previously published under title: From Black Muslims to Muslims. II. Title.

BP221 .M373 2000
297.8'09—dc21

                                                                                    00-021823

⊖™ The paper used in this publication meets the minimum requirements of American National Standard for Information Sciences—Permanence of Paper for Printed Library Materials, ANSI/NISO Z39.48–1992. Manufactured in the United States of America.

This book is dedicated to my three queens
Johnnie, Mecca, and Cynthia
thank you for allowing me to share your throne

and to my brother, Tuck Jesse Hanna,
and all the homeboys on the street corners of America
who had their dreams die too young

and to my father,
Clifton Hugo Marsh

Contents

Tables

Preface

I would like to thank Scarecrow Press for the opportunity to revisit the "Nation" and produce a second edition of the original work published in 1984. This work has become a great scholarly adventure. Observation of the Nation of Islam during the crucial years of transition has been the ultimate living picture show.

The quest to document the changes in the Nation of Islam has become a magnificent obsession. This study has enabled me to live and interact with history and touch the pulse of the organization. It has enabled me to smell the aroma of the Nation and lay prone on mother earth with my ear to the ground and listen for its giant footsteps. As a scholar and student, I care very little what people think about Minister Farrakhan and the Nation of Islam. This research has given me the privilege of documenting and studying the oldest, most powerful, and most significant black nationalist organization in the country.

The second edition is much improved and expanded. It includes four new chapters. Chapter 7 is an analysis of the continuing legacy of African nationalist social thought from 1815 to 1994. This chapter places Minister Farrakhan in a historical context and examines his addition to the African nationalist legacy of founding fathers like Cuffee, Delaney, Garvey, Wilmont Blyden, and Dr. W. E. B. DuBois.

Chapter 8 is a historical and philosophical analysis of the ideological dispute between Imam W. D. Muhammad and Minister Louis Farrakhan. This chapter details the ideological split between the two leaders during the period of 1974 to 1980.

Chapter 9 is concerned with growth, development, and change of the American Muslim Mission (AMM) and the Nation of Islam from 1980 to 1990. During this period, I analyzed the dissolution of the AMM by Imam W. D. Muhammad. Furthermore, during this period we witnessed the growth and surge in power and influence of the Nation of Islam under the leadership of Minister Louis Farrakhan.

Finally, in chapter 10 I discuss the most recent significant developments of the Nation of Islam from the halls of the United States Congress to the 1994 Saviour's Day in Accra, Ghana. During the last ten years, since the first edition was published, the Nation of Islam has expanded its influence and supplemented its mission to include gang violence, housing, health care, domestic violence, substance abuse, and ridding public housing units of the drug menace.

In every urban community I visited, from Los Angeles to New York City, I walked through rubble, decay, and despair. People of African descent are surviving as if they were residents of a Third World country. Walking tall and strong, the Muslims rejuvenated the community and lectured residents for immoral behavior, while praising them for doing the right thing.

Muslim men stand like giant bow-tied beacons of strength, shining their lights into the lost souls of black men and women in America. They exhort, "Up, you mighty race! Africa for Africans at home and abroad." Prescriptions of gigantic doses of racial pride and self-help have enabled the Muslims to rehabilitate urban communities. These Muslims have attacked social problems with an awesome, passionate zeal.

Elijah Muhammad carried the red, black, and green flag for forty-five years. In 1975, after Elijah Muhammad's death, Imam W. D. Muhammad dismantled the Nation of Islam. In 1977, Minister Louis Farrakhan left the World Community of Al-Islam in the West and resurrected the Nation of Islam. Without Minister Farrakhan blowing his hot, passionate breath into the lungs of the "Nation," it would have died a slow, quiet death. Minister Farrakhan rose from the ashes of the Nation of Islam and willed the "Black Muslims" back to life.

For his noble efforts, Minister Farrakhan not only entered the Black Nationalist Hall of Fame, he kicked down the doors of history. Minister Farrakhan's efforts would have made the founding fathers proud. Marcus Garvey, Noble Drew Ali, Delaney, Blyden, Cuffee, DuBois, and Master Fard Muhammad would wrap themselves in a red, black, and green blanket, while they sleep peacefully and dream of Minister Farrakhan.

The Honorable Elijah Muhammad's legacy and message to black men and women live in the heart, mind, and soul of his spiritual son, Minister Louis Farrakhan. His passion for the mission is strong and rock-solid. Minister Farrakhan has stepped into the footprints of great African nationalist leaders and filled them with his own remarkable impression.

I would like to thank Imam Warith Deen Muhammad for his interview in 1979. The interview provided me with valuable data to apply during the transition period. I would like to thank Mr. Simeon Booker for arranging the interview with Dr. Muhammad. Special thanks to Dr. Abdul Alim Muhammad, national spokesman for the Nation of Islam for his interview in 1994. Dr. Muhammad gave me "a wake-up call." I will always cherish and remember my interview with Dr. Muhammad. Special thanks to the Coalition for the Remembrance of Elijah (CROE) of Chicago and the valuable data they provided me. A very special thanks to the rank and file members of the Nation of Islam for allowing me to become a small part of their ever-changing world.

A very special thank you to Dr. Margo King for introducing me to Mr. Kermit Eady, president/founder of the Black United Fund of New York.

Thanks to Mr. Eady for the interview with sister Karriemah P. Muhammad, aide to Minister Louis Farrakhan.

I would like to thank Morris Brown College for allowing me valuable release time to complete my research. The staff of the Schomburg Center for Research in Black Culture in New York City, were also a very valuable resource.

A very special thank you to Ms. Rita Ordansa for providing me with hours of administrative assistance. Ms. Ordansa is without a doubt the most valuable player in this research effort and I would have been lost without her dedication, talent, integrity, and her belief in my vision and ideals. I would like to say a special prayer and thank you to Dr. Frank M. Reid III, pastor of Bethel A.M.E. Church in Baltimore for his support.

I have been blessed with a loving cadre of student assistants who believe in me and supported my work. Ms. Yvette Jefferson was a McNair Scholar student from Coppin State College. Mr. Otta Omom and Mr. Thomas Long were former members of the Nation of Islam. Mr. Omom and Mr. Long "pulled my coat" all through the research process. Thanks, brothers. A special thank you goes out to Ms. Gail Stokes who helped prepare the references, and Ms. Eva Griffin who served as the editor for the manuscript.

A special thank you to "my main man" Lou Moore, his wife Debra, and their children, Akil, Din, and Akary during my stay at the Schomburg Library. I would like to give praise to the Honorable Elijah Muhammad for his wisdom, courage, and will to carry the legacy of African nationalist thought for forty-five years.

It is often said that behind every great man there is a great woman. This humble scholar has the honor and privilege to associate with three women who have never walked behind me.

I would like to thank my three queens, who are the most responsible for the support needed to complete two volumes of scholarly pursuits. To Johnnie Hill-Marsh, the mother of my child and my Queen Mother, thank you for resurrecting my soul from the ashes of Watts during the fall of 1974 in Cortland, New York. Johnnie, thank you for allowing me to lay on the top of pyramids and drink honey from the milky way. Thank you, Ms. Cynthia Newbille for loving me, believing in me, and allowing me to cruise down the Nile River on your dreams while you fed me grapes from the Garden of Eden. To my daughter Mecca for insisting, demanding that I be the Daddy you always dreamed of. Mecca, thank you for the pleasure of being your Dad and the honor of watching you flower into womanhood.

Finally, a very special thanks to my Dad, Clifton Hugo Marsh. Thank you Dad, for standing tall, for being strong, and for teaching me to take giant steps.

Introduction

"My father, Elijah Muhammad made me. He went away and allowed the nation to be destroyed. I stood up seventeen years ago to rebuild the house of my father. He told me the two of us will be backing you up. That's why you can't get to me. I got some heavy backup. I got the Mahdi and the Messiah. You'll never kill me! You will never destroy this house! Jesus said, on this rock I built my house. He wasn't talkin' about no church, he was talkin' about the Nation of Islam. On my faith he built this house. My faith is firm like a rock, unshakeable in God. You all talk God, I live him!"

—Minister Louis Farrakhan
Saviour's Day, February 26, 1994
UIC Pavilion, Chicago Illinois

In 1977, Minister Louis Farrakhan was excommunicated from the World Community of Al-Islam in the West. Once he was excommunicated, Minister Farrakhan began to resurrect and rebuild the "house" of his spiritual father, the Honorable Elijah Muhammad. It was inevitable that Minister Farrakhan would depart from the course charted by W. D. Muhammad. Minister Farrakhan's resurrection of the Nation of Islam was a second birth for the organization. The black nationalist Nation of Islam was slowly dying under the orthodox leadership of W. D. Muhammad.

In 1933, Elijah Muhammad assumed leadership of the Nation of Islam. The Honorable Elijah Muhammad perceived Master Fard Muhammad as God in person, and Elijah Muhammad was his messenger for forty-two years until his death in 1975.

The organization has undergone many changes since the publication of the first book in 1984. The first edition was entitled *From Black Muslims to Muslims: The Transition from Separatism to Islam, 1930–1980.* The book detailed fifty years of the Nation of Islam's birth, development, and change.

It was extremely interesting to observe the Nation of Islam change during the transition of leadership to W. D. Muhammad. However, the biological son was dismantling, destroying, and dissolving the oldest, most powerful black nationalist organization in the United States.

During this period of history the Nation of Islam became lost under the leadership of W. D. Muhammad. It seemed that prior to 1977, the world was ready to close the book of life on Elijah Muhammad's beloved nation. All social scientists (including myself) were ready to write the final chapter (an obituary if you will) for the Nation of Islam.

None of us in the academic community knew or were aware of the black nationalist passion burning in the heart of Minister Louis Farrakhan. It was he who stepped in and forced the death grip from the throat of his spiritual father, the Honorable Elijah Muhammad. In 1977, Minister Louis Farrakhan resurrected/found the Nation of Islam and began to breath life into a dying movement. Therefore, Minister Farrakhan has forced the social-scientific community to reexamine the new nation. The sociological and historical developments over the last fifteen years since the publication of the first edition has forced me to radically change the second edition.

The second edition is entitled *From Black Muslims to Muslims: The Resurrection, Transformation, and Change of the Lost-Found Nation of Islam in America, 1930–1995*. I believe this title accurately reflects the in-depth and comprehensive analysis provided in the second edition. The first book was a mere 150 pages long. The second edition is a robust 223 pages and includes four new chapters. The second edition enabled me to observe the Nation's resurrection and provided many exciting opportunities to update the new edition.

Even as I write this introduction, the "Nation" is in the news. Thirty years after the murder of Malcolm X, his memory, image, and legacy haunts the Nation and Minister Louis Farrakhan. Qubilah Shabazz, 34-year-old daughter of Malcolm X, pleaded innocent of charges to plot the murder of Minister Louis Farrakhan in federal court in Minnesota on January 18, 1995. Ms. Shabazz allegedly used the telephone and traveled interstate to hire Michael Summers (a.k.a Fitzpatrick) to kill Minister Farrakhan to avenge the murder of her father over thirty years ago.

The men who were arrested and convicted of the murder of Malcolm X have served over two decades in prison and have been released. An ironic twist of Malcolm's murder is the fact that both he and his convicted assassins eventually embraced orthodox Islam. Malcolm's assassins underwent a religious conversion in prison and now Talmadge Hayer is called Majahid Abdul Halim. Halim, as of 1990, was participating in a work-release program at Edgecombe Correctional Facility in New York. Norman Butler is now Muhammad Abdul-Aziz; he was released from Ossining Correctional Facility in June of 1985. Thomas 15X has changed his name to Khalil Islam and he was released from Ossining Correctional Facility in February of 1987.

It seems very curious that the legend of Malcolm X is being used as a weapon against Minister Farrakhan and the Nation of Islam. Malcolm X was more feared in the 1960s than Minister Farrakhan is in the 1990s. The public embrace of Malcolm should not be in conflict with Minister Farrakhan's mission.

Remember, Malcolm was also a student of the Honorable Elijah Muhammad and Malcolm fought for the same ideals as Minister Farrakhan. Both Malcolm and Farrakhan fought to fulfill the Pan-African vision of the founding fathers: one God, one aim, one destiny! . . . Up, you mighty race! . . . Africa for Africans at home and abroad.

It is an honor and a pleasure to reintroduce the Nation to the world. I have worked very hard in pursuit of a personal quest to make the second edition a great improvement over the first. My quest has also been an adventurous expedition to follow in the magnificent footprints of Dr. C. Eric Lincoln and Dr. Essien Udom. These two men blazed the trail to lead the way to document the heartbeat of the Nation of Islam. When I wrote the first edition I felt dwarfed walking in their giant footsteps. The years between the first and second edition have matured and enabled me to work on my craft and improve my skill. This second edition will enable me to leave my own giant footprints in the sand.

Chapter 1

Black Nationalism as a Social Movement

This chapter develops a social movement framework in order to analyze the socioeconomic conditions that make it conducive for a black nationalist movement to emerge and to discuss the black nationalist perspective in the United States.

Black nationalism has been a consistent theme throughout the history of the African presence in America. Black nationalism had become a viable change mechanism when African Americans perceived the social, economic, and political conditions in the United States to be intolerable and inflexible to change by traditional means.

The problem for over twenty million African Americans is, How can former slaves achieve equality within a capitalist economy and a predominantly white society? People of African descent are subjected to unequal distribution of rewards, political power, and opportunities, which systematically restricts their chances to succeed as a group. By organizing in a social movement, African Americans want to change the conditions of racial and class inequality.

Social Movement Definition

A social movement is a large, organized group of people committed to collective goals and ideals to preserve or change the existing political-economic structure and human relations in society. This definition distinguishes social movements from other groups and group activities, such as lobbies, crowds, and tactics.

Lobby

A lobby is an organized group exerting political, economic, and ideological pressure within traditional channels to influence the public legislative process in order to create policy sympathetic to the group's interests.

Crowd Activity

Riots, panic, and mob behavior are spontaneous, unorganized, and leaderless. Individuals do not consciously join these kinds of activities

1

to achieve specific goals, nor are they sustained to change political and economic institutions.

Tactics

Tactics are defined as interaction by groups of people to bring their grievances to the attention of the public and governing elites. Demonstrations, rallies, and boycotts are organized to achieve the goals of the movement.

Social movements are concerned with changing the power relationships and the basic socioeconomic institutions. Individuals organize to improve their status as a group in society. People join movements for "some kind of change to be achieved, some innovation to be made or a previous condition to be restored."[1]

Underlying Assumptions

There are several underlying assumptions associated with the social movement definition. Movements are organized and have a structure; there is a consciousness shared among individuals that their socioeconomic problems can be solved more effectively in groups. The solution to social problems is believed to lie in the preservation of, or a change in, the means of production and governance of the society. Four areas will be covered in the following discussion: economic order, class, minority group status, and the political order.

The Economic Order

In our definition of a social movement, one underlying assumption is that certain groups in society are dissatisfied with their economic status and the governance of society. The motivation for the creation of a social movement is often found in the economic order.

The economic order is the system a society uses to produce and distribute goods and services. The forces of production include natural resources, expertise, tools, and labor. The interaction of individuals in this process is called the relations of production.

The United States is a capitalist society, which means the ownership of the means of production and distribution are operated for profit. The wealth derived from the profit is controlled by an elite class, which is comprised of a small segment of the total population. The members of the elite class create corporations to safeguard their economic interests. The corporations are "administratively and politically interrelated; together [they] hold the keys to economic decisions."[2] A "Capitalist society contains groups that are unequal in their participation in the productive system. As in all class societies, there is a dominant class that appropriates a surplus produced by a subordinate class."[3]

In the system of stratification, individuals are placed in the class system according to their occupation in the division of labor. The occupation represents different life chances to acquire income, property, higher education, and job opportunities. The primary components of the stratification system are occupation, economic class, social prestige, and power. An occupation represents a marketable skill and a specific function in the division of labor.

Occupation is the link between the individual, the class system, status, and power, "as well as to skill and function; to understand the occupations composing any social stratum, we must consider them in terms of each of these interrelated dimensions."[4]

Since the production of goods is less expensive than the workers' wages, this creates surplus wealth, or profit, for the employer. When surplus wealth is not distributed equally among various groups in society, a system of inequality emerges. The unequal groups are classes composed of people with different access to social rewards and opportunities by virtue of their rank in the economic order.

A class "is a set of people who share similar life choices because of their similar class situations."[5] The "combination of the division of labor with super and subordination makes up that basic configuration of social positions, strata and classes in the social system."[6] The individuals in the subordinate classes sell their skills and talent in the labor market and "in these occupations men work for someone else on someone else's property."[7]

The Working Class

Individuals who own no segments of the means of production and have no controlling voice in the governing of society comprise the working class. Members of the working class trade their skills, talent, and labor for a wage paid by the employers. Traditionally, white collar workers have been the economic buffer between the working class and the economic elite.

The white collar worker is in a similar property-class as the blue collar worker. White collar workers "have no direct fiscal tie to the means of production, no prime claims upon the proceeds from property. Like factory workers, they work for those who do own such means of livelihood."[8] The working class in the United States is comprised of four main segments: 1) blue-collar workers, which include semiskilled and skilled workers; 2) white-collar workers, which include clericals, professional, and technical individuals, and sales managers; 3) proprietors of small business, owners of "Mom and Pop" stores, or small business ventures that employ few or no employees, and physicians in private practice; and

4) reserve labor force, which includes unskilled and unemployed members of society. Members of this fourth group have limited opportunities and lack skills, hence they are always on the fringe of the labor market.

Minority Group Status

Minority group individuals, by virtue of unique physical or cultural characteristics that differ from the dominant racial, ethnic, or religious group, are subjected to different and unequal treatment and become victims of collective institutional discrimination. The presence of a minority group in society implies the existence of a corresponding dominant group with higher social status and greater privileges. Minority status carries with it the exclusion from full participation in life of society.[9]

Once a person of African descent achieves a better economic status, that person is denied the social rewards which normally accompany upward mobility. C. Wright Mills said, "Prestige involves two persons: one to claim it and another to honor the claim." Minority group status is not honored in the United States. Middle-class and professional blacks are subject to the same social ostracism as working class and poor blacks in a society which treats them equally in the prestige system. Prestige is often a birthright; the black child, regardless of individual achievement, "will not receive the deference which the white child may successfully claim. Race, nationality and family prestige is based on, or at least limited by, descent."[10]

Political Order

The political order is controlled by a segment of the population called the governing elite. The Marxist term "ruling class" applies only to an economic fact that small groups of people own large sums of wealth; the term does not address military and political power.

The modern governing elite in the United States is comprised of the economic elite, leaders of the military, and government officials. The power to make "decisions of national and international consequences are now so clearly seated in political, military and economic institutions, that other areas of society seem off to the side, and on occasion, readily subordinated to these."[11]

The modern state is large and complicated, "however, it still has the same core function to be a machine for insuring a smooth transfer of wealth from a producing class to an appropriating class."[12] The governing elite controls production of ideas through the major institutions in society, such as religious institutions, school systems, mass media, judicial systems, and government agencies.

These institutions reinforce the ideas that are compatible with the interest of the governing elite, define what behavior is legitimate, and establish the norms for individuals to emulate. The ideologies the state produces "tend to explain and justify the existing class structure."[13]

Most members of the working class fulfill their economic role with little awareness of how it affects their social status, class, and interpersonal relations. In order for individuals to be organized, there must be a common consciousness shared by the group that their individual socioeconomic problems are a result of the economic order and manipulation by the governing elite. There are certain social conditions which "encourage people to change their view of themselves and their world, to object to and challenge arrangements which they may have accepted previously."[14]

Social Change

Social Conditions

Economic inequality and institutional racism benefit white workers and are socioeconomic obstacles to proletariat unity. This structural relationship encourages competition within the working class which escalates into racial conflict. "The white groups tend to view their interests in a particularly united way when confronted with blacks making demands which are seen as threatening to vested interests."[15] The coalition between major corporations and the American labor movement has effectively co-opted and institutionalized the leadership to reinforce the interest of the economic elite. These socioeconomic realities have forced black leaders to organize around racial issues versus class solidarity.

Historically, black nationalist movements have occurred during periods of change in society, such as migration, a changing job market, and during wars. "Only in war time have labor shortages been sufficiently severe to induce employers to open up previously closed occupations to blacks and to provide employment to many black youths and women [who had been unable] to get regular jobs."[16]

Social changes in the United States create a push/pull effect. The push is the social, political, and economic conditions in the United States. The pull is the attraction to Africa as a homeland. "Changes in political behavior and beliefs do not occur separately from economic change."[17] The gradual increase in the standard of living ferments a sense of optimism. When economic, political, and social conditions do not continue to improve as expected, individuals become frustrated, and anger and discontent arise.

The social conditions previously discussed raise the expectations of blacks that equality and political power are attainable in the United States. When they are not achieved, the attraction to Africa becomes a possible solution. If the "deprived can readily see who is responsible for their condition, that group may soon be defined as the enemy and becomes the focus for the discontent."[18]

Group Consciousness

Changes in an individual's consciousness are a result of transformation in the society; "it accompanies reorganization of the individual's life situation as a result of and in response to structural transformation. It profoundly affects an individual's personality and world view."[19]

A political mentality or group consciousness is affected by the person's position in stratified systems. A group consciousness is likely to occur among homogeneous groups in regard to class, occupation, and prestige. The majority of blacks work in low-paying occupations, creating similar interests, working conditions, and life chances. The economic position allows them frequent communication to discuss grievances. Social isolation, as residents of segregated communities and minority status, add to this cohesiveness. By living under similar conditions, blacks "begin to seek a similarity of interest with one another, interaction among them intensifies; they start to share a common perspective and group consciousness emerges."[20] African American minority group status and economic deprivation become the basis for political action.

Organization

Leadership

Integrationist leaders representing "traditional" civil rights organizations are often responsive to corporate interests and not the needs of the black masses. The co-optation of leaders hinders any attempt to relieve the grievances of the black community. This kind of leadership benefits the status of certain individuals, "but it does not speak to the alleviation of the multitude of social problems shared by the masses."[21] Professional blacks are subjects of political powerlessness similar to their working class or unemployed brethren. Institutional racism and economic inequality place a limit on black upward mobility and the number of black people to fill roles in the division of labor. The precarious socioeconomic status of being black and middle class motivates some blacks to become dissidents and leaders of nationalist movements. The "intellectual elite deserving radical social change must depend on the deprived masses for support by aligning his interest with that of the masses; [through this move] strong impetus for change is affected."[22]

The "leaders encourage group members to question the present distribution of social goods and legitimacy of existing authority structure and they work out practical means of attaining the goal."[23] Organizations usually have a charismatic leader, an organizer, and an intellectual. All three types have unique functions within the organization, but charismatic leadership attracts the masses. The charismatic leader appeals to the emotions and ideals of the alienated. He or she leads by the pure force of his/her personality, "by virtue of which he/she was set apart from ordinary men and treated as endowed with supernatural superhuman powers."[24]

Ideology

The charismatic leader is able to articulate an ideology which offers political solutions to socioeconomic problems. An ideology is a belief system that provides a world view which reinforces the cause of a particular class or group. It is "a coherent set of ideas and guidelines for altering the authority structure."[25] The ideology organizes individuals into a cohesive body and enables the movement to overcome socioeconomic differences; that is, age, class, regional, race, and religious differences. Individuals join a social movement because "it offers answers to certain dissatisfactions prompted by societal conditions in relation to their unique experiences."[26]

The ideology provides a perspective for individuals to link personal injustice to institutional inequality thereby encouraging commitment to the organization's goals. The organization provides protection, security, sense of identity, and economic well-being.

Large groups of individuals and economic resources are valuable tools to attack social problems by rational means. Each individual is assigned specific functions and everyone's role is clearly defined; organization enables the group to pursue its objectives.

Types of Social Movements

There are five basic types of social movements which vary according to goals and objectives: 1) revolutionary movements, 2) reform movements, 3) backlash movements, 4) apolitical movements, and 5) separatist movements. People of African descent have participated in a majority of these movements, adding a black perspective to accommodate their unique socioeconomic problems. A black nationalist social movement is an organized effort to create a collective consciousness and racial/cultural pride, and it may or may not desire to control a sovereign territory. Some nationalists acknowledge that blacks have similar economic, political, and social problems as a group, but they have no desire to have a separate state or emigrate to Africa. All separatists are nationalists, but not all nationalists believe in separatism.

African American nationalists have taken two basic stands: First, some nationalists have a psychic identity with Africa, but desire to remain in America. These individuals may or may not desire land within the United States (a nation-within-a-nation). Second, other nationalists feel freedom cannot be achieved in America and desire to emigrate to Africa. In the framework of previous discussions, black nationalism can now be defined as an "ideological formulation, i.e., subjective reconstruction of reality in black terms; a social strategy containing proposals and programs of reconstruction and a collective vocation, that is, a struggle for community."[27]

An examination of black nationalism shows that it is a body of political thought and behavior, ranging from simple expressions of racial solidarity to the more sophisticated ideologies of Pan-Africanism. Between these extremes lie many varieties of black nationalism.

Revolutionary Movements

Revolutionary movements are concerned with overturning present governing elite and seizing control of the state in order to change the means of production and the redistribution of wealth in society.

Revolutionary black nationalists perceive the black communities as colonies in the United States. They believe that these colonies should be organized and serve as the vanguard force to overthrow the existing political and economic order, thereby bringing about liberation for all oppressed people. Revolutionary nationalists perceive the African American community as a nation, but that politically it does not control its own destiny. Such nationalists as Huey P. Newton and Bobby Seale, founders of the Black Panther party, proclaimed African Americans must identify with people of color throughout the world as an international majority instead of an American minority. Revolutionary nationalists perceived the economic and racial problems in America to be linked with the international problems of imperialism, colonialism, and exploitation of foreign labor and natural resources.

The revolutions of Third World people in China, Angola, Mozambique, Cuba, Algiers, and Vietnam encouraged the nationalists to suggest that African Americans align themselves with these people as comrades in an international struggle against racism and capitalism.

Reform Movements

Reform movements would like the distribution of wealth and governance of society to remain the same. They are concerned with manipulating specific institutions, attitudes, or laws which deny them access to social rewards and privileges.

Cultural Nationalism

Cultural nationalists feel blacks represent a distinct and separate culture from that of the white society. It is this cultural link with other blacks that forms a major portion of the ideology. Glorification of African art, literature, philosophy and history are essential to liberate the Afro-psyche from the traditions of Western civilization. Also, the assertion of a distinct life-style and world view in such ways as assuming African or Arabic names, wearing African clothes, and speaking African languages is essential to becoming free.

Cultural nationalists believe racial pride in themselves as a group comes before political change. They advocate creating black institutions, rituals, and holidays to celebrate black unity and African heritage.

The cultural nationalists "are concerned with returning to the old African culture, thereby regaining their identity and freedom. In other words, they feel that the African culture will automatically bring political freedom."[28]

Religious Nationalism

Religious nationalists perceive religion as a viable change mechanism. They perceive Christ or Muhammad as black leaders of nonwhite people against the rule of white nations.

One of the most dynamic black nationalists was Edward W. Blyden, born in 1832 in St. Thomas, Virgin Islands. He emigrated to Liberia on January 26, 1851. Blyden is significant because he was the earliest nationalist thinker to articulate a definite black nationalist ideology. Blyden's influence covers politics ("back to Africa"), economics (African socialism), and religion (urged the belief in Islam). Blyden worked and lived in Liberia for over forty years as a teacher, builder of educational institutions, and political leader. Blyden was the first nationalist to combine a "back to Africa" theme with African socialism and Islam as a religion to create African unity. Blyden concluded, that "Christianity, which focused on changing African values, had destructive and deleterious influence on Africans. He considered Islam more appropriate to the basic African life-style."[29] Blyden encouraged exchange and cooperation with Islamic states of Africa with the mutual aim of incorporating them into the Negro Republic.[30]

Blyden learned and instructed his students in Arabic and urged them to work as emissaries to Islamic nations.

Economic Nationalism

Economic nationalists advocate controlling the community's economic interest by establishing business enterprises. They may call for cooperative or capitalist ownership; the central theme is that community control of business enterprises is essential to the real development and growth of the community itself.

Pan-Africanism

Pan-Africanism is a movement toward economic cooperation, cultural awareness, and international political solidarity among people of African descent.

W.E.B. DuBois was instrumental in developing Pan-Africanism. DuBois and Henry Sylvester Williams protested European colonization of Africa through the Pan-African Congress held in 1900, 1921, 1923, 1927, and 1945. The conferences articulated several concerns: colonization of Africa, human rights in southern Africa, exploitation of blacks living in predominantly white societies, and self-government for nations in the West Indies.

The Pan-African Congress fostered the idea that "various groups of Africans, quite separate in origin, became so united in experience and so exposed to the impact of new cultures that they began to think of Africa as one idea and one land."[31]

Backlash Movements

These movements develop as a result of progressive changes in the society. Individuals join to resist change and maintain the existing social, economic, and political relationships. People of African descent have been victimized by backlash movements, which often emerge when blacks and other minorities appear to be making progress. The Ku Klux Klan, John Birch Society, and American Nazi Party are examples of backlash movements.

Apolitical Movements

Apolitical movements are not concerned with economic inequality or political power in society. There is a release of tension, collective flight, and self-expression with no plans to change the existing social order.

Historically, religious-oriented, "pie in the sky"-type organizations like "Father Divine," "Sweet Daddy Grace," and Reverend Ike have offered solutions to economic and political oppression through prayer and ceremonies. Apolitical movements help people cope and adapt to the situation instead of changing it.

Separatist Movements

Separatism is the belief that people of African descent cannot attain freedom and equality in the United States; therefore, the solution is to acquire a separate state. There are two forms of separatism: (a) territorial separatism (nation within a nation) and (b) the back-to-Africa movement.

Territorial Separatism

Organizations such as the Nation of Islam and the Republic of New Africa have asked for territory within the boundaries of the United States, a nation within a nation.

Nationalists of this persuasion feel oppressed in the United States, but have no strong inclination to immigrate to Africa. The nation-within-a-nation concept depends upon the economic and military support as well as goodwill of the parent nation (United States). Territorial separatists assume the parent nation and the black states could coexist peacefully without exploitation by the dominant power.

Emigration—Back to Africa

A consistent and strong theme in African American social thought has been the conclusion that blacks could never achieve equality in America and the only solution is to leave. Emigration has been viewed as an alternative when the American ideal of equality seemed unattainable. There was more of a dissatisfaction with the American society than there was a desire to live in Africa.

Marcus Garvey was the leader of a return-to-Africa movement. He founded the Universal Negro Improvement Association in 1916. Garvey planned to transplant the black American community in Africa, but the emigration theme did not originate with Garvey.

Paul Cuffee was an influential emigrationist. Cuffee wanted to transport black farmers, mechanics, and artisans to Sierra Leone and establish commercial and political intercourse with African states. With $4,000 of his own funds, Cuffee transported thirty-eight African Americans to Sierra Leone in 1815. The American Colonization Society was founded four years after Cuffee's death in 1821. The first settlement was called Monrovia in honor of President Monroe.

In 1858 Henry Highland Garnet became president of the African Civilization Society. Its goal was to establish in West Africa, "a grand center of negro nationality from which shall flow the streams of commercial, intellectual and political power which shall make colored people everywhere respected."[32]

Martin R. Delaney merged his National Emigration Conference with Garnet's African Civilization Society in May 1861 to raise funds to promote resettlement in the Niger Valley. Martin Delaney felt black Americans were culturally unique, "as the Poles in Russia, the Hungarians in Austria, the Welsh, Irish and Scotch in the British dominions."[33] The ambitious plans of Garnet and Delaney were stalled by the Civil

War; they felt if blacks participated in the war it would uplift their status as a group.

Edward Wilmont Blyden, a West Indian, migrated to Monrovia in 1851. Blyden firmly believed that blacks could never be equal to whites in the United States. Blyden was very critical of American blacks for delaying emigration plans in hopes of achieving equality in the United States. He said, "Half the time and energy that will be spent by them in struggles against caste, if devoted to the building up of a home and nationality of their own, would produce results immeasurably more useful and satisfactory."[34]

Blyden performed extensive research on Africa, its people, and the culture. Blyden was the first black nationalist to investigate the economic base of the African social systems. Blyden concluded it was "socialistic, cooperative and equitable an ideal for which Europe was desperately striving as the answers to the ills created by individualism and unscrupulous competition."[35] These ideas place Blyden above all nationalists before him or since. Blyden lived in Africa; studied the society; and incorporated Islam, African Socialism, and emigration in his world view.

Blyden's world view and self-esteem were not influenced by the flux of the economic marketplace. Nationalists felt driven out of America by oppressive conditions rather than a desire to live in Africa. This strong attraction to Africa is what separated Blyden and Marcus Garvey from other nationalists.

Organization Transformation

The transformation of the Nation of Islam to the World Community of Al-Islam in the West is consistent with the general trend of social movement development. There are three stages associated with the transformation: the formation stage (organization founded by Master Fard Muhammad), the formalization stage (development of ideology and institutions by Elijah Muhammad), and traditionalization (the change from separatism to Islam by Wallace D. Muhammad).

During the formation stage of a movement, social conditions create perilous circumstances in which individuals seek a solution by following a charismatic leader. When the movement attains a social and economic base, the charismatic leader depends less on charisma and more on a bureaucratic structure. The creation of a formal bureaucracy is the beginning of the formalization stage. During this stage Elijah Muhammad succeeded Master Fard Muhammad as the "Messenger of Allah" and began to create a distinct black separatist doctrine and a formal bureaucracy. Elijah Muhammad's death on February 25, 1975, was the start of the traditionalization stage.

Wallace D. Muhammad succeeded his father as leader of the Nation of Islam. He changed its name to the World Community of Al-Islam in the West. The name change is more than symbolic; it reflects an alteration in structure, doctrine, rituals, leadership, and goals. The traditionalization stage under Wallace D. Muhammad is a "diffusion of goals, in which a pragmatic leadership replaces unattainable goals." This stage is "always in the direction of greater conservatism."[36] The leadership during this stage usually revises the goals to accommodate the dominant group. Elijah Muhammad wanted to establish a nation within a nation, although this was almost impossible to attain in the United States. Wallace Muhammad is trying to achieve more realistic goals, such as ideological reform (within the organization), restoration of urban areas through employment, and trade with Islamic governments.

This chapter has outlined the economic and political system in the United States. It can be concluded that the structure of inequality is not enough to motivate certain groups in society to join a social movement. Certain periods in history are more conducive to rebellion than others. For example, Master Fard Muhammad's presence in Detroit during the Depression enabled him to capitalize on the discontent experienced by many African Americans.

A significant number of the early converts of the Nation of Islam were recent migrants from the southern section of the United States. The new migrants became potential recruits when their expectations of economic mobility and political power were not met.

Chapter two is an analysis of American social conditions between 1914 and 1930. We shall see why international and domestic conditions prompted many African Americans to investigate separatism as a solution to inequality in the United States.

Notes

1. Rudolph Heberle, *Social Movements* (New York: Appleton-Century-Crofts, 1951), p. 6.

2. C. Wright Mills, *Power, Politics and People* (New York: Ballantine Books, 1963), p. 28.

3. Roberta Ash-Garner, *Social Movements in America* (Chicago: Rand-McNally, 1977), p. 17.

4. Mills, *Power,* p. 307.

5. Ibid.

6. Anthony Oberschall, *Social Conflict and Social Movements* (Englewood Cliffs, N.J.: Prentice-Hall, 1973), p. 33.

7. Mills, *Power,* p. 307.

8. Ibid., p. 308.

9. George E. Simpson and Milton J. Yinger, *Racial and Cultural Minorities* (New York: Harper and Row, 1965), p. 16.

10. Mills, *Power,* p. 311.

11. Ibid., p. 27.

12. Ash-Garner, *Social Movements,* p. 4.

13. Ibid.

14. Irving Krauss, *Stratification Class and Conflict* (New York: The Free Press, 1976), p. 21.

15. Charles V. Hamilton and Stokely Carmichael, *Black Power* (New York: Vintage Books, 1967), p. 7.

16. Victor Perlo, *Economics of Racism U.S.A.* (New York: International Publishers, 1975), p. 56.

17. Roberta Ash-Garner, *Social Change* (Chicago: Rand-McNally, 1977), p. vii.

18. Krauss, *Stratification,* p. 21.

19. Ash-Garner, *Social Change,* p. 47.

20. Krauss, *Stratification,* p. 16.

21. Hamilton and Carmichael, *Black Power,* p. 12.

22. Ron E. Roberts and Robert M. Kloss, *Social Movements* (Saint Louis, Mo.: V.I. Mosby Company, 1974), p. 177.

23. Krauss, *Stratification,* p. 22.

24. Max Weber, *The Theory of Social and Economic Organization* (New York: Oxford University Press, 1977), p. 358.

25. Krauss, *Stratification,* p. 22.

26. Raymond Hall, *Black Separatism and Social Reality* (New York: Pergamon Press, 1977), p. 13.

27. M. Ron Karenga, "Afro-American Nationalism, Beyond Mystification and Misconception," *Black Books Bulletin,* Vol. 6, No. 1 (Spring 1979), p. 25.

28. Roberts and Kloss, *Social Movements,* p. 47.

29. James Turner, "Blyden, Black Nationalism and Emigration Schemes," *Black Books Bulletin,* Vol. 6, No. 1, (Spring 1979), p. 25.

30. Hollis Lynch, *Edward Wilmont Blyden* (London: Oxford Press, 1967), p. 46.

31. W.E.B. DuBois, *The World and Africa* (New York: Viking Press, 1947), p. 7.

32. Lynch, *Blyden,* pp. 23–24.

33. Martin D. Delaney, *The Condition, Elevation, Emigration and Destiny of the Colored People of the United States, Politically Considered* (New York: Arno Press, 1968), Appendix.

34. Lynch, *Blyden*, p. 35.
35. Ibid.
36. Joseph H. Gusfield, *Protest, Reform and Revolt* (New York: John Wiley and Sons, 1970), p. 110.

Chapter 2

Social Conditions, 1914–1930

Social movements arise in society during periods of social change. The period 1914–1930 represents one of the most dynamic periods in the history of the United States.

Social conditions that provoked discontent among blacks were World War I and the Depression. They caused migration of blacks to the North and race riots following World War I. When conditions were improving during this era, African Americans expected their status to continue to improve. When they experienced a drop in status after the war, frustration, anxiety, and discontent arose. (During this era African Americans improved their status, but relative to the white population they did not improve at all.) This disparity between the two groups remains the same today, thereby retarding attempts for equality within the work force and society in general.

With the arrival of World War I blacks were confronted with a question concerning citizenship in the United States. Should they help save democracy in France while they were denied participation in the democratic process in Alabama and New York City?

African Americans' confidence in the government to improve the group's status in the military was bolstered when the Wilson administration appointed Emmett J. Scott to be Negro advisor to the secretary of war. Scott had been a confidential secretary to Booker T. Washington for eighteen years. His functions were to urge equal and impartial application of the selective service system and to create programs that promoted morale among black soldiers and civilians as well.

Black men fought bravely against tremendous physical and psychological odds to prove their loyalty as Americans and their valor as soldiers. In the face of all practical evidence prior to, during, and after World War I, however, there were widespread stereotypes restricting blacks' participation in the U.S. military.

The United States' involvement in World War I required massive recruitment in order to succeed. Congress passed and President Wilson signed the Selective Service Law on May 18, 1917, which required all able-bodied American men between 21 and 31 years old to register with their local draft boards.

The draft consumed some of the best possible labor and "there is little doubt of southern reluctance to have black farm labor drafted. In fact, it was not uncommon policy for draft boards to take blacks who owned their own land while exempting those who worked for white sharecroppers or tenants."[1] Draft boards

> regularly inducted blacks who were physically unfit while excluding whites with similar disabilities. Blacks entitled to a deferment were railroaded into the army, while whites with no legitimate excuse for exemption were allowed to escape the requirements of the draft system.[2]

There were 404,384 black troops in the military—most were in the Army. Out of these were 1,353 commissioned officers trained in segregated facilities. Tables 2.1 and 2.2 reveal the differences in selective service classifications and inductions, comparing white with black. In Table 2.1, Class 1 included those men available for active duty. Deferred status included those who were exempt from military service.

Out of a total of 10,640,846 people registered for the draft, blacks comprised 10.13 percent; 1,078,331 blacks registered for the draft from June 5, 1917, to September 11, 1918. Of the 1,078,331 blacks registered, 556,917 were ranked for Class I; that is, 51.65 percent of the black men examined were fit for military service. There were 521,414 blacks who received military deferments, which made 48.35 percent of the black men ineligible for military duty. Compared with white men, 9,562,515 registered for the draft during the same time period and 3,110,659 were given the Class I status, which made only 32.53 percent of the whites ineligible for the draft, while 6,541,856 were deferred, which made 67.4 percent of the white men who were registered ineligible for military service.

Table 2.1
Black and White Classifications Compared

Total Blacks and Whites Registered	Number	Percent of Classified
June 5, 1917–Sept. 11, 1918	10,640,846	—
Total Blacks Registered	1,078,331	100.00
Class I	556,917	51.65
Deferred Classes	521,414	48.35
Total Whites Registered	9,562,515	100.00
Class I	3,110,659	32.53
Deferred Classes	6,451,856	67.47
Percentage Accepted for Service		
(Calls before December 15, 1917)		
Black		36.23
White		24.75

Source: Second report of the Provost Marshal General to the Secretary of War on the Operations of the Selective System to December 20, 1918. Washington, D.C.: Government Printing Office, 1919.

Table 2.2
Black and White Inductions Compared

Total Black and White Inductions	Number	Percent of Inductions
June 5, 1912–Nov. 11, 1918	2,810,296	100.00
Black	367,710	13.08
White	2,442,586	86.92

Source: Second report of the Provost Marshal General to the Secretary of War on the Operations of the Selective Service System to December 20, 1918. Washington, D.C.: Government Printing Office, 1919.

Blacks accepted for service comprised 36.23 percent, while 24.75 percent of the whites were called for active duty. These data apparently amazed Emmett Scott; he offered the following criticism: "The Provost Marshal offered more or less elaborate explanations of the reasons for the higher figures for colored registrants in Class I, but they do not seem now, to be tenable reasons."[3]

In Table 2.2 out of the 2,810,296 people drafted, 367,710 were black, which is 13.08 percent of the total inductions for the period of June 5, 1912, to November 11, 1918. Blacks comprised less than 10 percent of the total population, but were 13 percent of the inducted military force.

Along with the discriminatory practices of the draft policy in World War I, "intelligence testing was a new tool of the new science of psychology: in fact, the massing of men of war gave psychologists their real chance to develop and validate the test."[4]

These tests, seemingly scientific, helped "validate" blacks' inferiority as a race and incompetence as fighting men. The army assigned blacks to stevedore regiments and labor battalions because it was commonly believed that blacks were only suited for manual labor.

Discrimination by the United States government was clear. Out of approximately 350,000 blacks drafted, only 40,000 became combat soldiers. Blacks inducted into the armed services were segregated from white soldiers during their training and they also experienced segregation during active duty.

The induction of blacks as fighting men created the unique problem of who would lead them. The American government had the answer: white men, of course! In the following government document, the leadership of the 92nd Division was appointed:

> October 24, the War Department establishes the 92nd Division, National Army; colored selective service men from the United States at large are to be organized into the component units at various northern stations. General and field officers in the technical branches and in the field artillery above the grade of first lieutenant are to be white."[5]

The army made a concerted effort to exclude blacks from the Officers' ranks. Through the efforts of the National Association for the Advancement of Colored People (NAACP) and various pressure groups, a compromise was created to train and recruit black officers.

There were fourteen training camps for whites, and in conjunction with the government's policy on segregation, a separate training camp was created for blacks. Led by Joel Spingarn, president of the NAACP, and James Weldon Johnson, a leading NAACP official,

> a central committee of Negro college men to seek officer training opportunities was formed, with headquarters at Howard University in Washington D.C. One thousand Negro college students pledged themselves to enter officers training camp for Negroes, which accommodated 1,250 men and was formally opened at Des Moines, Iowa.[6]

Even though the government trained these troops and officers, their role as efficient fighting personnel was played down during the conflict. Many of these black officers were not given an opportunity to lead their men. After a short time in combat they were usually replaced by white officers. Efficiency boards were created to weed out black officers. Such boards could act on the mere opinion of a field officer.

The majority of the inefficiency charges by these boards were based on "race and nature" and not on incompetence of the individual officer.

The first African Americans to arrive in France were the labor battalions comprising approximately 150,000 men. Most of the combat officers and troops served in the all-black 92nd and 93rd infantry divisions. The 93rd Division consisted of all-black national guard units, the 9th-Illinois, the 15th-New York, and units from the District of Columbia, Maryland, Ohio, Tennessee, and Massachusetts. The division never functioned as a military unit and was forced into action by the severe need for reinforcements in the French army. The 93rd Division landed in France on January 1, 1918, and was integrated into the French army. Equipped as French units,

> carrying French rifles and eating French rations, they knew an equality denied them by their own military. They operated in the area of Meuse Argonne near Saint Mihiel Champagne and in the Oise-Aisne Offensive from the early summer of 1918 to the end of the war.[7]

The men of the 93rd distinguished themselves in battle, and 540 officers and troops were decorated by the American and French governments. The 93rd Division suffered 2,583 causalities, of which 574 were killed and 2,009 wounded.

The 92nd was unprepared for combat. The division trained in sections and never assembled as a whole unit until the last days of the war. It was given "the most ignorant and physically disqualified Negroes in the United States, with 40 percent of its men illiterate. Its white officers were unsympathetic to the Negro men and hostile to the Negro officers."[8]

The most alarming note of institutional discrimination by the United States government occurred during August of 1918. The general headquarters of the American army at Chaiemont, the French military mission, sent out racist propaganda to French governors and mayors where black troops were stationed. The document, entitled "Secret Information Concerning Black American Troops," concerned the American attitude toward blacks, "warning against social recognition, stating that Negroes were prone to deeds of violence and were threatening America with degeneration. The white troops backed this propaganda by warnings and tales wherever they preceded the blacks."[9]

The effort by the United States government to discredit black troops in the eyes of the French was unsuccessful. The French government saw fit to look out for the welfare of the black soldiers. Generally, blacks moved about freely in France without rigid social barriers. The real concern of the U.S. government underlying the "secret document" was that the humane treatment blacks received would turn them bitter toward American racism when they returned home. To reinforce the subordinate behavior expected of black soldiers upon their return to America, the secretary of war sent Robert R. Moton, successor to Booker T. Washington at Tuskegee University, to speak to the troops. The black soldiers who heard Dr. Moton "reported that he told them not to expect in the United States the kind of freedom they had enjoyed in France and that they must remain content with the same position they had always occupied in the United States."[10]

Black people who remained at home during the war were in store for a dramatic change in their lives. The great migration between 1916 and 1918 was a movement motivated by various political and economic conditions created by the war efforts. These conditions made it attractive for black people to migrate to the North. It is estimated that 300,000 blacks moved north during the peak migratory years, 1916 to 1918.

World War I also created dramatic changes in American industrial production. The northern industrialists experienced a business boom; the production of munitions and military goods for the allies increased the demand for unskilled and semiskilled laborers. The draft and the cessation of European immigration created a severe labor shortage since for years foreign immigration had constituted the chief source of unskilled labor for northern industry.

There was a great need for unskilled workers in heavy industry, and blacks in rural and urban areas of the South were recruited. The employment of blacks as cheap labor had always been an important part of the southern agricultural economy. During the war, northern industrialists actively pursued this cheap labor market.

[The] 3,000,000 Negroes engaged in agricultural pursuits constituted in [1909] 30 percent of the rural population of the south and 40 percent of all southern agricultural workers. Their skill and industry govern, to a large degree, the prosperity of the southern farmer.[11]

The plantation tenant system kept blacks under the control of agricultural capitalists. Black landownership was extremely hard to achieve. The black prospective buyer had to be acceptable to the white community, acquire a white sponsor, and was allowed to purchase only acreage that was undesirable to whites. The independent black farmer was rare;

historically he has lacked enough cash to finance his operations, and so often sold himself into debt at ruinous interest rates. He also lacked enough land to diversify and so gambled heavily on cotton. Over a span of some four decades, more than half the black farm owners were squeezed off the land.[12]

Below the independent landowners were the tenants who did not own anything but their own labor. The black tenant worked on a specified number of acres, and depending upon the harvest, he was to receive a certain percentage of the produce to feed his family and to sell on the open market. He had to do so under a very special set of rules. Until recent times he was often required to make all his purchases through the plantation commissary. If he lacked cash, which was almost always, he was extended credit at exorbitant interest. The debts were secured by a lien, which usually extended to anything the cropper owned and to all his future produce.

If a tenant were so much in debt that he could never pay the landlord off, the easiest way out would be to move to another plantation. But,

many a time he found himself having invested a full season's work without having received anything near the wages he would have earned had he been a wage laborer with full employment. On such occasions at least, he had to face long months of semi-starvation for himself and his family.[13]

Table 2.3 illustrates the class positions of blacks in the agricultural economy. Between 1910 and 1930 the percentage of black farm owners dropped 3.8 percent from 24.0 percent in 1910 to 20.2 percent in 1930. The largest contingent of black farm owners was in 1920, when 212,365 black people owned small farms.

The majority of blacks were tenant farmers. From 1910 to 1930, the black tenant farm population increased from 75.9 percent to 79.7 percent, a difference of 3.9 percent. Black tenant farmers reached a peak in population of 701,471 people in 1920. The smallest agricultural class among blacks was the farm manager. This class comprised 0.1 percent in 1930, 0.2 percent in 1920 and 0.1 percent in 1910. The black farmer

Table 2.3
Number of Black Operators by Tenure and Sections

	Number of Farm Operators			Percent Distribution		
	1930	1920	1910	1930	1920	1910
Owners	176,130	212,365	211,087	20.2	32.2	24.0
Tenants	694,004	701,471	668,559	79.7	76.6	75.9
Managers	805	1,759	1,190	.1	.2	.1

Source: Negroes in the United States, 1920–1932, U.S. Department of Commerce, Bureau of Census, Government Printing Office, Washington, D.C.

was unable to compete with his white counterpart and usually his farming enterprise produced just enough to meet family needs and pay off debts. He could not garner enough profit to improve the farm or expand his production.

The farm manager kept watch over the field tenants and acted as a liaison between the black field hand, and the plantation owner. The masses of blacks were tenant farmers, 79.7 percent of whom were unskilled. The tenants were locked in an agricultural economy that offered no opportunity for advancement and a decent way of life. The law of the land was on the side of the landlord who could place liens against his produce and sell the property of the tenant to meet payment on any debts.

Along with economic deprivation, a natural disaster occurred which precipitated mass migration. The Cotton Belt of the South was struck first with drought and then heavy rains: the boll weevil set upon the cotton crops.

[As] a result, many of the farmers were almost ruined and many decided to change from cotton to food products. These food products were peanuts, corn, velvet beans, oats, sorghum, and sweet potatoes, which required only 70 to 80 percent of the labor which all cotton crop requires.[14]

With the heavy rains, the invasion of the boll weevil, and the new mechanizations developed to harvest peanuts, corn, and sweet potatoes, many black tenants were unemployed, and the few independent black landowners were forced to mechanize or go out of business.

The economic repression of blacks in the South was fortified by political powerlessness and social segregation. Politically, African Americans were rendered powerless through the literacy test, the poll tax, the grandfather clause, and other unethical methods to keep blacks from voting and exercising political power.

The social and economic factors for the great migration to the North were taking hold. Blacks were dispossessed, unskilled workers in a changing agricultural economy.

In 1915 Henry Ford revolutionized American industry by creating an eight-hour day and a five-dollar daily minimum wage. Such work hours and wages were encouraging figures for blacks who worked in the fields for hours earning as little as seventy-five cents per day or less.

Migration northward was assisted by labor agents and the black press, which capitalized on the discontent to offer appealing alternatives to the southern way of life.

Robert Abbott, editor and publisher of the *Chicago Defender,* was the most vocal advocate of migration. The paper editorialized the plight of southern blacks with headlines that played up the negative aspects of southern life while exclaiming the virtues of northern living. Repeated stories of those who were leaving the South or who were already in the North conveyed the excitement of a mass movement under way and created an atmosphere of religious hysteria.

The *Defender* was helped a great deal by "negroes already in the north writing letters to relatives and friends in the south. Such letters were often passed on by word of mouth among the illiterates."[15]

Labor agents, backed by northern industrial concerns, were instrumental in recruiting as many as twenty percent of the black workers who migrated.

There were many cases of mass transport. Steel mills and railroads sent special trains to the South to transport workers to the North. The fee and expenses for the transportation by rail was charged against the worker's future wages.

Table 2.4 illustrates the rapid increase of black residents in thirteen major northern cities. All of these urban centers experienced dramatic population changes. For example, New York City in 1910 had a total of 91,709 black residents; by 1920, 152,467 blacks resided in New York City, an increase of 60,758 people, or 66.3 percent. Chicago, Illinois, in 1910 had a black population of 44,103; ten years later 109,458 blacks lived in Chicago, an astronomical increase in 148.2 percent. Detroit, Michigan, the hub of the automobile industry in 1910, had a black population of only 5,741. By 1920 there were 40,838 black residents in Detroit. Black migration to the North was an attempt to acquire better occupational opportunities in the war-inflated economy.

Black industrial employment during World War I was concentrated in a few fields. Blacks were iron and steel workers, meat packers, ship builders, and automobile workers. There were always positions open in the "traditional" black occupations as domestics, maintenance men, and road construction workers. Racist hiring practices, labor unions, and resentful white workers effectively retarded black workers' opportunities. Owners "of northern industry were not very willing to hire negro workers except when orders were piling up, and European immigrant laborers could not be had because of the war or legal restrictions on immigration."[16]

Table 2.4
Cities Having a Black Population of 19,000 or More in 1930 with Comparative Figures for 1920 and 1910

City	1930	1920	1910	1920–1930		1910–1920	
				Number	Percent	Number	Percent
New York, N.Y.	327,706	152,467	91,709	175,239	114.9%	60,758	66.3%
Chicago, Ill.	233,903	109,458	44,103	124,445	113.7%	65,355	148.2%
Philadelphia, Pa.	219,599	134,229	84,459	85,370	63.3%	49,770	58.9%
Baltimore, Md.	142,106	108,322	84,749	33,784	31.2%	23,573	27.8%
Washington, D.C.	132,068	109,966	94,446	22,102	20.1%	15,520	16.4%
Detroit, Mich.	120,066	40,838	5,741	79,228	194.0%	35,097	611.3%
St. Louis, Mo.	93,580	69,854	43,960	23,726	34.0%	25,894	58.9%
Cleveland, Ohio	71,899	34,451	8,448	37,448	108.7%	26,003	307.8%
Pittsburgh, Pa.	47,818	30,079	19,639	17,739	59.0%	10,440	53.2%
Newark, N.J.	38,880	16,977	9,475	21,903	129.0%	7,502	79.2%
Boston, Mass.	20,514	16,350	13,564	4,225	25.8%	2,786	20.5%
East St. Louis, Ill.	11,536	7,437	5,882	4,099	55.1%	1,555	26.4%

Source: Negroes in the United States, 1920–1932, Bureau of the Census, U.S. Government Printing Office, 1935.

Employment statistics show a steady increase in black employment, but blacks dominated only three areas: agriculture, domestic and personal service, and high rates of employment in the manufacturing and mechanical industries. These three occupations employed 89 percent of the black population in 1910: agriculture, 54.8 percent; manufacturing and mechanical industries, 12.6 percent; domestic and personal service, 21.6 percent. In 1920 the same three occupations employed 84.9 percent of the black population: agriculture, 44.2 percent; manufacturing and mechanical industries, 18.7 percent; and domestic services, 22.0 percent. In 1930 these occupations employed 83.3 percent: agriculture, 36.1 percent; manufacturing and mechanical industries, 18.6 percent; and domestic and personal service, 28.6 percent.*

These figures reveal that there was some advancement during this period, but there was no upward mobility. Blacks were hired in "traditional black jobs" as field hands and sharecroppers in agriculture and as maids, butlers, and servants in domestic services. The manufacturing and mechanical industries were the highest employer of blacks in "nontraditional" jobs.

On November 11, 1918, World War I ended and many able-bodied black and white men returned to the United States industrial centers seeking employment. The influx of servicemen to the job market caused much unemployment among blacks once more.

The economic inequality blacks were suffering in northern industry was augmented by segregated housing conditions which made the new black community a municipal problem for many urban centers. The manufacturing and railroad interest which spearheaded the transportation of blacks to the North ignored the social welfare of the men. "They saw them crowded into wretched cabins, without water or any of the conveniences of life, their wives and children condemned to live in the disreputable quarters of the town and made no effort to lift them out of the mire."[17]

Soon the industrial centers became crowded and blacks moved into previously all-white districts; competition and the diminishing job market brought blacks and whites into violent conflicts. There were approximately eighteen major interracial disturbances between 1915 and 1919.

Toward the end of the World War I interracial violence had spread throughout America. Such headlines as "Race Riot in East St. Louis," "Nine Killed in Chicago," and "Riot in Nation's Capital" were frequent in newspapers during this period. The social conditions "needed for a 'race war' were created by whites while relegating blacks to subordinate positions."[18]

---

*Negroes in the United States, 1920–1932, Bureau of the Census, U.S. Government Printing Office, 1935.

When the Depression began in 1929, millions of Americans were not capable of supporting themselves and needed relief payments. By 1934, 17 percent of whites and 38 percent of blacks were incapable of self-support. The Depression pushed millions out of work; the relief rolls and the bread lines grew longer. The Depression added to the distress of blacks seeking freedom from want; "added to denials of freedom and democracy was the specter of starvation."[19]

Conditions of American society between 1914 and 1930 changed the character of the black population. The social changes transformed a large segment of the black population from rural farmhands to urban workers.

Such major urban centers as Detroit, Cleveland, Philadelphia, Newark, Chicago, and New York City experienced rapid increases of their black population. Housing conditions as previously discussed, coupled with competition with whites for jobs, touched off racial violence throughout the United States.

These social conditions made black nationalism an attractive alternative for African Americans. The Nation of Islam began in the black community of Detroit in 1930 during an era of hunger, discontent, anguish, and disillusionment. "So it was that in Detroit there appeared in the black ghetto a mysterious messiah called W. D. Fard Muhammad. His mission was to wake the dead Nation in the West."[20]

Chapter three will investigate the origin and development of the Nation of Islam's ideology and leadership. The chapter will also analyze the relationship between the Nation of Islam and the Moorish Science Temple.

Notes

1. Arthur E. Barbeau and Henry Florette, *The Unknown Soldiers* (Philadelphia: Temple University Press, 1974), p. 37.

2. Jack D. Foner, *Blacks and the Military in American History* (New York: Praeger Publishers, 1974), p. 112.

3. Emmett J. Scott, "The Participation of Negroes in World War I," *Journal of Negro Education XII,* (Summer 1943), p. 35.

4. Barbeau and Florette, *Unknown Soldiers,* p. 44.

5. Historical Section, Army War College, *Order of Battle of the United States Land Forces in the World War* (Washington, D.C.: Government Printing Office, 1931), p. 431.

6. Emmett J. Scott, *Scott's Official History of the American Negro in the World War* (Chicago: L. W. Walters, 1919), p. 82.

7. Foner, *Blacks and the Military,* p. 123.

8. Ulysses Lee, *The Employment of Negro Troops U.S. Army in World War II* (Washington D.C.: U.S. Army, 1966), p. 10.

9. W.E.B. DuBois, "An Essay toward a History of the Black Man in the Great War," *The Crisis,* Vol. 18 (May–October 1919), p. 70.

10. John H. Franklin, *From Slavery to Freedom* (New York: Random House, 1969), p. 469.

11. U.S. Bureau of Education, *Negro Education in the United States* (Washington D.C.: U.S. Printing Office, 1917), p. 73

12. George W. Groh, *The Black Migration* (New York: Weybright & Talley, 1972), p. 32.

13. Gunnar Myrdal, *An American Dilemma* (New York: Harper and Brothers, 1944), p. 246.

14. Thomas J. Woofter, *Negro Migration* (New York: Negro Universities Press, 1969), p. 79.

15. Myrdal, *American Dilemma,* p. 194.

16. Ibid., p. 195.

17. Allen Grimshaw, *Racial Violence in the United States* (Chicago: Aldine, 1969), p. 63.

18. Paul Mitchell, ed., *Race Riots in Black and White* (Englewood Cliffs, N.J.: Prentice Hall, 1970), p. 1–2.

19. Franklin, *From Slavery,* p. 496.

20. Eric C. Lincoln, *The Black Muslims in America* (Canada: Saunders of Toronto, 1961), p. xxv.

Chapter 3

The Moorish Science Temple, 1913–1929

"Fard Muhammad studied Noble Drew Ali's approach to introduce the Koran to the black community. Professor Fard introduced the whole text of the Koran, in the very inception of the Nation of Islam. To introduce it he had to put it in the package of Drew Ali."

—Imam Wallace D. Muhammad
Chief Minister, World Community of
Al-Islam in the West

Social conditions after the Depression left Americans in general and the African American community in particular in a state of disorganization. High unemployment, low wages, discrimination in housing, and the treatment black servicemen received after World War I created discontent among African Americans. These social and economic factors made it conducive for a black nationalist movement to emerge as a vehicle for social reform.

The Nation of Islam evolved from the Moorish Science Organization, founded by Timothy Drew, who was born in North Carolina in 1886. (See Table 3.1) Drew was a semiliterate migrant to Newark, New Jersey, who worked as a train expressman before starting the first Moorish Science Temple there in 1913.

Drew came upon two revelations which radically influenced his thinking. "He encountered some forms of Oriental philosophy and was impressed with its racial catholicity."[1] According to the legend of the movement, Timothy Drew made a pilgrimage to North Africa "where he received a mission from the King of Morocco to teach Islam to the Negroes in the United States."[2] Drew had to pass a test to prove he was the prophet of Allah. The test involved the pyramids of Egypt, in which Drew was allegedly released inside and had to find his way out. Drew "mastered the pyramids and they knew he was the prophet; he came back to the Temple in New Jersey in 1913."[3]

Timothy Drew changed his name to Noble Drew Ali and began to spread his doctrine in basements, empty lots, and street corners of Newark, New Jersey. Noble Drew Ali had very little formal education, but "a certain magnetic charm, a sincerity of purpose and a real determination to lead his people out of the difficulties of racial prejudice and discrimination brought him followers."[4]

Table 3.1
Evolution of the Moorish Science Temple and the National of Islam

Moorish American
Science Temple

(Newark 1913)

NOBLE DREW ALI
(b. Timothy Drew)

Drew Ali dies (1929)

JOHN GIVENS EL and W. D. FARD

(each claims to be reincarnation of Noble Drew Ali)

Moors remain faithful to:

JOHN GIVENS EL	W. D. FARD
(Chicago 1930)	(Detroit 1930)
	Fard disappears (1933)

Two factions developed:

Fard as prophet,	Fard as Allah,
ABDUL MUHAMMAD	ELIJAH MUHAMMAD establishes headquarters in Chicago
	Nation of Islam

Nationality

Marcus Garvey's Universal Negro Improvement Association (UNIA) and Drew Ali's Moorish Science Temple flourished about the same time, though Garvey had many more followers than Ali. Garvey started the UNIA in Jamaica 1914 and founded a branch in Harlem in 1916.

Members of the Moorish Science Temple believe that Marcus Garvey "was a forerunner to plant the seed in the people and prepare them to be received by Noble Drew Ali."[5] Unlike Garvey, however, Drew Ali did not call for emigration to Africa. Drew Ali's nationalism was purely psychological.

Noble Drew Ali and his followers "sought a psychic escape by changing their names and the symbols of their culture; [they] hoped to change their social fortunes."[6] Drew Ali advocated that true emancipation would come through knowledge of black Americans' African heritage and by becoming Muslims. He also felt that Christianity was for Europeans and Islam was for people of African descent. Peace on earth is not possible, according to Ali, until each racial group has its own "true religion."

Noble Drew Ali advocated that individuals must know themselves and their nationality before they can know Allah. Drew Ali founded the Moorish Science Temple upon the idea that African Americans are Asiatics, specifically Moors, whose ancestors had come from Morocco. Moorish Americans were "descendants of the ancient Moabites who inhabited the northwestern and southwestern shores of Africa."[7] Drew Ali also taught his members to believe that when a star and crescent moon were seen in the sky, "this betokened the arrival of the day of the Asiatics and the destruction of the Europeans."[8]

Noble Drew Ali's doctrine inspired Master Fard Muhammad to create similar value systems for the nation of Islam. (See Table 3.2) During an interview with Imam Wallace D. Muhammad, he explained how Master Fard Muhammad taught members of the Nation of Islam that "we were Black Asiatics and that's what Drew Ali taught his people. Master Fard Muhammad taught us we were descendants from a great Islamic Kingdom and Drew Ali taught his people the same."[9] Drew Ali taught that people of African descent were subjugated to white domination because they used names like colored, black, or Ethiopian. Noble Drew Ali provided African-Americans ". . . with a new national origin that made them part of a far-flung Moorish Nation that had somehow made its way to North America."[10]

Noble Drew Ali's philosophy was published in his 64-page Holy Koran, a pamphlet consisting of principles from the Islamic Quran, the Christian Bible, some of Marcus Garvey's African nationalist ideas, and Drew Ali's own historical interpretations. The Holy Koran is regarded as a book to be read only by his followers.

The Holy Koran proclaimed that Noble Drew Ali was a prophet, ordained by Allah to carry the message of Islam to people of African descent in America. Membership in Ali's Moorish Science Temple was restricted to Asiatics only, by which he meant any person who is non-Caucasian. Moorish Americans, however, were overwhelmingly comprised of black people.

Table 3.2
Organizational Comparisons between the Moorish Science Temple
and the Nation of Islam

	Moorish Science Temple	Nation of Islam
Nationality	Moorish Americans	Asiatic-Black
Prophet	Noble Drew Ali	Elijah Muhammad
Religion	Islam	Islam
Land	No desire for separate state, psychological separation through Moorish status	Separate state
Sacred Text	Koran created by Noble Drew Ali	Islamic Quran and Christian Bible
God	Allah	Allah in the form of Fard Muhammad
Race	Asiatics	Asiatic Blacks (Tribe of Shabazz)
Place of Worship	Temple	Mosque
Heaven	In the mind	On earth
Separation of Sexes	Yes	Yes
Names	Bey, El	X—replaces slave name because real name is unknown
Dress	Men—fez worn during official functions, beards and mustaches allowed, suit and tie optional Women—turbans optional, no makeup, pants, long dresses to shoe tops	Men—suit and ties, clean-shaven Women—head covered, no makeup, long dresses to shoe tops
Citizenship	United States of America	Nation of Islam, Nation within a Nation

Rituals and Practices

When attending services in the temple, men and women are segregated. At all times male members wear a red fez with a black tassel. Men are allowed to wear beards, and when not attending official functions they may dress casually. The Fruit of Islam's uniforms in the Nation of Islam are fashioned after the Moorish Americans; "the dress Master Fard Muhammad originally gave male members of the Fruit of Islam is the same dress Drew Ali's people had."[11] Moorish American marriages are monogamous and divorce is rarely permitted. In most cases the husband is the only source of financial support and women are expected to be housewives.

Women wear pants or long dresses and no makeup. A turban is worn only with long dresses. It is not considered appropriate to wear pants with the turban. On Fridays (their Sabbath) women must wear long white dresses which fall below the knee when seated. On Sunday and Wednesday night meetings (8:00–10:00 P.M.), they are free to dress as they please, but they should never wear revealing clothes. Sunday School is conducted for children from 5 P.M. to 7 P.M.

Moorish Americans pray three times daily — at sunrise, noon, and sunset. When praying, members stand facing the east toward Mecca. They use two words of greeting, "peace" and "Islam" with the right hand raised and palm out. Moorish Americans attach special significance to their dress, especially the fez and turban. They believe the "fez is the first headdress worn by man and the turban the first headdress worn by woman. The fez and turban symbolize that knowledge is embedded within them and these wraps protect the wearer."[12] Moorish Americans also adhere to a strict vegetarian diet. No meat or eggs are to be eaten, but fish and vegetables are prescribed. Smoking, drinking liquor, straightening the hair, and using cosmetics are forbidden. Sports and games, attendance at motion pictures, and secular dancing are also discouraged.

Drew Ali created a Moorish flag which is red with a green five-pointed star in the center. The points on the star represent truth, love, peace, justice, and freedom. The Moorish flag is usually next to the American flag in all meetings. Moorish Americans are "loyal citizens of the United States and pledge allegiance to its flag."[13]

Organization

The Temple is the main organizational unit of the Moorish Science Movement. The national headquarters located in Chicago, originally had a membership of 10,000. Drew Ali established temples in Detroit, Harlem, Pittsburgh, Philadelphia, Kansas City, West Virginia, Brooklyn, Richmond (Virginia), South Carolina, and Augusta (Georgia). Overall membership is approximately 30,000. Financial support for the organization is derived from dues collected at the various temples and numerous businesses. Leaders of the temples are called grand sheiks. Beneath the sheiks are ministers, elders, and stewards. Rank-and-file members are referred to as brothers and sisters. All Moorish Americans must attach the term "El" or "Bey" to their names.

Free National Name

To become a member of the Moorish Science Temple individuals must affirm their desire to follow Noble Drew Ali and pay an initiation fee of $1.00. New members are given a free national name and a nationality card.

Moorish Americans refer to the El or Bey as their "free national name." The national name represents "African heritage which allows you to be a citizen in the international affair. In the affairs of nations those people not of a nation receive no consideration."[14] Moorish Americans are required to carry a nationality card which bears the following inscription:

(Replica of Star and Crescent)   Unity   (replica of Circle "7")

(Replica of Clasped Hands)

MEMBER'S NAME

This is your nationality and identification card for the Moorish Science Temple of America, and birthright for the Moorish Americans. We honor all the divine prophets, Jesus, Mohammad, Buddha, and Confucious. May the blessings of God of our father Allah, be upon you that carry this card. I do hereby declare that you are a Muslim under the Divine Law of the Holy Koran of Mecca—Love, Truth, Peace, Freedom, and Justice. "I am a citizen of the USA."

Noble Drew Ali, The Prophet
3810 Wabash Avenue
Chicago, Illinois

Moorish Americans believed the sight of the nationality card would stop individual and institutional oppression by white Americans. Members of the Moorish Science Temple began accosting "the white enemy on the streets, showing their membership card and buttons, and proclaiming in the name of their prophet, Noble Drew Ali, that they had been freed of European domination."[15] Soon after these altercations Drew Ali ordered his followers to stop "flashing your cards at Europeans."

Noble Drew Ali Reincarnated

In 1929, Drew Ali began to designate more power to his subordinates. His subordinates began to exploit the members by selling herbs, magic charms, and literature on the movement to the extent that some of them became wealthy. Drew Ali attempted to stop this dishonest practice and became a pawn in the struggle for power.

One of his sheiks, Claude Greene, a former butler of philanthropist Julius Rosenwald, challenged Drew Ali's leadership. Current members of the Moorish Science Temple advocate that Sheik Claude Greene was a minor character in the splintering of the organization. Noble Drew Ali was reputed to have taught four men and instructed them to carry out his mission. Elijah Muhammad was one of them. "Daddy Grace, Father Divine and Carlos Cookman, none of them did what Noble Drew Ali asked them to. All they wanted was that gold for themselves."[16]

During the conflict between the factions Sheik Claude Greene was shot to death on March 15, 1929, in the office at the Unity Club. Drew Ali was not in Chicago at the time; nevertheless, he was arrested and charged with the murder. Drew Ali was released on bond and died a few weeks later.

All theories of his death point to two circumstances. He either died from injuries inflicted by police during his imprisonment or was killed by followers loyal to Sheik Claude Greene.

The story of Noble Drew Ali's death is told differently by members of the Moorish Science Temple. George Bey, a Moorish American for twenty-five years and minister of Temple No. 7 in Richmond, Virginia, said "his health went bad on him; as far as I know he died a natural death."[17]

When Drew Ali died and Marcus Garvey was deported, there was a severe leadership crisis within the black nationalist movement. Two men, Master Fard Muhammad and John Givens El, attempted to solve the problem by claiming to be Noble Drew Ali reincarnated.

John Givens El was Noble Drew Ali's chauffeur. It is reputed that while he was working on Drew Ali's automobile, shortly after Ali's death, he fainted. John Givens El's eyes were examined; "He had the sign of the star and crescent in his eyes and they knew right then he was the prophet reincarnated into his chauffeur,"[18]

Those who believed John Givens El are the present-day Moorish Americans. Those who believed Master Fard Muhammad's reincarnation comprised what came to be known as the Nation of Islam.

The following chapter is a discussion of the Nation of Islam's doctrine under the leadership of Master Fard Muhammad and Chief Assistant, Elijah Muhammad.

Notes

1. Arthur F. Fauset, *Black Gods of the Metropolis* (Philadelphia: University of Pennsylvania Press, 1944), p. 41.

2. E. U. Essien-Udom, *Black Nationalism: A Search for an Identity in America* (Chicago: University of Chicago Press, 1962), p. 34.

3. Interview, Sam Bey, Member of Moorish Science Temple, Richmond, Virginia, August 4, 1976.

4. Fauset, *Black Gods,* p. 42.

5. Interview, Minister George Bey of Moorish Science Temple, Richmond, Virginia, August 4, 1976.

6. Eric C. Lincoln, *The Black Muslims in America* (Canada: Saunders of Toronto, 1961), p. 52.

7. Drew Ali, *The Holy Koran of the Moorish Holy Temple of Science* (Chicago: privately published, no date).

8. Fauset, *Black Gods,* p. 42.

9. Interview, Imam Wallace D. Muhammad, Chicago, Illinois, July 25, 1979.

10. Theodore Draper, *The Rediscovery of Black Nationalism* (New York: Viking Press, 1969), p. 70–71.

11. Interview, Imam Wallace D. Muhammad.

12. Interview, Frank Bey, Moorish Science Temple, August 4, 1976.

13. Draper, *Rediscovery,* p. 71.

14. Interview, Bill El, Moorish Science Temple, August 4, 1976.

15. Arna Bontemps and Jack Conroy, *They Seek a City* (New York: Doubleday, 1945), p. 176.

16. Interview, Minister George Bey.

17. Ibid.

18. Interview, Sam Bey, November 12, 1975.

Chapter 4

The Nation of Islam, 1930–1959

"The Nation of Islam was a religion and a social movement organization. In fact, the religion as it was introduced to the membership was more a social reform philosophy than Orthodox Islam."
—Imam Wallace D. Muhammad
Chief Minister, WCIW

During the summer of 1930, Master Fard Muhammad, often referred to as Professor Fard, appeared in the Paradise Valley community of Detroit, Michigan, claiming to be Noble Drew Ali reincarnated. Master Fard's mission was to gain freedom, justice, and equality for people of African descent residing in the United States. Master Fard proclaimed himself the leader of the Nation of Islam with remedies to cure problems in the African American community: "social problems, lack of economic development, undisciplined family life and alcoholism."[1]

Master Fard Muhammad claimed he was born in Mecca on February 26, 1877. His light color and Oriental features fostered the belief that he was an Arab. Fard maintained he was of royal ancestry, "the son of a wealthy member of the tribe of Kareish to which the prophet Muhammad belonged."[2] Master Fard was reputed to have received an education at the University of California and spent several years studying in England to "be trained for a diplomatic career in the service of the kingdom of Hejaz."[3]

Master Fard Muhammad earned a living as a street peddler. He pushed a cart along the streets selling silks and artifacts door-to-door. Master Fard claimed the silks and clothing were like the garb worn by blacks in their original homeland, Africa. When Master Fard gained access to people's homes, he discussed three concepts which became the foundation of his ideology: "Allah is God, the white man is the devil and the so-called Negroes are the Asiatic Black people, the cream of the planet earth."[4]

Master Fard Muhammad taught from the Bible until he introduced the Quran to his membership. Master Fard published two documents containing his doctrine, *Teachings for the Lost-Found Nation in a Mathematical Way* and *Secret Ritual of the Nation of Islam,* which were orally transmitted. Freedom, justice, and equality could not be achieved in the United States, Master Fard felt, until blacks regained their true religion (Islam), their language (Arabic), and a separate autonomous state.

Gradually Master Fard Muhammad introduced himself to his followers as a "Christ figure to displace the old Christ that Christianity gave black people."[5] Master Fard was accepted as a Christ figure because he convinced his followers "that Christianity is geared toward the enslavement of the individual's mind. It demands the imagination of a child to accept something unseen and immaterial."[6]

To reinforce his Christ image Master Fard often mesmerized his followers with feats of magic. Once, members placed strands of their hair in a pile and Master Fard took a strand of hair from his head and with it lifted all of them up. Followers interpreted this to mean "Lift me up and I will draw all men unto me."[7] Often Master Fard would attend sermons and his hair would be completely gray; "he would appear the next time and [have] no gray hair. He made it a purpose to draw their attention to that."[8]

Master Fard perceived Christianity as the white man's religion, one that didn't offer solutions to social problems or development of the "Asiatic Nation." Members of the Nation of Islam also believe that white people have learned to be evil and, therefore, it is not in their nature to accept Islam and become Muslims. However, Islam is the nature of black people. Master Fard Muhammad also perceived a "natural" conflict between Islam and Christianity. This conflict would ultimately be resolved through the Battle of Armageddon, which he defined as a religious war between Muslims and Christians.

Master Fard began to arrange more meetings in private homes and gathered a small devoted group of followers. The former peddler assumed the role of the prophet. Membership at the house meetings became so large that his followers rented a hall which they called their temple. At that point the Nation of Islam was born.

Between 1930 and 1933, Master Fard Muhammad recruited 8,000 followers among Detroit blacks. The rapid growth of Fard's organization made it necessary for Master Fard to train several ministers to help manage the organization's affairs. One of the first ministers was an unemployed auto worker named Elijah Poole.

Elijah Poole was born in Sandersville, Georgia, on October 7, 1898. His father, Wallace Poole, was a Baptist minister and a sharecropper who supported a wife and thirteen children. Elijah attended public schools in Georgia. He "learned only the bare rudiments of reading, writing, and arithmetic before he had to go to the fields to help his family earn a living."[9]

Elijah Poole worked in Sandersville and in Macon, Georgia, as a laborer for the Southern Railroad. Later he was employed as a builder for the Cherokee Brick Company and was appointed foreman in 1919. While Poole was employed in Macon, he met and married Clara Evans. In 1923, Elijah, Clara, and their two sons (Emmanuel and Nathaniel) moved to Detroit. The Poole family increased to four more sons (Herbert, Elijah II, Wallace, Akbar) and two daughters (Ethel and Lotta).

Elijah Poole worked for the Chevrolet Auto Plant in Detroit from 1923 to 1929. The Depression caused the family to go on relief for two years, from 1929 to 1931.

One night in 1931, Elijah Poole attended one of Master Fard Muhammad's sermons. While talking to Master Fard after the meeting, Poole said, "I know who you are, you're God himself." Master Fard whispered to Poole, "That's right, but don't tell it now. It is not yet time for me to be known."[10]

Shortly after Poole encountered Master Fard, he began to study Islam. Elijah Poole became a minister and was given the name Kariem and eventually adopted the name Elijah Muhammad. Elijah Muhammad was so devoted to Master Fard that he was named the Chief Minister of Islam and became Master Fard's eventual successor.

Elijah Muhammad was the son of a Baptist minister; that is one reason why "Master Fard Muhammad chose him because he was so learned in the Bible. The people were already bible oriented."[11]

In 1932, Elijah Muhammad moved to Chicago where he established Temple No. 2. He returned to Detroit to aid Master Fard, who had been imprisoned that year. Released and ordered out of Detroit on May 26, 1933, Master Fard went to Temple No. 2 in Chicago and was arrested again. After a series of police confrontations, Master Fard gradually withdrew from the organization. When Master Fard left, Elijah Muhammad taught his followers that Master Fard was God in person. Master Fard's absence fortified the belief that he was God momentarily assuming a human form to alleviate the oppression suffered by African Americans. Elijah Muhammad was almost "single-handedly responsible for the deification of Fard and for the perpetuation of his teachings in the early years after Fard disappeared."[12] One of the ministers of the organization, Abdul Muhammad, organized a group of Muslims loyal to the constitution of the United States. A different faction which believed Master Fard was Allah, established an organization in Chicago in 1934 under the guidance of Elijah Muhammad. The Detroit Temple eventually became a branch of Elijah Muhammad's organization.

Temple No. 2 became the main headquarters for the Nation of Islam after Master Fard's disappearance. Temple No. 2 in Chicago was located at 5335 South Greenwood Avenue and adjacent to it is the University of Islam at 5333 South Greenwood Avenue. In his role as messenger of Allah, Elijah Muhammad became the master architect to develop the ideology started by Master Fard Muhammad.

Elijah Muhammad ran his organization as the absolute authority. Muhammad appointed ministers of each temple; he also appointed supreme captains who were responsible to him. Beneath the supreme captains were captains, then first, second and third lieutenants. The temples were not autonomous; all order had to be cleared through Elijah Muhammad.

Nationality

Individuals interested in becoming members of the Nation of Islam were required to send the following letter to the Chicago headquarters address:

Mr. E. Muhammad
4847 S. Woodlawn Avenue
Chicago 15, Illinois

Dear Mr. Muhammad:

I have been attending the teachings of Islam by one of your Ministers. I believe in It, and I bear witness that there is no God but Allah, and that Muhammad is Thy Servant and Apostle. I desire to reclaim my Own. Please give me my Original name. My slave name is as follows:

Name

Address

City and State

After forwarding this letter, the prospective member was required to answer several questions concerning marital status, number of children, and age. When this procedure was completed individuals were assigned their X. The Nation of Islam requires members to change their last names to X in order to rid themselves of their "slave names." The X also stands for the unknown identity associated with the African ancestry. Each member of a temple is assigned an X. If there are two people with the same first name, a number of attached to the X. For example, if James X is a member of Temple No. 2 and James Smith becomes a Muslim and also joins Temple No. 2, he is designated James IX.

Members of the Nation of Islam referred to their nationality as Asiatics, "descendants of the original black nation of Asia, of the Great Asiatic nation, from the continent of Africa."[13]

Within the Asiatic nation is a group known as the "Tribe of Shabazz," which they believed originated in Africa when a great explosion divided the earth from the moon some 60 trillion years ago. The Tribe of Shabazz discovered "the best part of our planet to live on, the rich Nile Valley of Egypt and the present seat of the Holy City, Mecca."[14] Elijah Muhammad's Tribe of Shabazz is an attempt to equip black Americans with an African identity. The Nation of Islam helped the membership to believe "at least in fantasy, the glorious history of Black Afro-Asia."[15]

The Tribe of Shabazz (people of African descent) were enslaved for four hundred years. African Americans constitute the Nation of Islam. Master Fard Muhammad and his messenger Elijah Muhammad were sent to relocate the "lost-found nation" in an independent state. Elijah Muhammad renounced his citizenship and urged his followers to do the same. Muhammad taught that, "we [so-called negroes] are not and cannot be American Citizens, since we are not Americans by nature or race."[16]

The Devil

The "white man is the devil" theme propagated by the Nation of Islam was a direct inspiration from the teachings of Noble Drew Ali. Drew Ali "identified white people with the embodiment of evil in Scripture, which is Satan."[17]

Drew Ali interpreted the Bible to define whites "as the rider on the pale horse," which was a symbol of death. He "took that out of the Bible to identify the white man as the pale horse, whose rider is death."[18] Master Fard Muhammad was a student of comparative religious studies. He was able to detect "what the average follower of Drew Ali couldn't. The Caucasian race is the embodiment of evil. Fard came out in plain language and said they are devils."[19]

Part of the Muslim doctrine created the Tribe of Shabazz; another segment introduced an elaborate mythology which depicted the devil as white people. The doctrine describes a scientist named Yacub, who was a descendant of the Tribe of Shabazz 6800 years ago in the Holy City of Mecca. Yacub ran into conflict with Meccan authorities and was exiled with 59,999 of his followers to an island called Patmos in the Aegean Sea. There Yacub created a vengeful plot to enslave the Tribe of Shabazz. Yacub was skilled in genetics, and through crossbreeding he supposedly developed the white race.

It took Yacub several stages to create whites out of the black race. First he created the brown; two hundred years later he created the red race from brown. It took two hundred more years to create the yellow race from the red, and more than six thousand years ago he created the white race out of the yellow.

The first white person Yacub created was Adam and soon Eve followed. Adam's descendants, "at first walking on all fours and living in caves and trees (also mating with beast) stayed on Patmos for six hundred years before they escaped to the mainland."[20]

After two thousand years, Allah raised up Moses to civilize the white race, but even Moses found this task difficult. Yacub's white race was destined to rule for six thousand years until 1914.

Separatism

Members of the Nation of Islam believed that their organization was a black nation within the United States and that Muslims were citizens of Mecca who saluted the Islamic flag.

Muslims believed that African Americans must free themselves physically (a separate state) and psychologically (Asiatics). Separation "can take a psychological, a religious and an economic form even if it cannot express itself in the ultimate guise of a national territory."[21]

Vertical (upward) mobility in the United States' system is limited by institutional racism and economic inequality. Elijah Muhammad felt the solution was not integration into the system, but separation. Charles 4X Jackson, a Muslim, compared Elijah Muhammad to Moses. He said, "Elijah is Moses, he is the one saying 'Pharaoh, let my people go.' He's saying, 'Let's separate, we want to leave the white man.' "[22]

The program of the Nation of Islam made an appeal for a separate state, but if a separate state was not obtained, they demanded equal employment opportunity and justice for African Americans.

Elijah Muhammad advocated, "We have as much right to the soil as the white man. Why should we claim the land of our Black brother in Africa; our destiny is right here in America."[23] Elijah Muhammad explained his position as follows:

> We want to establish a separate state or territory to ourselves in this country or elsewhere. Our former slave masters are obligated to maintain, to supply our needs in this zone or territory for the next twenty-five years, until we are able to produce and supply our own needs."[24]

A separate state within the United States is a fantasy. For internal security reasons the government would not allow it, a reality Elijah Muhammad himself was aware of. Elijah Muhammad admitted, "They will never give us three or four states. That I probably know, but that doesn't hinder you and me from asking for it."[25]

Self-Help

Elijah Muhammad's economic program is an attempt to encourage self-help through collective ownership of business. Members must adhere to a strict moral and economic code which will foster thrift, capital gain, independence and self-respect. Muslims pray five times a day, eat once a day, and abstain from pork, alcohol, tobacco, narcotics, gambling, sports, long vacations from work, and sleeping more than is necessary for health.

Each individual within the organization is responsible for his or her own behavior and must assist others in adhering to the code of ethics. "Doing your own thing" is not permitted. Sharon Shabazz, a Muslim official, says lack of discipline is "destroying the moral fiber of the whole country. Alcohol, smoking whether it's dope or cigarettes, it destroys the moral standard, the physical being and the society."[26]

Muslims advocate complete economic independence from white America. But until they achieve a "state," their economic survival depends on the establishment of a black business industry which provides jobs for members and consumable supplies and services to the community. Muslims are encouraged to pool their resources and invest in the black business.

To accomplish economic security for the Nation of Islam, Elijah Muhammad created an "Economic Blueprint" which consists of five propositions:

1. Recognize the necessity for unity and group operation (activities).
2. Pool your resources, physically as well as financially.
3. Stop wanton criticism, of everything that is black-owned and black-operated.
4. Keep in mind—jealousy destroys from within.
5. Work hard in a collective manner.[27]

Muslims also regularly give part of their income to the nation of Islam. These contributions are given as "alms" (for the "cause of Islam"). The author has attended several meetings and witnessed a literal competition between members giving what they could afford. From the highest bill to the smallest copper coin, each cent which was donated to the cause received a loud "Praise Allah!"

The University of Islam

Established in the 1930s by Elijah Muhammad, the University of Islam provided schooling for students in grades four through twelve. During its first years of operation, the Detroit Board of Education attempted to close the University of Islam and return the students to public schools. Several Muslim teachers, including Elijah Muhammad, were arrested for contributing to the delinquency of minors. The court released the Muslims and suspended the sentences.

Currently the institution is known as Clara Muhammad School. The curriculum includes African and African American history, language skills, math, science and Islamic relations. Observance of dietary laws is encouraged and there is a Parent-Teacher Association. Muslim children go to school fifty weeks a year with no vacation (except for holidays Muslims observe). There is no sport or play; rest, snack, and free periods are eliminated.

The girls, clad in long dresses, their heads mostly covered by scarves, attend school in the morning from 8:00 to 11:00 A.M. They are taught the same academic subjects as boys. To supplement their formal education, they attend the "Muslim Girls in Training" course (MGT), which teaches basic domestic skills—housekeeping, child-rearing, and hygiene.

There is a junior MGT for young women between the ages of 15 and 19. Originally, the 15- to 19-year-old group was called the General Civilization Class. Women in the organization were required to adhere to the following rules, referred to as "Laws of Islam":

1. Do not use lipstick or makeup.
2. Do not wear hair up unless wearing long dress.
3. Do not smoke or drink alcohol.
4. Do not commit adultery.
5. Do not use pork in any form.
6. Do not cook in aluminum utensils.
7. Do not wear heels over 1½ inches.
8. Do not dance with anyone except one's husband.

Young boys are expected to be members of the Fruit of Islam, which is divided into age groups: for children and adolescents from 1 to 16 years old, from 16 to 35 years old, and men over 35. Each temple has a unit of the Fruit of Islam. A captain leads it and has a staff composed of several lieutenants, drill masters, and secretaries. Members are also trained in self-defense techniques. The purpose of the Fruit of Islam is three-fold:

1. to protect organizational officials and property;
2. to reinforce the doctrine and objective of the organization;
3. to prepare for the race war known as Armageddon.

There is a nominal tuition charge at the University of Islam. The organization also provides adult education classes for its members.

The period from 1935 to 1946 represented difficult times in the development of the Nation of Islam. When the United States entered World War II, Elijah Muhammad was arrested and found guilty for refusing to comply with the Selective Service Act. Elijah Muhammad, his son Emmanuel, and several other Muslims were charged "with evading the draft and influencing others to do so, and also with maintaining relations with the Japanese government. The later indictment more or less petered out."[28]

Elijah Muhammad was sentenced to the federal penitentiary in Milan, Michigan, and served four years, from 1942 to 1946. Elijah and Emmanuel established a temple in the penitentiary, where they held services on Wednesday and Friday evenings and Sunday afternoons. They made many converts in prison. Many Muslims would leave one prison and convert others; once released, they would joint the temple in their communities.

While Elijah and Emmanuel were in prison, Clara Muhammad, Elijah's wife, was instrumental in keeping the movement together. Clara Muhammad was the supreme secretary of the movement during Elijah Muhammad's incarceration. The "orders came from him [Elijah Muhammad] to her to the ministers and captains. She was executing his decision for him while he was in prison."[29]

Elijah Muhammad's imprisonment appeared a martyrdom to his followers and it enhanced his position upon his release from the federal penitentiary. He returned to Chicago as the undisputed leader of the Nation of Islam.

When Elijah Muhammad was paroled from prison, there was one temple each in Detroit, Chicago, Milwaukee, and Washington, D.C. In the 1950s the Nation of Islam began to establish temples throughout the country. A primary reason for expansion of the organization was the recruitment of a former inmate named Malcolm Little. In 1948 Malcolm Little was serving a ten-year prison term for grand larceny in the Norfolk Prison Colony in Massachusetts. During this time his older brother, Philbert, joined the Nation of Islam and began to correspond with him on the "natural religion for the black man." Malcolm began to correspond with Elijah Muhammad and read Muslim literature. Malcolm, known as Satan by fellow inmates because of his antireligious beliefs, began to pray to Allah. One night Malcolm had a vision "of a man with a light-brown skin, an Asiatic countenance and oily black hair sitting beside his prison bed."[30] Malcolm believed the man in his vision was Master Fard Muhammad.

During the spring of 1952 Malcolm Little was paroled from prison and went to Detroit Temple No. 1. He joined the Nation of Islam and received his X. Malcolm "came right out of prison and became a minister; he didn't take on the thinking and behavior of the old conservative ministerial body."[31] Minister Malcolm "became a familiar figure on Harlem street corners, holding large audiences spellbound."[32]

In 1959 Malcolm X created the organization's newspaper, *Muhammad Speaks,* which was an extension of Elijah Muhammad's column in the *Pittsburgh Courier,* the *Los Angeles Herald Dispatch,* the *Chicago Defender,* and the *Chicago News Crusader.* It had a circulation of over 500,000. During the same year, Malcolm X was appointed national spokesman by Elijah Muhammad. Elijah Muhammad recognized the appeal of the tall, handsome, and articulate Malcolm X and often told his older ministers, "You're teaching the same thing we taught in the thirties. Malcolm X is in modern times; he knows how to help me."[33] Malcolm X emerged as the major voice of the Nation of Islam. His appointment as national spokesman made Malcolm X a leading figure in the organization. Elijah Muhammad "welcomed this new blood. He gave Malcolm free reign to preach his doctrine.[34] Slowly Malcolm X began to alter the doctrine and influence membership on the virtues of Orthodox Islam. The transformation from black Muslims to Muslims began in the early 1960s with the emerging leadership of Malcolm X.

Chapter five will describe the contribution of Malcolm X to the development of the Nation of Islam.

Program and Position

What Muslims Want:

1. We want freedom. We want a full, complete freedom.
2. We want justice, equal justice under the law. We want justice applied equally regardless of creed, class or color.
3. We want equality of opportunity.
4. We want our people in America whose parents or grandparents were descendants from slaves to be allowed to establish a separate state or territory of their own.
5. We want freedom of all believers of Islam now held in federal prison.
6. We want an immediate end to the police brutality and mob attacks against the so-called Negroes throughout the United States.
7. As long as we are not allowed to establish a state or territory of our own, we demand not only equal justice under the laws of the United States, but equal employment opportunities now!
8. We want the government of the United States to exempt our people from all taxation as long as we are deprived of equal justice under the laws of the land.
9. We want equal education—but separate schools, up to sixteen for boys and eighteen for girls on the condition that the girls be sent to women's colleges and universities. We want all black children educated, taught, and trained by their own teachers.

What Muslims Believe:

1. We believe in the one God whose proper name is Allah.
2. We believe in the Holy Koran and in the scriptures of all the prophets of God.

3. We believe in the truth of the Bible, but we believe that it has been tampered with and must be reinterpreted so that mankind will not be snared by the falsehoods that have been added to it.
4. We believe in Allah's prophets and the scriptures they brought to the people.
5. We believe in the resurrection of the dead—not in physical resurrection—but in mental resurrection. We believe that the so-called Negroes are most in need of mental resurrection. Therefore, they will be resurrected first. Furthermore, we believe we are the people of God's choice.
6. We believe in the judgment. We believe this first judgment will take place as God revealed, in America.
7. We believe this is the time in history for the separation of the so-called Negroes and the so-called white Americans.
8. We believe in justice for all, whether in God or not; we believe as others, that we are due equal justice as human beings. We believe in equality—as a nation—of equals. We do not believe that we are equal with our slave masters in the status of "freed slaves." We recognize and respect American citizens as independent people and we respect their laws which govern this nation.
9. We believe that the offer of integration is hypocritical and is made by those who are trying to deceive the black people into believing that their 400-year-old open enemies of freedom, justice, and equality are, all of a sudden, their "friends."
10. We believe that intermarriage or race-mixing should be prohibited.
11. We believe that we who declared ourselves to be righteous Muslims should not participate in wars which take the lives of humans.
12. We believe our women should be respected and protected as the women of other nationalities are respected and protected.
13. We believe that Allah (God) appeared in the person of Master W. Fard Muhammad, July 1930; the long awaited "Messiah" of the Christians and the "Mahdi" of the Muslims.

Notes

1. Interview, Imam Wallace D. Muhammad, Chicago, Illinois, July 25, 1979.
2. Arna Bontemps and Jack Conroy, *They Seek a City* (New York: Doubleday, 1945), p. 217.
3. Ibid.
4. Interview, Charles 4X Jackson, member of the Nation of Islam, Los Angeles, California, April 4, 1970.

5. Interview, Imam Wallace D. Muhammad.

6. Interview, James 2X Jones, member of the Nation of Islam, Richmond, Virginia, July 5, 1976.

7. Interview, Imam Wallace D. Muhammad.

8. Ibid.

9. Elijah Muhammad, *Message to the Blackman in America* (Chicago: Muhammad's Mosque No. 2, 1965), pp. 178–179.

10. *Muhammad Speaks,* Special Issue, April 1972.

11. Interview, Imam Wallace D. Muhammad.

12. Eric C. Lincoln, *The Black Muslims in America* (Canada: Saunders in Toronto, 1961), p. 15.

13. Theodore Draper, *The Rediscovery of Black Nationalism* (New York: Viking Press, 1969), p. 79.

14. Muhammad, *Message,* p. 120.

15. Lincoln, *Black Muslims,* p. 13.

16. Muhammad, *Message,* p. 183.

17. Interview, Imam Wallace D. Muhammad.

18. Ibid.

19. Ibid.

20. Bontemps and Conroy, *They Seek,* p. 228.

21. Draper, *Rediscovery,* p. 84.

22. Interview, Charles 4X Jackson.

23. Muhammad, *Message,* p. xiv.

24. Ibid.

25. E. U. Essien-Udom, *Black Nationalism: A Search for an Identity in America* (Chicago: University of Chicago Press, 1962), p. 286.

26. Interview, Sharon Shabazz, Nation of Islam, New York City, December 16, 1975.

27. Muhammad, *Message,* p. 174.

28. Bontemps and Conroy, *They Seek,* p. 224.

29. Interview, Imam Wallace D. Muhammad.

30. Draper, *Rediscovery,* p. 84.

31. Interview, Imam Wallace D. Muhammad.

32. Bontemps and Conroy, *They Seek,* p. 232.

33. Interview, Imam Wallace D. Muhammad.

34. Ibid.

Chapter 5

Minister Malcolm X Shabazz, 1925–1965

"Minister Malcolm's contribution to the changes that took place in the Nation of Islam goes further back than my own. When I was a young man, maybe the early twenties, Malcolm X was an influence in my life."
— Imam Wallace D. Muhammad,
Chief Minister, WCIW

Malcolm X Shabazz was a leading spokesman in the struggle for human rights. His influence and charisma transcended the Nation of Islam and the domicile of the United States.

By the time Minister Malcolm X met his death via an assassin's bullet, he had become an international leader. Imam Wallace D. Muhammad's quote above attests to Malcolm's significance in the alteration of the Nation of Islam's ideology. Malcolm X Shabazz was the chief spokesman and traveling representative of Elijah Muhammad for twelve years. Malcolm's dynamic personality and articulate speaking was instrumental in recruiting, organizing temples, and providing exposure domestically and internationally for the Nation of Islam. Most of Malcolm's career was associated with developing and propagating the ideology of the Nation of Islam.

Malcolm brought youth, individuality, and often conflict during the caucuses of Elijah Muhammad's ministerial body. Initially, Elijah Muhammad welcomed and encouraged Malcolm. Eventually Malcolm's intellectual growth and the changing current of the African American and Third World struggle drove a wedge between Malcolm and Elijah Muhammad.

Malcolm adopted three names during his life; each represented an evolutionary stage in his ideological development and life-style. "Pulled from the mud" by a religious conversion in prison, Malcolm Little, or "Detroit Red," as he was known, was a pimp, racketeer, and dope pusher. After his acceptance of the Nation of Islam's doctrine, Malcolm X became a black nationalist devoted to the separatist teachings of Elijah Muhammad. When he defected from the Black Muslims and accepted Orthodox Islam, Malcolm then adopted the name El Hajj Malik El-Shabazz.

Malcolm described his life as one of changes. Where Malcolm would have gone ideologically, had he not been assassinated, can only be guessed. He was in the process of developing his new perspective before his death. Where he came from and what he did in his lifetime is a remarkable biography.

Malcolm Little was born May 19, 1925, in Omaha, Nebraska. His father, the Reverend Earl Little, was tall (six feet four inches) and "very, very dark." Malcolm's mother, Louise, was born in Grenada, which was then a British colony in the Caribbean.

The Little family consisted of eight children; Earl supported them as a free-lance Baptist minister. He also was an organizer for Marcus Garvey's Universal Negro Improvement Association. Young Malcolm often accompanied his father to UNIA meetings and was impressed as the Garveyites exclaimed, "Africa for Africans and Ethiopia Awake."

Reverend Little raised the ire of the local white community because of his attempts to organize black people in Omaha. Their home was burned to the ground one evening by the Ku Klux Klan while he was away.

Shortly after the birth of Malcolm, the Littles moved to Milwaukee and eventually to Lansing, Michigan. When Malcolm was six years old his father was murdered. "He was attacked and then laid across some tracks for a street car to run over him."[1] Malcolm believed that he would die a violent death too, as so many men in his family had.

Louise Little raised her eight children during the Depression. Eventually, the strain of poverty and the dehumanizing welfare system rendered Mrs. Little helpless. She suffered "a complete breakdown and the court orders were finally signed. They took her to the state mental hospital at Kalamazoo."[2] Mrs. Little remained in the hospital for twenty-six years. The children were supported in state institutions, boarding homes, or lived with relatives.

During his elementary school years, Malcolm Little was an exceptional student. He was the only black person in his class at Mason Junior High School and was elected class president in the seventh grade. Malcolm participated in basketball and, urged on by the success of his brother Philbert, boxed as a bantam weight. Malcolm's height and raw-boned frame enabled him to deceive the officials into believing he was sixteen years old—even though he was just thirteen at that time. His boxing career ended when he was knocked out twice by the "same white boy."

During a Careers Day at Mason Junior High, Malcolm was reprimanded by his counselor for aspiring to become a lawyer. The school counselor suggested carpentry as a realistic occupation for a "nigger."

From that moment on, Malcolm became alienated from school, Lansing, and white America. He began corresponding with his older sister Ella in Boston, requesting to live with her. Ella gained official custody of Malcolm, transferring him from Michigan to Massachusetts.

The move from Lansing to Boston was the beginning of Malcolm's street education which catapulted him into a life of crime. Between the ages of fifteen and twenty-one, Malcolm spent his life in the ghettos of Boston and Harlem engaged in part-time "legal" employment—drugs, gambling, and hustling.

Ella lived in the Sugar Hill section of Roxbury, which was largely black middle-class, but the life-style of the urban poor and working class attracted young Malcolm like a magnet.

Malcolm's first job was shining shoes in the Roseland State Ballroom where he unscuffed the toes of great musicians like Duke Ellington, Count Basie, Lionel Hampton, and Lester Young. While employed at Roseland, Malcolm began to smoke marijuana, play numbers, wear zoot suits, "conk" his hair red, and dance a frantic Lindy Hop. Malcolm left Roseland and was employed by the railroad as the fourth cook on the *Yankee Clipper,* which traveled between Boston and New York City. Malcolm's first visit to Harlem narcotized him. In Small's Paradise Bar, Malcolm said that he was "awed within the first five minutes in Small's; I had left Boston and Roxbury forever."[3]

In 1942, at the age of seventeen, he quit his railroad job and became a waiter in Small's. Malcolm Little was on his way to becoming "one of the most depraved, parasitical hustlers among New York's eight million people."[4] Malcolm was eventually fired and barred from Small's for procuring a prostitute for a serviceman while in the restaurant.

When Malcolm was dismissed from Small's, he turned to crime for full-time employment and acquired the name "Detroit Red." Initially, he sold reefers (marijuana cigarettes), but within six months Malcolm began to engage in armed robbery. Armed with a .32, .38, or .45 caliber pistol and snorting cocaine for courage, "Detroit Red" prowled the streets looking for victims.

Malcolm was almost twenty-one before he was arrested and sentenced to up to ten years on a burglary charge. In February of 1946 Malcolm Little was sent to Charlestown State Prison and in 1948 he was transferred to the Norfolk Prison Colony. He served a total of six years in prison.

Malcolm Little underwent a religious conversion in prison, with encouraging words from his family to "face east and pray to Allah." Malcolm began to investigate the Nation of Islam and correspond with Elijah Muhammad. Malcolm spent most of his time studying, researching, and developing his penmanship. He took correspondence courses in English and Latin, and developed his vocabulary by memorizing a dictionary. Malcolm developed his political consciousness by reading volumes of African and African American history and Oriental philosophy. He eventually led prison debates and discussion groups, which enhanced his public speaking.

Malcolm Little was released on parole at the age of twenty-seven, after six years in prison. When he was released in August of 1952, he was a "Black Muslim," although he had not acquired his X. By writing Elijah Muhammad weekly and being counseled by his brothers, Wilfred and Philbert, "Detroit Red" became a devoted follower of

Elijah Muhammad. He spent the next twelve years totally devoted to the Nation of Islam and mesmerized by Elijah Muhammad.

Throughout his career as a Muslim, Malcolm was a diligent recruiter, tireless worker (he routinely worked eighteen-hour days), and devout Muslim. His Pan-African ideology and Orthodox Islamic beliefs developed later in his career as he studied and traveled domestically and abroad.

Malcolm moved to Detroit after his parole to live with his brother Wilfred. There he received his X in Temple No. 1, the original temple organized by Master Fard Muhammad. The Detroit Temple was located in a storefront at 1470 Frederick Street. Most of Muhammad's temples were located in the urban black community. During the early years of the Nation of Islam, the organization owned very little property, so most of the temples were rented halls, frequently on the second floor of a commercial establishment. The Chicago headquarters and the Washington, D.C. temples are notable exceptions since they were built and owned by the Nation of Islam.

It was the practice each month for the Detroit Temple to motorcade caravan-style to Chicago to hear sermons by Elijah Muhammad. The Sunday before Labor Day in 1952, a two-car caravan transported Malcolm X and several ministers to Chicago.

During this period Malcolm was employed by the Garwood Furniture Company and later as an assembly worker with the Ford Motor Company. Every evening after work Malcolm walked the ghetto looking for new recruits in bars, poolrooms, and on street corners.

Malcolm's aggressive tactics tripled the membership and in a few months he led a caravan of twenty-five automobiles to Chicago to hear Elijah Muhammad speak. Needless to say, Elijah Muhammad was very pleased by the increased membership generated by the converted ex-convict, Malcolm X. During the summer of 1953, Malcolm X was appointed assistant minister of Temple No. 1 and became a full-time minister for the Nation of Islam.

In larger temples, ministers devote all their time to organization activities. The minister receives support from donations made by temple members and his home, car, and family necessities are supplied by the temple membership. Ministers in smaller temples work a full-time job to support themselves.

Malcolm X began to serve as Elijah Muhammad's prime minister throughout the United States, going from city to city preaching, recruiting, and establishing new temples. In the 1950s a period of expansion began for the Nation of Islam. Malcolm X helped to establish most of the one hundred temples in the United States. He was "criss-crossing through North America, sometimes as often as four times a week."[5] From Detroit, Malcolm X was sent to Boston to organize Temple No. 11.

In March 1954 Malcolm moved from Boston to Philadelphia, and in three months Temple No. 12 was opened in the City of Brotherly Love. From Philadelphia, Malcolm X moved to New York City and became minister of Temple No. 7.

Malcolm X returned to New York, where a few short years before his colleagues had been West Indian Archie, Sammy the Pimp, and Cadillac Drake. Clean-shaven and walking tall in suit and tie, his former friends in crime exclaimed in disbelief, "Red, my man! This can't be you!"

From the storefront of Temple No. 7 Malcolm roamed the borough of Manhattan, recruiting on street corners, in Christian churches, and in other nationalist groups. On weekdays he traveled by bus and train to preach in other parts of the country. Many times he preached in private homes until the membership became large enough to rent a temple.

Malcolm's impatience with older, more conservative ministers and the pace of the development of the organization provoked Elijah Muhammad to chastise him often.

Malcolm wanted to recruit more followers, build more temples, and hire better ministers. Malcolm believed that he increased the membership from four hundred to forty thousand in the few years after he joined. Elijah Muhammad needed Malcolm's charisma and organizational skills, but he also had to temper his enthusiasm.

The only thing that kept Malcolm under control during his early years was his complete devotion and trust in Elijah Muhammad and Malcolm's own ideological development. Though chastising Malcolm as he did, Elijah Muhammad continued to support Malcolm's evangelistic style.

In 1955, Malcolm organized Temple No. 15 in Atlanta, Georgia. To reward and assist the young minister, the Nation of Islam supplied him with a new 1956 Chevrolet. Malcolm X put thirty thousand miles on the automobile in five months. In 1957, Elijah Muhammad sent Malcolm X west where he organized the Los Angeles Temple.

Prior to Malcolm's tenure, the Nation of Islam was successful in recruiting poor and working-class black people, but few educated and skilled individuals joined their ranks. By 1957, the Nation of Islam began to attract the educated, academics, people with vocational skills, civil servants, nurses, clerks, and salespersons. A more remarkable metamorphosis appeared among the ministers of the Nation of Islam. Elijah Muhammad was often perturbed over his inability to attract younger educated people in general, and younger educated ministers in particular.

Imam Wallace D. Muhammad explained how Malcolm persuaded the youth to follow Elijah Muhammad: "Malcolm's new thinking, courage, and youth attracted most of the young people into following the Honorable Elijah Muhammad and I was one of them."[6]

In examining the education and background of the nine most active ministers, there is a distinct difference between the type of ministers active prior to Malcolm and the type that joined the organization after Malcolm.

Four of the nine ministers were members of the Nation of Islam prior to 1953: James 3X Anderson, Chicago; James 3X McGregor, Newark; Isaiah Karriem Edwards, Baltimore; and Wilfred X Little (Malcolm's brother), Detroit.

Anderson, McGregor, and Edwards became Muslims in the early 1940s and each served a prison term for refusing to register for the military draft. Each had been a Muslim for years before attaining the status of minister. The fourth minister was Malcolm's brother Wilfred who, though a member of the Nation of Islam prior to 1953, had not yet risen to a leadership position.The remaining five of the nine leading ministers joined the Nation of Islam after Malcolm became a leading official. They were Lonnie 3X Cross, Washington, D.C.; Bernard X Cushmere, San Francisco; John Shabazz, Los Angeles; Jeremiah X Pugh, Philadelphia; and Louis X Walcott, who eventually succeeded Malcolm X as national spokesman, Boston. All of these ministers had at least a high school or college education, one being a Ph.D. and a former college professor. Louis X Walcott was a former calypso singer, poet, and playwright. Their average age was thirty-three. Seven of the nine ministers owned their conversion to Malcolm and were assisted by him in gaining their leadership status.

The influential ministerial body was significant, but still subordinate to Elijah Muhammad and the Nation of Islam's hierarchy stationed in Chicago. The organization's elite leaders consisted of most of the members of Elijah Muhammad's immediate family: Hassan Sharrieff, Elijah Muhammad's grandson, was in charge of public relations; Herbert Muhammad—publisher of *Muhammad Speaks*; Elijah Muhammad, Jr.—assistant supreme captain of the Fruit of Islam; Raymond Shariff, Elijah's son-in-law (married Elijah's daughter Ethel)—supreme captain of the Fruit of Islam; and Wallace Muhammad—minister-at-large. Elijah Muhammad's daughter Lottie Fagan and sons Emmanuel and Nathaniel were also devoted to their father and his message. The only nonfamily member among national leaders was John Ali, who was the national secretary.

Through Malcolm's training and recruitment of top ministers, he was indirectly shaping the destiny of the organization. The family hierarchy, however, was devoted to Elijah Muhammad.

During this period, Elijah Muhammad's very ambitious three-year economic plan began to bear fruit. Numerous small-business service enterprises began to emerge under the aegis of the Nation of Islam: bakeries, restaurants, dress shops, barbershops, grocery stores, and cleaning establishments. The businesses derived most of their income from members of the organization and from residents of the black community patronizing the Muslim enterprises.

On January 14, 1958, Malcolm X married Sister Betty X, a tall, brown-skinned beauty and former student at Tuskegee Institute in Alabama. The family grew to include four daughters, Attilah (1958), Qubilah (1960), Ilyasah (1962), and Amilah (1964).

In 1959, the media played an important role in providing the Nation of Islam and Malcolm X with national and international recognition. Newsman Mike Wallace, with the help of a black writer, Louis Lomax, persuaded the Nation of Islam to participate in a television documentary entitled, "The Hate That Hate Produced," which brought the organization into homes of millions of television viewers. Also, Malcolm began to speak before a wider audience by appearing on college campuses, radio, and television talk shows. The organization received coverage in *Life, Look, Newsweek,* and *Reader's Digest.*

Malcolm was still a devoted and obedient follower of Elijah Muhammad, echoing his doctrine wherever he spoke. Beginning each response with "The Honorable Elijah Muhammad teaches us," he would espouse the virtues of separation for the black man in America as the only solution.

Malcolm X believed that the American economic and political system was unequal and unjust and that to integrate into such a system would do nothing for the masses of poor and working-class blacks. Only through separation (not segregation, which results in white control of the black community) would true equality be created because "separation is that which is done voluntarily by two equals for the good of both."[7]

Malcolm also felt that Christianity assisted in the subordination of blacks and still insisted "Christianity is the white man's religion. The Bible in the . . . white man's hands and his interpretations of it, have been the greatest single ideological weapon for enslaving millions of non-white human beings."[8]

On matters of race, Malcolm still parroted the doctrine initiated by Master Fard Muhammad and carried on by Elijah Muhammad. Malcolm still believed that "Our enemy is the white man!" and he equated the "enemy" with the devil. "Oh yes, that devil is our enemy," he would preach.

As late as 1959, he broadened the concept from purely race and color classification to actions and behavior. Malcolm explained, "We are not speaking of any individual white man. We are speaking of the collective white man's historical record. The white man's collective cruelties, evils, and deeds, that have seen him act like a devil toward the non-white man."[9]

Because Elijah Muhammad was confined to Phoenix, Arizona, in 1959 for his bronchial condition, he was unable to regulate the decision-making and administrative duties of the Nation of Islam. He carried on the work through his family members and loyal ministers and eventually appointed Malcolm X national spokesman. Elijah gave Malcolm the opportunity to make his own decisions in governing the affairs of the Nation of Islam. Malcolm stated, "He said that my guideline should be whatever I felt was wise—whatever was in the general good interests of our Nation of Islam."[10]

Entering the 1960s, the stage was set for Malcolm to emerge from the shadow of Elijah Muhammad and become an international leader. There were several reasons for Malcolm's prominence during that decade. Malcolm's appointment as national spokesman provided a platform for him as the charismatic leader. The increased administrative and decision-making duties gave Malcolm more power to utilize the numerous institutions within the Nation of Islam. Media coverage of the organization's activities provided massive exposure and Malcolm was the natural focal point.

The rise of black nationalism in the 1960s in the United States came during the escalation of the Vietnam War and liberation struggles in Colonial Africa. The nationalist leaders perceived the African American struggle in world solidarity as a struggle against colonialism, racism, and capitalist expansionism. The Nation of Islam was the oldest and most powerful black nationalist organization in the United States. Malcolm X became the "Prince of the Black Revolution."

With the mood of nationalism sweeping black America, Malcolm felt the Nation of Islam should be active in leading a frontline struggle. Malcolm was convinced that "the Nation of Islam could be even a greater force in the American Black man's overall struggle if we engaged in more action."[11] Elijah Muhammad advocated that Muslims should not become involved in the "white man's politics" and insisted that members invest their time on self-improvement. Malcolm perceived the self-improvement position as making the Nation of Islam a separate, closed community within the black community. Malcolm even considered voting as a means of achieving power. He said, "The polls are one place where every black man could fight the black man's cause with dignity and power."[12]

In April 1960, Elijah Muhammad's son Wallace was sentenced to prison for three years for failure to report for hospital work as a conscientious objector. For the next three years, Elijah Muhammad spent over $20,000 in legal fees appealing the decision. On November 4, 1961, Wallace entered prison. Even before he entered prison Wallace had doubts about his father's version of Islam. Wallace also questioned his father's interpretation of Fard Muhammad as Allah. Wallace had seen many of Fard's writings in which he referred to himself as the messenger of Allah.

The same year that Wallace went to prison, Malcolm began to encounter jealousy and hostility within the hierarchy of the Nation of

Islam. Most of the problems emanated from the national headquarters in Chicago. Rumors were spread that "Malcolm is trying to take over the Nation." He was accused of taking credit for Elijah Muhammad's teachings and building a financial empire. The media, black leaders, and even several Muslims were giving Malcolm credit for the progress of the Nation of Islam.

In response to the rumors and accusations, Malcolm began refusing interviews and public addresses. He often urged the media, "Please use Mr. Muhammad's picture instead of mine." By 1962, Malcolm noticed he appeared less and less in the organization's newspaper, *Muhammad Speaks*. Herbert Muhammad, the publisher of the paper, instructed editors to "print as little as possible about Malcolm." Malcolm began to resent these efforts after the hard work he had performed for the organization. Eventually, he received no coverage at all in *Muhammad Speaks*. In addition, the Chicago headquarters began to discourage him from holding rallies and public speaking engagements.

In January 10, 1963, Wallace D. Muhammad was paroled from Sandstone Correctional Institution. While in prison, Wallace meditated, discussed, and wrote about Islam, and made comparisons with his father's version of the religion. Wallace consulted several relatives and organization members (including Malcolm X) to clarify his doubts about his father's teachings. Wallace regularly attended Nation of Islam functions and taught classes at the University of Islam. Wallace stirred up more controversy concerning his father's activities both nationally and in Chicago.

During the same year, Elijah Muhammad became a subject of rumors concerning his morality. A UPI press release stated that testimony by two of Elijah Muhammad's former secretaries, Miss Rosary and Miss Williams, indicated that they had sexual relationships with Mr. Muhammad since 1957. Each woman alleged that Elijah Muhammad had fathered their children. Malcolm X had utmost faith in Elijah Muhammad and perceived him as the symbol of moral and spiritual reform for African Americans. These rumors forced Malcolm to discuss morality less during public speaking engagements and concentrate on social doctrine, current events, and politics.

To satisfy his own curiosity and possibly stop the rumors, Malcolm X launched his own investigation. He interviewed the membership, family members, and three former secretaries; they all confirmed the rumors.

For advice, Malcolm X confided in Wallace D. Muhammad. Wallace and Malcolm reviewed the Quran and the Bible for documentation and biblical justification for Elijah Muhammad's actions. With Wallace's help Malcolm found Koran and Bible passages that might be taught to the membership as the fulfillment of prophecy. Malcolm visited Elijah Muhammad in Chicago and asked him about the accusations by the two secretaries. Elijah Muhammad was pleased with Malcolm's Quranic and biblical research. He replied,

> I'm David, when you read about how David took another man's wife, I'm that David. You read about Noah, who got drunk—that's me. You read about Lot, who went and laid up with his own daughter. I have fulfilled all those things.[13]

Malcolm's concern was interpreted as spreading dissension and fanning flames of discontent. Resentment and hostility toward Malcolm rapidly increased among numerous members of the "Royal Family." When it appeared Malcolm was becoming more powerful and influential than Elijah Muhammad, the leadership in Chicago began to sever Malcolm's powers within the organization. Malcolm was being forced out of the leadership circle and eventually the organization. Malcolm was aggressive, eager, and articulate and was often moving faster than Elijah Muhammad wished, as well as moving in political directions that Elijah Muhammad did not approve. Malcolm was gaining more and more prominence within the organization. Domestically and abroad, he became better known than any black leader in the United States, including Elijah Muhammad.

Malcolm X's ideological growth began to ripen by 1963. He started to question more and more the Nation of Islam's doctrine, political activities (or lack of them), and religious beliefs. Malcolm began to detour from Elijah Muhammad's doctrine and addressed social and economic issues oppressing black people domestically and internationally. He began to speak out against the United States government for its involvement in the Vietnam War and the lack of commitment toward solving domestic problems.

On November 22, 1963, President John F. Kennedy was assassinated. Afterwards, Elijah Muhammad issued a directive to all Muslim ministers to refrain from commenting on his death. In a speaking engagement in New York's Manhattan Center during a question and answer period, Malcolm X was asked his opinion of the assassination. He replied, "I saw it as a case of chickens coming home to roost. I said, it was the same thing as had happened with Medger Evers, with Patrice Lumumba, with Madam Nhu's husband."[14]

Malcolm X was silenced for ninety days by Elijah Muhammad for making these remarks. For a month after the silencing, many conferences were held between Malcolm, Elijah Muhammad, and national leaders. The differences between Malcolm and the Nation of Islam became more pronounced. Elijah Muhammad removed Malcolm as a minister of Temple No. 7 in New York in January 1964. The same month, Muhammad excommunicated his son Wallace for working closely with Malcolm.

Wallace explained the excommunication: "I was charged with trying to influence Malcolm's theological thinking and with giving him personal private knowledge of the Honorable Elijah Muhammad's living."[15] Wallace protested the excommunication to no avail. He wanted to face his accusers, but Muhammad declared, "Malcolm X is not facing his accusers either."

The following month, a young Louisville boxer was training in Miami, Florida, to fight Sonny Liston for the heavyweight championship of the world. The young challenger, Cassius Clay, invited Malcolm X and his family to his training camp to honor Malcolm and Betty on their sixth wedding anniversary. Malcolm had known Cassius as early as 1962 when Cassius and his brother Rudolph came to Detroit to hear Elijah Muhammad speak; they consequently became close friends.

Young Clay won a gold medal in the 1960 Rome Olympics. When he returned home to Kentucky, he and his friend, Ronnie King, were refused service in a restaurant because they were black. After leaving the restaurant, Clay and King were attacked by a white motorcycle gang which Clay and King fought off. Discouraged and angry, Clay heaved his gold medal into the Ohio River as a silent protest. Clay became interested in the Nation of Islam shortly afterward. In 1962, Cassius and Rudolph attended several Nation of Islam functions throughout the country. Cassius even spoke before a Nation of Islam rally in January 1964 while training for the Sonny Liston fight.

Clay's "I-am-the-greatest" antics brought him considerable news coverage. Prior to the fight with Sonny Liston on February 25, 1964, no one gave Cassius Clay a chance to survive with his life, much less win the fight. Prior to the fight, in Clay's dressing room, Malcolm X gave young Clay a religious pep talk. Malcolm yelled, "This fight is truth; it's the Cross and the Crescent fighting."[16] Malcolm terminated his pep talk with a question to Clay. He peered into his sweat-soaked face and asked, "Do you think Allah has brought about all this, intending for you to leave the ring anything but a champion?"[17] Malcolm and the young contender faced east and prayed to Allah.

Malcolm X left Cassius Clay's dressing room and took a seat among eight thousand fans at Miami's Convention Hall. The "Louisville Lip" shocked the sports world and won by a technical knockout. The bleeding and exhausted Sonny Liston was unable to leave his stool to answer the bell for the seventh round. After the fight, Clay announced, "I believe in the religion of Islam which means I believe there is no God but Allah and Muhammad is his apostle."[18]

Soon after the fight, newspapers carried pictures with Malcolm X introducing Cassius Clay to numerous African diplomats in the United Nations. Malcolm and Clay rode through Harlem and other parts of the country with Malcolm as the champion's friend and religious advisor.

On March 6, 1964, Elijah Muhammad bestowed on Clay the name Muhammad Ali. Malcolm predicted that Muhammad Ali would "develop into a major world figure."

By 1964, Malcolm X and the Nation of Islam's marriage of twelve years was breaking up. Malcolm felt that he would remain suspended and eventually be "isolated," excluded from all Muslim functions. Malcolm also began receiving rumors of his assassination and suspected a zealous follower of Elijah Muhammad might kill him as his religious duty.

On March 8, 1964, Malcolm announced that he was leaving the Nation of Islam to establish his own organization, based upon Orthodox Islamic principles, called the Muslim Mosque Inc. with an associate political body, the Organization of Afro-American Unity. Malcolm's organization consisted of approximately fifty former Nation of Islam members. The headquarters for his organization was the Hotel Theresa on 125th Street and Seventh Avenue in Harlem. The organization of Afro-American unity was a "nonreligious and nonsectarian group organized to unite Afro-Americans for a constructive program toward attainment of human rights."[19] The OAAU was an all-black organization whose ultimate objective was to "help create a society in which there could be an honest white-black brotherhood."[20] Malcolm was willing to work with white people and requested their financial support. He urged whites to confront racism in their own communities to create a brotherhood of all races; however, Malcolm did not permit whites to join the OAAU. He was convinced there could be no black and white coalitions before black solidarity was achieved. Ultimately, black and white organizations would have solidarity, but only after African Americans had been organized. Malcolm traveled extensively to Africa and his ideological growth accelerated.

In April 1964, Malcolm X made the pilgrimage, known as the Hajj, to the Holy City of Mecca. Muslims are obligated to take at least one pilgrimage in their lifetime, if financially able. During his pilgrimage, Malcolm began to alter his perspective on the Nation of Islam's doctrine and Islam practiced by Muslims throughout the world. Malcolm was embarrassed because, as a Muslim minister, he did not know the prayer ritual, nor did he practice the "Pillars of Islam" and other Islamic principles. He was impressed with the spirit of brotherhood, lack of color-consciousness, and nonracist attitudes among Muslims. He met with Islamic scholars and read volumes of literature on the religion.

The following month, Malcolm X went on an eighteen-week trip through Africa and had private audiences with several African heads of state. In Egypt Malcolm was the guest of King Faisal and also talked to Gamal Abdel Nasser of Egypt, President Julius K. Nyerere of Tanzania, President Nnamai Asikiwe of Nigeria, Dr. Kwame Nkrumah of Ghana,

President Jomo Kenyatta of Kenya, and Prime Minister Dr. Milton Obote of Uganda. Malcolm's travels convinced him that Islam as taught by Elijah Muhammad was out of sync with 800 million Muslims worldwide. His discussions with Wallace D. Muhammad made Malcolm suspect that the Nation of Islam was an unorthodox brand of Islam. The Hajj reinforced his suspicions and resulted in his conversion to Orthodox Islam.

When Malcolm X returned to the United States in June 1964, he found there was still dissension within the ranks of the "Royal Family" of Muhammad. On June 21, 1964, Elijah Muhammad's grandson Hassan Sharrieff was expelled from the organization and denounced as a hypocrite for deviating from Elijah Muhammad's teachings. On January 1, 1965, another of Elijah Muhammad's sons was expelled; Akbar Muhammad's expulsion followed after he refused to denounce Wallace and Malcolm as hyprocrites. Instead of denouncing Malcolm and Wallace, he praised them. Akbar was a student of Islamic law at Al Azhar University in Cairo, Egypt, He referred to his father's brand of Islam as "homemade" and not an accurate reflection of the religion. Eventually Akbar and his family returned to Egypt.

The conflict within the Nation of Islam convinced Malcolm X he was correct in his analysis of the organization and his political and ideological development. Malcolm changed his name to El-Hajj Malik El-Shabazz after he accepted Orthodox Islam. Malcolm felt true Islam unites people rather than separating them as Elijah Muhammad's teaching advocated.

Betty Shabazz, Malcolm X's wife, described her husband's change: "He went to Mecca as a Black Muslim and there he became only a Muslim. He felt all men were human beings; we must judge a man on his deeds."[21] Malcolm Shabazz felt that the Muslim world's religious community and the societies built upon Islamic principles had eliminated racism. He began to separate whiteness as a color from attitudes and actions. Malcolm truly believed color and race were irrelevant in the Muslim world, but "if one encountered any difference based on attitudes toward color this directly reflected the degree of Western influence."[22]

Malcolm Shabazz's changed attitude toward white people was based upon his international travels and observing other social systems and economic means of production. By virtue of his observations he believed that capitalism and racism are related by reinforcing racial inequality for private gain. It was not white people per se who were inherently evil, but the United States' political, economic, and social system which was demonic. Malcolm said, "The American political, economic and social atmosphere . . . automatically nourishes a racist psychology in the white man."[23]

Malcolm Shabazz's travels through Africa convinced him to change his perspective on black nationalism. Africans in Algiers, Morocco, Arabia, Egypt, Iraq, and other parts of the continent were Africans but not "Black" in the strict anthropological sense. Black nationalism as a political ideology was separating Malcolm and his organization from millions of people in the Muslim world. To alleviate the ideological conflict, Malcolm advocated Pan-Africanism as the solution to the African American problem. In Ghana, Malcolm talked to Dr. Kwame Nkrumah who "agreed that Pan-Africanism was the key also to the problems of those of African heritage."[24] Malcolm wanted to internationalize the plight of African Americans. He was convinced of the inherent limitations of moral pressure and an "Americanized" struggle. Perceiving the race question as a domestic problem, leaders were limited to resolutions within the confines of the United States, where blacks sought support from the same officials, organizations, and institutions that were oppressing them. Malcolm linked the African American struggle with cultural and philosophical ties in Africa. Malcolm explained his Pan-African perspective as follows:

> It was time for all Afro-Americans to join the world's Pan-Africanists. Physically, we Afro-Americans might remain in America, fighting for our constitutional rights, but that philosophically and culturally we Afro-Americans badly needed to return to Africa and to develop a working unity in the framework of Pan-Africanism.[25]

Malcolm perceived the plight of the African American as similar to that of blacks in South Africa. The cross-cultural likeness of oppression qualified the United States' "race problem" as a denial of human rights and not merely a civil rights violation. Malcolm Shabazz wanted to present the cause of African Americans before the United Nations. Malcolm explained, "The American black man needed to recognize that he had a strong air-tight case to take the United States before the United Nations on a formal accusation of denial of human rights."[26] He went purely beyond a Pan-African perspective to include the Third World. He often spoke of Latin American "brothers" and 800 million Chinese "brothers" supporting such a United nations resolution. Minister Malcolm Shabazz did not live long enough to work toward these ideals.

On February 21, 1965, at 2:00 P.M., Malcolm Shabazz arrived at the Audubon Ballroom in New York City to speak to approximately five hundred people. He greeted the audience with "Al-salaam alaikum" ("Peace be unto you"). "Wa-alaikum salaam" ("And unto you be peace"), answered the crowd. Then, in approximately the eight row from the stage a fight started. "Hold it! Hold it! Don't get excited," Malcolm pleaded. Three men in the front row stood and pointed guns at him and fired. The bullets hit him in the head and chest with such force that he was pushed over the chairs behind him. Sixteen gunshot pellets and revolver slugs dotted his shirt with blood. Malcolm laid on the stage, his mouth wide open and his teeth bared. His wife, Betty Shabazz, pushed her way through the crowd of people surrounding his body, fell to her knees, grabbed his chest and cried, "They killed him." He was rushed to the Vanderbilt Clinic one block away and at 3:00 P.M., Minister El-Hajj Malik El-Shabazz was pronounced dead.

The autopsy performed by Dr. Milton Helper, chief medical examiner, revealed Shabazz died from shotgun wounds in the heart, inflicted by a sawed-off shotgun, and he had wounds from .45 and .38 caliber pistols. Assistant Chief Inspector Joseph Coyle, in charge of Manhattan North Detectives, described the killing as a "well-planned conspiracy." Following Shabazz's assassination, three men were arrested and accused of his murder: Talmadge Hayer, age 22; Thomas 15X Johnson, age 30; and Norman 3X Butler, age 26.

The three men charged with the murder of Minister El-Hajj Malik El-Shabazz were former Muslims, which created suspicion that the Nation of Islam had him killed. Imam Wallace D. Muhammad felt that the former Muslims were used: "I don't believe that the Nation of Islam planned the assassination of Malcolm X. I believe outsiders assassinated Malcolm X and members were used."[27]

Talmadge Hayer admitted he purchased the guns (a 12-gauge shotgun, a .45 caliber pistol, and a Luger) "hot" from the street underworld. Hayer and his colleagues investigated the Audubon Ballroom on two occasions before the night Malcolm was killed. They attended one of Malcolm's rallies to see if they would be searched. He halted all searching of people who attended his OAAU rallies because it reminded him too much of Elijah Muhammad and the Nation of Islam. He dismissed the search by saying, "If I can't be safe with my own kind, where can I be?" Hayer attended a dance on February 20, 1965, to observe the exits for escape routes. The signal for the murder to begin was when Malcolm greeted the audience with "Al-salaam alaikum." Initially, Hayer refused to say who his co-assassins were. The police, equipped with eyewitness descriptions of the assailants, arrested Johnson and Butler because they matched the descriptions. There was such circumstantial evidence as their "strong man image" in New York's Fruit of Islam. Also, both men were out on bail for attempting to kill Benjamin Brown, who had defected from the Nation of Islam and founded a rival organization in the Bronx. Neither Johnson nor Butler confessed to killing Malcolm X; Hayer is the only confessed assassin and he implicated the other two. The three men were sentenced to life in prison. They were sent to Sing Sing and later shipped upstate to Dannemora and maintained in solitary confinement. For most of the 15 years of their incarceration, they had been separated from each other—Hayer at Napanoch, Johnson at Dannemora, and Butler at Sing Sing.

In the autumn of 1977, Talmadge Hayer confessed to Nuriddin Faiz, a Muslim prison chaplain, that he had lied and Butler and Johnson were innocent. Hayer named four men who were still active Muslims living in New Jersey. Faiz contacted Defense Attorney William Kunstler, who agreed to take the case for Johnson and Butler. Hayer supplied the names, addresses, detailed descriptions, and occupations of the four who, he now claimed, assisted him. Kunstler attempted to have the case reopened based upon Hayer's sworn testimony.

In 1978, Kunstler was refused a new trial by Judge Harold Rathway, who ruled Hayer's new testimony did not constitute enough evidence for another trial. The District Attorney's office of New York also resisted Attorney Kunstler's legal pleas.

Kunstler petitioned the House of Representatives in the spring of 1979 via the Congressional Black Caucus. The Black Caucus was discussing the virtues and merits of Kunstler's petitions. It was Attorney Kunstler's view that the Federal Bureau of Investigation and the New York City police played a supporting role in Malcolm's death. The FBI had Malcolm and other leaders in the Nation of Islam under surveillance for years as an "internal security risk" and also infiltrated the organization with paid informants.

Hayer may have told the truth. Whoever killed Malcolm X, whether they were Muslims or agents of the state as others had suggested, there are many riddles which remain unsolved. Why weren't there searches at the door? Had Malcolm become so unrealistic that he thought his "own kind" wouldn't attempt to kill him? Why did he refuse police protection? Why weren't the armed guards on stage? Why didn't Malcolm arm himself? How could three members of the Nation of Islam as well-known as Hayer, Johnson, and Butler were to Malcolm and his organization slip into the room without being noticed? Many of these questions will go unanswered and we can only guess why Malcolm and his colleagues made such tragic mistakes.

There could have been inside help within Malcolm's organization to set him up which enabled the assassination to occur so smoothly. Many of the mistakes Malcolm made concerning his own personal security may relate to drastic changes he had undergone during the year. Malcolm was fresh from the Hajj in Africa where he experienced genuine love and forgot that he may have been loved all over the world except in the United States. He had allowed himself the luxury of false consciousness concerning his security; also, since he accepted Orthodox Islam, he might have assumed "Allah will protect me" and neglected to protect himself. It is ironic that El-Hajj Malik El-Shabazz made these fundamental errors because "Detroit Red" never would have allowed himself to be put in such a situation. Another ironic twist of Malcolm's murder is the fact that both he and his convicted assassins eventually moved away from Elijah Muhammad's doctrine and embraced Orthodox Islam. His assassins underwent a religious conversion in prison and now Talmadge Hayer is called Majahid Abdul Halim, Norman Butler is Muhammad Abdul-Aziz, and Thomas 15X has changed his name to Khalil Islam.

We cannot say with any certainty where Malcolm was headed ideologically. His assassination put an abrupt halt to the process of redefining his perspective. It would be foolish to predict his direction and use it to support a specific ideology. It would be just as foolish not to use his life as a lesson, his leadership as an example, and his original approach to human rights to instruct others on their own development. He made enormous contributions to Pan-Africanism, as an advocate of human rights, and toward efforts to acquire equality for people of African descent living in the United States. We have chronicled Malcolm's influence on the Nation of Islam. Many of the changes that were created in the Nation of Islam can directly be attributed to El-Hajj Malik El-Shabazz. Muhammad Akbar, a Muslim official, explains just one of his contributions:

> The primary influence in terms of changes was he foresaw the natural evolution of the movement. Malcolm saw the way Muslims were in the east. He came back with the description of what was supposed to be an Islamic community. He visualized the ultimate form of the organization was more like the Orthodox Islamic world.[28]

After the death of Malcolm Shabazz, his close friend Wallace D. Muhammad eventually succeeded his father, Elijah Muhammad. Wallace initiated many of the changes Malcolm had advocated. The following chapter will detail the alteration in the image and doctrine of the former Black Muslim to an Orthodox Islamic religious organization.

Notes

1. Malcolm X, *The Autobiography of Malcolm X* (New York: Grove Press, 1964; New York: Ballantine Books, 1973, 1977), p. 10.

2. Ibid., p. 26

3. Ibid., p. 73

4. Ibid., p. 75

5. Ibid., p. 290

6. Interview, Imam Wallace D. Muhammad, Chicago, Illinois, July 25, 1979.

7. Ibid.

8. Malcolm X, *Autobiography,* pp. 241–242.

9. Ibid., p. 266

10. Ibid., p. 265

11. Ibid.

12. Ibid., p. 313.

13. Ibid., p. 299
14. Ibid., p. 301.
15. Interview, Imam Wallace D. Muhammad.
16. Malcolm X, *Autobiography,* p. 301.
17. Ibid.
18. Ibid.
19. Ibid., p. 416.
20. Ibid., p. 375.
21. *Pittsburgh Courier,* March 6, 1965, p. 4.
22. Malcolm X, *Autobiography,* p. 375.
23. Ibid., p. 371.
24. Ibid., p. 357.
25. Ibid., p. 350.
26. Ibid., p. 361.
27. Interview, Imam Wallace D. Muhammad.
28. Interview, Muhammad Akbar, April 21, 1977.

Chapter 6

The Nation of Islam and the World Community of Al-Islam in the West 1965–1980

"The W.C.I.W. is an organized social movement and a religion but in line with the Quranic teachings. The old Nation of Islam was not in line with the Quranic teachings."

—Imam Wallace D. Muhammad

After the assassination of Malcolm X, it was feared his death would be the catalyst for a "holy war" between the nationalists loyal to him and the followers of Elijah Muhammad who was placed under heavy guard in his Chicago residence. The Fruit of Islam and Chicago police officers kept the University of Islam and *Muhammad Speaks* newspaper under constant surveillance.

When Malcolm announced his split from the Nation of Islam on March 8, 1964, he began to build his organization until his death on February 21, 1965. One year was not enough time to establish formal bureaucracy which would sustain his charisma and ideas after his death. One member of the OAAU expressed what most others felt: "He was the spirit, the force and the fiber of the movement; without him there is no movement."[1]

On February 23, 1965, in an apparent retaliation for Malcolm's murder, the Harlem Mosque No. 7 at 102 W. 116th Street was firebombed; a Mosque in San Francisco was also firebombed. These two incidents created alarm that other acts of vengeance would follow.

Three days later, on February 26, 1965, the Nation of Islam held their annual Savior's Day Convention in Chicago. Elijah Muhammad blamed Malcolm's death in his departure from the Nation of Islam's doctrine, saying, "We didn't want to kill Malcolm and we didn't try to. It was his foolishness, ignorance, and his preachings that brought him to his death."[2]

During the convention, Malcolm's brothers, Wilfred and Philbert, refused to attend Malcolm's funeral services, denounced their brother for "going astray," and pledged their allegiance to Elijah Muhammad and the Nation of Islam.

Elijah Muhammad received additional support from his son Wallace D. Muhammad, who was accepted back into the organization during the Savior's Day Convention of 1965. Wallace returned to his father and asked for forgiveness. The reinstatement didn't last very long. Wallace said, "I was right back out. I was excommunicated three or four times and always for the same charge. I was not accepting the God image given to Fard Muhammad."[3]

After Wallace was suspended again in 1965, he remained inactive until he was readmitted in 1969. While he was suspended, the right to interact and communicate with members of his family was denied. During his suspension, he owned a bookstore and formed a study group called the Upliftment Society. Wallace also worked as a welder and operated a carpet and furniture cleaning business. He was accepted back into the organization in 1969, but did not regain his minister's status until 1974.

Entering the decade of the 1970s, the Nation of Islam continued to prosper in spite of the defections associated with Malcolm X, internal conflicts among the "royal family," and the deteriorating health of Elijah Muhammad. By the 1970s the organization grew to approximately one million members, of which 250,000 are currently active.

Under Elijah Muhammad's leadership, the organization managed to acquire 15,000 acres of farmland in several states, thousands of head of cattle and sheep, poultry and dairy farms, warehouses and cold storage facilities, the *Muhammad Speaks* newspaper, tractor-trailer fleets, aircraft, the Guaranty Bank and Trust Company, apartment complexes, and wholesale and retail businesses throughout America. The Nation of Islam also managed to organize over seventy-six Muhammad Mosques of Islam in the United States and abroad in Bermuda, Jamaica, Trinidad, Central America, England, Ghana, and the U.S. Virgin Islands. The Nation of Islam estimated that its business enterprises were valued at over $85 million by the late 1970s.

In 1974, Wallace D. Muhammad was accepted back into the ministry and assumed authority over the Chicago Mosque. Wallace was given complete freedom to preach as his wisdom dictated. He said, "I would actually test the support for me from the Honorable Elijah Muhammad. I would say things that I knew were different than some of the things taught under his leadership."[4]

Wallace and his father repeatedly engaged in ideological conflicts for over fourteen years. Finally, in 1974, Elijah Muhammad gave his consent to relinquish the "Black Muslims" doctrine for the Orthodox model presented by Wallace.

One fateful afternoon in 1974, officers of the Fruit of Islam brought a recording of one of Wallace's sermons to Elijah Muhammad; he summoned Wallace to listen with him. At one point during the recording Elijah Muhammad exclaimed, "My son's got it, my son can go anywhere on earth and preach."[5] With those words, uttered before Muslim officials, Elijah Muhammad began the transfer of power. Before the transfer was complete, he became seriously ill.

On January 29, 1975, Elijah Muhammad was admitted to Chicago's Mercy Hospital for a routine medical examination. On February 8, 1975, he was rushed into the intensive care unit after he was stricken with congestive heart failure. His condition continued to deteriorate. At 8:10 A.M. on February 25, 1975, he was pronounced dead by his physician, Dr. Charles Williams.

On February 25, 1975, at the annual Savior's Day Rally before 20,000 members and friends of the organization, Abas Rassoull, national secretary of the Nation of Islam, announced that Wallace D. Muhammad was chosen to lead the Nation of Islam. The appointment of Wallace D. Muhammad astonished the general public because he had kept a relatively low profile up to that point. However, members of the Nation of Islam knew as early as 1958 that Wallace would succeed his father.

Wallace D. Muhammad was born in Detroit, Michigan, on October 30, 1933. He received his entire elementary and high school education at the University of Islam in Chicago. He studied microbiology, English, history, and social sciences at Wilson and Loop Junior College in Chicago. He has been employed as a painter, carpet cleaner, grocery store and restaurant manager, and welder for U.S. Steel and Bethlehem Steel. He has operated his own bookstore and served as a lieutenant in the Fruit of Islam. In 1967, Wallace made a pilgrimage to Mecca and later two umaras (out-of-season pilgrimage). He was the minister of the Philadelphia Temple for three years, from 1958 to 1961. He was sentenced to three years in the Sandstone Minnesota Federal Correctional Institution for failing to report to Elgin State Hospital as required under the laws affecting conscientious objectors.

Why was Wallace D. Muhammad selected to lead, and not other members of the organization? The family of Elijah Muhammad was known as the "Royal Family" among members of the organization. Only members of the family could succeed Elijah Muhammad.

Wallace D. Muhammad was "chosen for the mission." He was chosen to succeed his father by Master Fard Muhammad who told Elijah that his seventh child would be a son and his eventual successor. "This new-born baby predicted by Master Fard Muhammad that [sic] he would be a male and it so happened the guess was right."[6]

The seventh child was a son and Elijah Muhammad named him Wallace D. Muhammad in honor of Master Fard Muhammad, the founder of the Nation of Islam. Imam Wallace D. Muhammad explained why he was chosen to lead: "I was chosen because a new baby, new birth—they wanted a Christ figure, someone with a mystery about [him]."[7]

With the death of Elijah Muhammad, Wallace was free to shape the movement as he saw fit. Elijah Muhammad's passing brought to an end the bulwark of black separatism, black identity and consciousness in the United States.

Through the reorganizing, denationalizing, decentralizing, and orthodoxing of the Nation of Islam into the World Community of Al-Islam in the West, Wallace D. Muhammad has changed the most powerful and feared black nationalist group into an Orthodox Islamic religion. He said that he is changing the religion "in a way which will gain acceptance in America; this is the kind of thinking I have to encourage in our membership."[8]

Wallace D. Muhammad engineered a series of conceptual changes which altered the character and structure of the Nation of Islam. He debunked the racial superiority doctrine of Elijah Muhammad; redefined Master Fard Muhammad as a wise man instead of "God in person"; restored Malcolm X to a position of respect and prominence in the organization; separated business from religious practices; ceased the demand for a separate state; began to honor the American Constitution, and brought the doctrine in line with Orthodox Islamic practices.

One of the first official acts of Imam Wallace D. Muhammad's administration was to reinterpret his father's role as "messenger of Allah." Wallace felt his father had not been speaking in the theological spirit of the Quran and the Bible. Instead, he felt his father had been saying of Master Fard, "A man came to me with solutions for your health problems, social problems and I am bringing you the message he gave to me."[9]

Imam Wallace D. Muhammad often read Master Fard's doctrine and therefore knew Elijah Muhammad was the person who defined Master Fard as God in person. Master Fard referred to himself as a messenger of God and Elijah Muhammad reinterpreted his message.

Wallace D. Muhammad redefined both men's contributions to the organization. Master Fard Muhammad is now recognized as the founder of the movement and not "God in person," as Elijah Muhammad had suggested. To coincide with Orthodox Islam, Wallace D. Muhammad defines "Allah as a supernatural being that acts out his wishes through his vessels on earth, those who submit to Allah."[10]

Elijah Muhammad believed African Americans were Asiatic descendants from the tribe of Shabazz. Wallace D. Muhammad had changed the Asiatic nationality to the term "Bilalians." Bilal was an Ethiopian Muslim who was born circa A.D. 600. Bilal was so firm in his convictions that when punished by the slave master after refusing to denounce Islam, he would cry, "Ahad!", "Ahad!" ("One, only one God").

By changing the name of their nationality, Wallace D. Muhammad created a spiritual and national bond with Islam as a religion and Africa as a continent. "They have a double connection with Bilal because he was a Muslim and he was also a so-called African."[11] The *Muhammad Speaks* newspaper was renamed the *Bilalian News,* effective November 1, 1975.

Another alteration in organization policy occurred when the organization changed its belief in the learned evil behavior of white people. Islam does not restrict its membership to one race nor does it advocate racial superiority. The racial doctrine that depicted whites as devils has been changed to describe a devil mentality which motivates individuals to commit evil deeds. Blacks as well as whites can be affected by a mentality. Minister Abdul Haleem Farrakhan explains the new doctrine: "What Honorable Elijah Muhammad gave us in physical terms had spiritual meaning. They didn't graft him physically [Yacub's creation of whites] but it's a mentality. There is no devil just limited to white flesh."[12]

For several years Elijah Muhammad advocated that the United States government should give the Nation of Islam several states to create a separate nation. It was Elijah Muhammad's belief that Muslims were not really citizens of the United States, because blacks were not given the privileges associated with citizenship status. Discrimination in employment, education, and housing denied blacks the opportunity to fully participate in the society. Until social economic conditions were changed, members of the Nation of Islam did not vote, run for office, or join the military.

Wallace D. Muhammad felt it was futile to demand a separate state within the United States. Keeping his vow to make Islam acceptable to the government and society at large and to enhance its image, he encouraged Muslims to honor the American flag and urged members to vote. He explained, "As citizens of the United States of America we are obligated to defend the USA. But if you yourself think it is wrong to go to war, that's between you and God."[13]

It was inevitable that Wallace D. Muhammad would restore Malcolm X Shabazz to a place of honor within the organization. Malcolm was instrumental in the development of the movement in his prime minister role for Elijah Muhammad. His charisma, recruitment efforts, and organizational skills helped propel the Nation of Islam from an obscure local group to a powerful religious organization with international connections. Many of the present members agreed with Malcolm's view of an Islamic community. Wallace reiterated this point: "Many people agreed with the stand Malcolm took but remained in the Nation of Islam. Although Malcolm left the Nation of Islam, I'm glad he remained a Muslim."[14] Malcolm and Wallace were close friends and they were both excommunicated by Elijah Muhammad almost simultaneously. Malcolm and Wallace maintained their friendship while exiled from the Nation of Islam. To respect his contribution to the development of the organization, the New York City Mosque was named Malcolm Shabazz Mosque No. 7.

Wallace D. Muhammad has also changed the rituals and dress of the membership and the decor of the buildings. Mosques are now referred to as "Masjids" and instead of anti-American, anti-Christian slogans on the walls, there are Arabic symbols. Tape-recorded sounds of Eastern music and Islamic prayers filter throughout the Masjid. People are no longer searched, but must leave their shoes at the front door. Seats have been replaced by carpet and everyone sits on the floor, although the seating is still segregated by sex. All adult males sit in the front; the young boys sit behind the men, followed by the women and girls. During services a local Imam leads the congregation in a prayer.

The worshipers were asked to stand facing the east with cupped hands before them and bowed heads while the minister prays in Arabic and then in English. The membership also believes in the two basic faiths of Islam: belief in the oneness of God and that Muhammad is the messenger and prophet of Allah.

WCIW also practices the devotional duties, or pillars of Islam (testimony, prayer, fasting, alms, and pilgrimage). Wallace D. Muhammad has brought the religious beliefs, rituals, and practices in line with Orthodox Islam.

Under Elijah Muhammad's leadership, there had been a strict dress and grooming code. Wallace D. Muhammad allows the members to wear anything they want so long as it is neat, clean, and does not degrade the religion. Women are allowed to wear pants and do not have to cover their heads except while attending Muslim functions. Muslim ministers, or Imams, often wear Eastern-style leisure suits with a high collar buttoned at the neck. National spokesman Louis Farrakhan explained the change as an emphasis on uniformity of mind, not dress: "The Honorable Elijah Muhammad was building us towards not a uniform dress but a uniformity of mind. And once we have uniformity of mind, we can dress any way that mind directs us."[15]

Women in the Nation of Islam under the administration of Elijah Muhammad had a subordinate role to men. Wallace D. Muhammad has changed that role, and in many cases women are placed over men in administrative positions.

There is also a change in the nature of the Muslim girls' training and general civilization class. Traditionally, the classes taught "the basic principles of keeping the house, taking care of children and taking care of her husband."[16] The class has been changed in name and substance, according to Sharon Shabazz. "The Muslim Women's Development Class, established by Wallace Muhammad, looks at life in a broader sense. She is encouraged as a woman to fulfill her mental capabilities."[17]

Wallace D. Muhammad studied the role of women during the early development of Islam; he believes the right of women to equal education is protected under Islamic law. Wallace justifies the new status by saying, "We cannot make any distinctions between men and women in terms of intelligence, spirituality or moral nature. Women are equal with men and they are not to be treated any differently."[18]

Under Elijah Muhammad, the organization managed numerous businesses. Wallace D. Muhammad has separated the spiritual from the business element of the organization. He has liquidated more than $6 million in long-term debts and tax obligations and has sold less profitable enterprises.

The business ventures were managed by ministers of local Masjids who also had religious duties to fulfill. Farms and other property have been leased to Muslims and non-Muslims. Wallace D. Muhammad explained the arrangement: "[T]hese individuals have a freehand to manage the income, monies and operation. We just look for him to show a profit. If he shows a profit, we want our share."[19]

By adhering to Orthodox Islam, there are economic and political benefits as well as spiritual ones. If Wallace D. Muhammad had followed his father's doctrine, the organization would still be alienated from the international Islamic community. The changes began to bear fruit early during Wallace's administration.

Egyptian president Anwar El Sadat arrived in Washington, D.C. on October 26, 1975. After his visit with President Gerald Ford, he traveled to Chicago where he had a private session with Imam Wallace D. Muhammad in Sadat's hotel suite in the Drake Hotel. The Egyptian government awarded the WCIW twelve scholarships to enable Muslim students to attend Egyptian universities.

During an interview Imam Wallace D. Muhammad was asked his opinion of the proposed peace agreement between Egypt and Israel. He replied, "The Islamic world leadership has much to gain from the political psychology of President Sadat. He is inviting his people to come away from an emotional response to the presence of Israel on Muslim land to a more philosophical, rational strategy."[20]

The change in doctrine has also made the organization more compatible with the government of the United States. In February 1979, the WCIW was awarded $22 million (the largest amount ever awarded to a black firm) by the Department of Commerce. The WCIW, in conjunction with American Pouch Foods Company, is producing precooked combat rations for the United States military. The contract will provide 400 jobs for Chicago residents.

Certain segments of the organization have resisted Wallace D. Muhammad's changes. The most significant development is the defection of international spokesman, Louis Abdul Farrakhan, who announced his departure in December 1977. Farrakhan disagreed with many changes initiated by Wallace and continues to follow the doctrine of Elijah Muhammad. Farrakhan felt the move to Orthodox Islam has caused a decrease in financial holdings and created a lack of discipline among the members. Farrakhan has formed another organization (the Nation of Islam) based upon the doctrine of Elijah Muhammad.

Louis Abdul Farrakhan publishes the newspaper *The Final Call,* which features Elijah Muhammad's picture and the traditional "want and beliefs" which comprise the program of the Nation of Islam. Farrakhan also sells publications written by Elijah Muhammad and refers to himself as "Elijah Muhammad's national representative."

Wallace D. Muhammad perceives Farrakhan's organization as political and not religious. He says, "I think he is trying to stay abreast politically with the Black Movement. Farrakhan has the ability and intelligence to speak and deal with the African problem in the context of man's problem on earth."[21]

The WCIW is comprised on 138 Masjids domestically and internationally (Jamaica, Bahamas, Bermuda, and Barbados). The Masjid represents the basic organization unit in the WCIW. The most important rank in each Masjid is the Imam (Minister). Imam Muhammad Akbar explains the change in the structure under Wallace D. Muhammad as "removal of autocratic centralized leadership of the organization. A shift to a more democratic and shared decision-making process. That has been the most radical change in the organization."[22] Under Elijah Muhammad, all power was centralized in Chicago; local Masjids had very little autonomy. (See Table 6.1 for a complete breakdown of WCIW's organizational structure.)

On September 12, 1978, Wallace D. Muhammad announced his resignation as spiritual leader of the organization to become an evangelist, or ambassador-at-large. He now speaks on behalf of the organization domestically and internationally. The governing of the organization is being administered by a council of six Imams. Each member has equal power nationally, but total power in his respective region; each Imam serves a one-year term. The Imams on the council in 1980 were Ali Rahid, New York City; Khalil Abdel Alim, Washington, D.C.; James Shabazz, Chicago; Ibrahim Kamel Udein, Houston; Ibrahim Pusha, Atlanta; and Karim Hasan, Los Angeles.

Wallace D. Muhammad provided seventeen nominations and the group's membership voted for six via telephone hookup. He requested the council to adhere to the teachings of the Quran, to become actively involved in the capitalistic system and committed to the government of the United States, and to maintain a position of neutrality on affairs of Arab nations. Wallace D. Muhammad, as ambassador-at-large, will be involved in public speaking and interviews to make the public more knowledgeable of the organization.

When Imam Wallace D. Muhammad was asked why he chose to fulfill the role of ambassador-at-large, he replied:

> I was not satisfied with the response in the ministerial body to my call for us to get out in the broader community and let our contributions be known. We are fighting the same evils that Christians are fighting. In fact, I have spoken outside the community more than I have spoken inside.[23]

Table 6.1
World Community of Al-Islam in the West, Organizational Structure

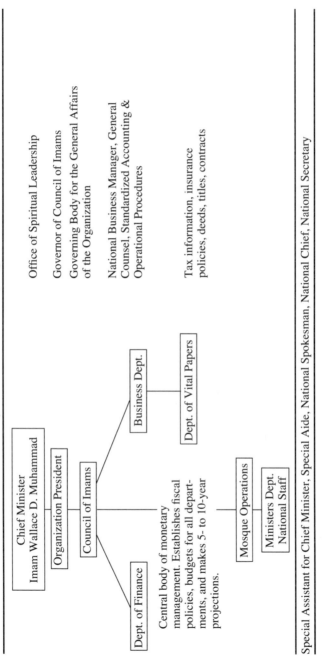

Office of Spiritual Leadership	
Governor of Council of Imams	
Governing Body for the General Affairs of the Organization	
National Business Manager, General Counsel, Standardized Accounting & Operational Procedures	
Tax information, insurance policies, deeds, titles, contracts	

Chief Minister
Imam Wallace D. Muhammad

Organization President

Council of Imams

Business Dept.

Dept. of Vital Papers

Dept. of Finance

Central body of monetary management. Establishes fiscal policies, budgets for all departments, and makes 5- to 10-year projections.

Mosque Operations

Ministers Dept.
National Staff

Special Assistant for Chief Minister, Special Aide, National Spokesman, National Chief, National Secretary

Table 6.1 (Continued)
Muslim Women's Development Class Director, Minister of Justice,
Assistant Minister of Education, Consultants on National Education Staff

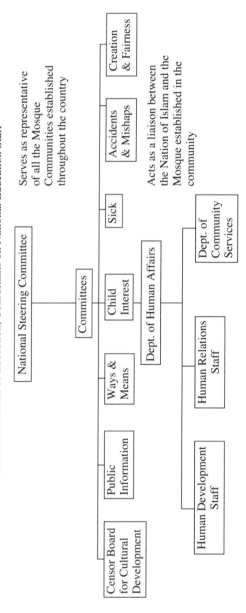

Wallace, in his role as spiritual leader, has managed to alter the doctrine, character, and direction of the former "Black Muslims." These changes enabled the World Community of Al-Islam in the West to be accepted by the Islamic World Community and also be accepted by the United States government. The organization is no longer considered a threat to internal security.

The transformation of the organization has been a reflection of the leadership during various stages of development. Master Fard Muhammad founded the organization during the Depression and Elijah Muhammad skillfully maneuvered the Nation of Islam into a position to aid the African American communities. The organization might still be a separatist movement without the influence of Malcolm X Shabazz on Wallace D. Muhammad and the entire Muslim community. Wallace's ideological struggles with his father ultimately led to the creation of the World Community of Al-Islam in the West. It is too early to predict if the changes will be beneficial. The WCIW is working toward an "accepted religion" status.

The majority of black people are still deprived of basic political-economic necessities. The same social problems the Nation of Islam tried to cure still exist. The WCIW is taking a different approach to remedy the social ills faced by millions of Americans.

Notes

1. *New York Post,* February 23, 1965.

2. *New York Post,* February 28, 1965.

3. Interview, Imam Wallace D. Muhammad, Chicago, Illinois, July 25, 1979.

4. Ibid.

5. Ibid.

6. Ibid.

7. Ibid.

8. Ibid.

9. Ibid.

10. Public Address, Imam Wallace D. Muhammad, Richmond, Virginia, April 1, 1977.

11. *Bilalian News,* October 24, 1976, p. 31.

12. Public Address, Louis Farrakhan, Richmond, Virginia, February 4, 1976.

13. Public Address, Imam Wallace D. Muhammad.

14. Ibid.

15. Public Address, Louis Farrakhan.

16. Interview, Sharon Shabazz, New York City, New York, December 16, 1975.

17. Ibid.

18. Interview, Imam Wallace D. Muhammad.

19. Ibid.

20. Ibid.

21. Ibid.

22. Interview (telephone), Muhammad Akbar, Chicago, Illinois, April 21, 1977.

23. Interview, Imam Wallace D. Muhammad.

Chapter 7

Minister Louis Farrakhan, National Representative of the Honorable Elijah Muhammad and the Nation of Islam: the Continuation of the African Nationalist Legacy, 1815–1994

> "Minister Louis Farrakhan is preaching a kind of moderate form of the early teachings. I would say, he has gone back in time. He has gone back further than the Honorable Elijah Muhammad himself was at the time of his death. To try to introduce again, Black Nationalist philosophy, I think he is trying to stay abreast politically with the Black movement."
> —Imam Warith Deen Muhammad,
> July 25, 1979[1]

In 1977, Minister Louis Farrakhan was excommunicated from the WCIW after the numerous changes initiated by Imam Warith Deen Muhammad (see chapter 6). Minister Louis Farrakhan's resurrection of the Nation of Islam in the name of the Honorable Elijah Muhammad continues an African nationalist/separatist legacy, which has its ideological roots in over two hundred years of African nationalist thought in the United States. A consistent and strong theme in African American social thought has been the conclusion that Africans could never achieve equality in America. Separatism and emigration have been utilized as an alternative when the American ideal of equality seemed unattainable. There was more of a dissatisfaction with the American society than there was a desire to live in Africa or a separate state. In a 1979 interview, Imam Warith Deen Muhammad proved to be a wise sage. Now fifteen years later in 1994, Minister Louis Farrakhan has adopted the ideology and program of the Honorable Elijah Muhammad to fit the social historical circumstances of his time. It is true that Minister Louis Farrakhan is "staying abreast" with the Black Nationalist Movement, but it is also true that Minister Louis Farrakhan is continuing an ideological legacy that is almost as old as the African presence in America. The black nationalist "tradition in the United States has been nurtured in a peculiar environment of political oppression and racial presumption and has developed unique qualities of its own, such as a special relationship with Africa and repeated efforts to emigrate from America."[2] During the historical epoch of each prominent nationalist leader the social, economic, and historical circumstances have created an inevitable conflict between the needs of the African American people and the social and economic problems caused by class and gender inequality, and institutional racism. Rationally speaking, "We must accept the fact that White racism was responsible for Black nationalist teaching; furthermore, we must acknowledge that this race teaching did serve a purpose for a people who were made to look upon themselves as subhuman."[3]

Table 7.1
Origin, Development, and Change
of African American Nationalism

1815
Paul Cuffee
Emigrationism Back to Africa
|
1851
Edward Wilmont Blyden
Emigrationism Back to Africa
|
1858
Henry Highland Garnet
Emigrationism Back to Africa
Founder of the African Civilization Society
|
1861
Martin Delaney
Emigrationism Back to Africa
Founder of the National Emigration Conference
|
1900
Pan-Africanism
Dr. W.E.B. DuBois and Henry Sylvester Williams
|
1913
Noble Drew Ali
Founder of the Moorish Science Temple
|
1916
Marcus Garvey
Founder of the Universal Negro
Improvement Association

Table 7.1 (Continued)

1929
Noble Drew Ali Dies

John Givens El   W. D. Fard
(Each claims to be the reincarnation of Noble Drew Ali)

John Givens El, Chicago 1930   W. D. Fard, Detroit 1930–1933
Present-Day Moorish Science   Nation of Islam
Temple

1933
Master W. D. Fard disappears
|
Two Factions Develop
|

Abdul Muhammad   Elijah Muhammad, Chicago
perceived Fard as a prophet   1933, Nation of Islam—Fard
                                        perceived as Allah (God) in
                                        person

1965   1975
| |
Malcolm X, El-Hajj Malik El-Shabazz   Elijah Muhammad dies,
Organization of African American   Imam Warith Deen Muhammad
Unity and Muslim Mosque, Inc.   assumes leadership, changes from
                                        Nation of Islam to World
                                        Community of Al-Islam in the West
                                        and eventually the American
                                        Muslim Mission. Dissolved in
                                        1985, autonomous mosque, no
                                        central leadership structure.

1977
|

Silas Muhammad   Minister Louis Farrakhan   John Muhammad
Nation of Islam   Excommunicated from the   brother of the
Headquarters,   American Muslim Mission.   Honorable Elijah
Atlanta, GA   Leads his own organization,   Muhammad, Nation
                      the Nation of Islam,   of Islam.
                      Headquarters, Chicago, IL

                                |

                Five Percenters   Emmanual A. Muhammad
                Claim Nation of Islam   Baltimore, MD, Nation of
                as their heritage.   Islam.

   The social conditions and historical circumstances have changed since
early nationalist leaders like Paul Cuffee in 1815 advocated "Back to
Africa." In 1994 Minister Louis Farrakhan and other African American
leaders are confronted with an assortment of social pathologies that were

unthinkable for early nationalist leaders like Cuffee, Delaney, Blyden, Garvey, and Noble Drew Ali. Drug addiction, the crack epidemic, gang violence, drive-by shootings, domestic violence, the endangered black man, AIDS, the deterioration of the African American family, homelessness, unemployment, police brutality, and a black prison population that is larger than even in South Africa.

The Honorable Elijah Muhammad — Advocate of the Self-Help Concept

Minister Louis Farrakhan's response to the socioeconomic ills of African Americans in 1994 is consistent with the "self-help" concept utilized by the Honorable Elijah Muhammad. Traditional civil rights organizations often have to rely on donations from nonblacks, corporate donations, and government grants to maintain financial stability. Muslims also deplore the use of alcohol and tobacco companies to subsidize black organizations and conventions. Minister Louis Farrakhan utilizes the self-help concepts learned from the Honorable Elijah Muhammad to solve the social and economic problems of African Americans.

In a 1994 editorial in the *Final Call* entitled *Are Black Leaders and Organizations Really Ours?*, Minister Louis Farrakhan says,

> The Honorable Elijah Muhammad taught us how to build organizations and nations. He taught us that if we would get up and show the world that we are willing to shoulder our own responsibility for freedom others would come to our side to help us. By the Grace of Allah (God), the Nation of Islam under the leadership of the Honorable Elijah Muhammad and his Minister, Louis Farrakhan, is moving in that direction.[4]

Elijah Muhammad's Health and Nutrition Program The Abundant Life Clinic

The self-help concept also insures that black leadership will be free of the ideological restraints and concerns of donors and wealthy benefactors. The Nation of Islam under Minister Louis Farrakhan also continues to use the health and nutrition ideas of the Honorable Elijah Muhammad. For many years he wrote about "proper food for body and mind" in the *Muhammad Speaks* newspaper, with excerpts from *How to Eat to Live* and *The Message to the Black Man in America*. The Honorable Elijah Muhammad often admonished his followers to "stay away from the hog, tobacco, alcohol and such foolishness." He believed in fasting and one meal a day to cleanse the body for a long and healthy life. Clearly, Minister Louis Farrakhan has followed this directive.

Dr. Abdul Alim Muhammad, national spokesman for Minister Louis Farrakhan and minister of health and human resources for the Nation of Islam, operates the Abundant Life Clinic in Washington, D.C. It is located in the Paradise Manor Public Housing Units. The apartment units were previously infested with drugs and drug dealers. The Nation of Islam's security organization, the Fruit of Islam, organized the people in the projects, maintained the units, and dispersed the drug dealers with immediate haste. Dr. Abdul Alim Muhammad explains the metamorphosis of the Paradise Manor Community:

> This is the original place where the dope busters, as they called us, got started. This place here, Paradise Manor, was considered one of the ten worst drug markets in America and we came in by the grace of Allah and cleaned it up so that we can set up a clinic and take care of the health needs of our people. That's the Nation of Islam.[5]

The Abundant Life Clinic is a nonprofit organization and was founded in 1986 by Dr. Abdul Alim Muhammad and Dr. Phulgenda Sinha. It is a medical foundation dedicated to alternative medical therapies. The Abundant Life Clinic's most revolutionary medical contribution is the successful low-dose oral alpha-interferon therapy for HIV disease. H. L. Aubrey, Ph.D., ASA, Abdul Alim Muhammad, M.D., and Barbara Justice, M.D., collaborated on an article entitled "The Efficacy of Multiple Sub-Type Low Dose Orally Absorbed Alpha-Interferon Therapy in Patients with HIV-Infection: A Clinical Retrospective Analysis."

The abstract of the article describes the HIV therapy as follows: "A clinical retrospective analysis of a randomly selected sample of fifty patients was conducted to test the clinical efficiency of immunex, a drug treatment for HIV infected patients. This drug is similar to and developmentally related to keniron, a drug developed by Koech et al., at the Kenyan Medical Research Institute."[6] There were fifty patients, thirty-nine were men (78%), and eleven were women (22%). The patients ranged between twenty and fifty-four years of age. The oral alpha interferon was 82% effective in reversing the signs and symptoms of HIV infection.

Early African American Nationalist Thought
"The Founding Fathers" 1815–1861

Minister Louis Farrakhan's charisma along with the Honorable Elijah Muhammad's ideology and the Nation of Islam as an agent for social change is an attempt to address, intervene, and try to solve the social problems that plague his era. Minister Louis Farrakhan's methods, ideas, and ideals were consistent with African nationalist thought throughout the African history in the United States. Minister Louis Farrakhan is aware of the problems black leaders face when working for African and African American independence. He reveals his empathy toward the founding fathers.

Many of the early architects of Africa's independence were brilliant men on a right course. However, the stronger their ideas for African unity and progress toward economic independence. These leaders one by one were cut down by the manipulative forces of Europe and America. It is deemed not in the best interest of Europe and America that Africa should be politically and economically free.[7]

Since the beginning of a large African presence on American soil, there have been calls for blacks to be repatriated to a homeland outside the borders of the United States. As early as "1714 a Native American believed to be a resident of New Jersey had proposed sending Negroes back to Africa; the idea did not die."[8]

The genesis for Minister Louis Farrakhan's black separatist perspective began with the black church. The black church was the first institution under slavery and during the pre-emancipation era that was allowed to exist and be supported by people of African descent. Religious separatism and separate church worship were the first expressions of separatism, racial solidarity, and African American empowerment. In the 1770s, "the First Separatist Baptist Church was founded at Silver Bliff, South Carolina. The first Black Episcopal Church, founded by Absalom Jones in the 1880s, emerged from the parishioners to allow Blacks to integrate their worship services, as did the founding in 1815 of the African Methodist Episcopal (A.M.E.) Church in Philadelphia by Richard Allen."[9] The early "religious separatists" were not black nationalist in the traditional sense of the word. Separate worship and religious rituals were out of necessity due to segregation and slavery.

The religious separation is exemplified recently by Archbishop George Stallings who in 1989 left the Roman Catholic Church to enable him to practice Afro-centric rituals, theology, and symbols within his African American Catholic congregation. Rev. Stallings' AACC has established the "Imani Temple" in six cities in the United States, and one in Lagos, Nigeria. Rev. Stallings' followers believe that Jesus and his mother, Mary, are black people who originated in Africa.

The early separatist believed that Africans in the United States constituted a nation-within-a-nation. Since the dominant racial group was European, it would be difficult if not impossible for the African American minority to achieve equality and freedom. The history of African American nationalism suggests that racial solidarity was essential to change the social conditions which oppressed blacks as a race and class.

Classical separatism and the advocacy of Back to Africa, began with Paul Cuffee in 1815. Separatism provided an opportunity for African Americans to build a black nation. Cuffee was a "free Black man" who used his own financial resources to settle thirty African Americans in Sierra Leone in 1815. "Immediately after reaching adulthood and acquiring wealth, Cuffee became engrossed in Africa and African repatriation. He dedicated his life and fortune to this venture."[10] Cuffee petitioned the legislatives of New Jersey to contact the United States Congress to emancipate the slaves and allow willing blacks to leave the United States. The petition led to the creation of the American Colonization Society.

Paul Cuffee's commitment to transport Africans to the west coast of Africa was a "Back to the Mother Land" solution to racial injustice in the United States. The attraction to Africa was one of the first developments of early nationalism and the desire for a specific territory and land base, in an attempt to form a sovereign government and independent state. Early separatists received encouragement from whites; the American Colonization Society (ACS), was formed to transport free blacks to Africa. Many white Americans supported their efforts, "because they felt that African Americans were inferior and their presence here was a drawback to the development of White American institutions and culture."[11]

African American separatism and emigrationism began to take three specific forms of social change: Back to Africa, emigrationism to Third World countries in the Caribbean or South America, and a nation-within-a-nation or territorial separatism. Paul Cuffee influenced other separatists to look to Africa for social, economic, and political salvation. Three other significant African nationalist/separatists also influenced the African American separatist ideology: Henry Highland Garnet, Martin Delaney, and Edward Wilmont Blyden. Each man added specific ideas to the ideology which would influence those nationalists which followed them, including Marcus Garvey, Noble Drew Ali, Rastafari, Master Fard Muhammad, and Minister Louis Farrakhan's mentor, the Honorable Elijah Muhammad.

Early separatists who desired to emigrate to a separate state were motivated by five reasons: "(1) Christian nationalism and trade, (2) the mission of civilization, (3) Africa as a land of riches, (4) the black need of a homeland for racial regeneration, and (5) economic depression in the United States."[12] Following Cuffee's emigration efforts, the period between 1845 and 1861, the socioeconomic push factors in America continued to be more oppressive. The Fugitive Slave Law of 1850 safeguarded slave owners. In the western part of the United States, the Kansas-Nebraska Act of 1854 permitted states to accept or reject slavery. The Dred Scott case of 1857 reinforced the property status of slaves without legal rights, and crossing state boundaries into a "free state" did not make the slave a free man or woman. During this period the pull to emigrate to Africa became extremely alluring. In one "decade Liberia had settled the unprecedented total of 2,029 immigrants, almost as many people as had been settled over the past three decades."[13]

In 1858, Henry Highland Garnet became president of the African Civilization Society. Garnet wanted to establish an independent state in West Africa. Nationalism or "negro nationality" was the foundation for economic/commercial and political power for blacks throughout the black diaspora. The goal of Garnet's African Civilization Society was "a grand center on Negro nationality, from which shall flow the streams of commercial, intellectual, and political power. Which shall make colored people everywhere respected."[14]

Martin Delaney merged his National Emigration Conference with Garnet's African Civilization Society in 1861 to promote emigration to Africa. Delaney felt that African Americans were as culturally unique as the "Poles in Russia or the Hungarians in Austria." The culturally unique aspect of Africans residing in America was a source of pride, hope, and salvation for the race. Delaney was the first African American nationalist to advocate that African Americans are a "nation-within-a-nation."

Delaney's National Emigration Conference met three times. During the first convention in 1854, they discussed an independent state in the Caribbean region. By the second convention in 1856, Delaney, along with his associates H. Whetford and James T. Halley, began to negotiate with leaders in south Central America and Haiti to relocate. By the third convention Africa became the promised land. Delaney's "ideal colony would be somewhere in Nigeria as he saw it as being a colony of White business interest."[15] He thought very little of Liberia.

Delaney and Wilmont Blyden were instrumental in defining a definite "Black separatist ideology." Edward Wilmont Blyden, a West Indian, immigrated to Monrovia in 1851. Blyden, like his contemporaries, firmly believed that Africans could never be equal to Europeans in the United States. Blyden advocated nation building, and economic cooperation based upon African socialism, which Blyden felt was equitable and more humane than the capitalist system. Furthermore, Blyden was one of the first early African American separatists to be very critical of Christianity and denounce it as a "destructive and deleterious influence" on Africans. Blyden encouraged African Americans to turn to the east, pray to Allah, and accept Islam as their religious belief.

Blyden's perceptions of Islam in Africa led him to believe that "Islam strengthened and hastened certain tendencies to independence and self-reliance already at work, and amalgamated its own forms with African ones."[16] Edward Wilmont Blyden dedicated his life to the unification of Africans at home and abroad. Perhaps, "it was, is this very race pride, this ability to clearly define oneself in relation to Africa that pulled men like Blyden to Africa rather than those like Delaney who felt compelled to leave America."[17]

The founding fathers of African American separatist thought established some basic ideological concepts, which were to become the foundation for future African American separatists. They are as follows:

1. The desire for a specific territory.
2. Belief in an African American cultural uniqueness.
3. Belief in a common culture based on similarities as African people.
4. The desire for an independent sovereign government.
5. Economic cooperation and African socialism.
6. Back to Africa and territorial separatism.
7. Islam as appropriate and beneficial to African psychological, spiritual, and political needs.
8. Africans in America as a part of an international African network or Pan-Africanism.
9. African Americans as a "nation-within-a-nation."

The Pan-African Perspective, 1990
Dr. W.E.B. DuBois

The Pan-African concept was utilized for social change by Dr. W.E.B. DuBois and Henry Sylvester Williams. DuBois and Williams protested European colonialism and imperialism through their Pan-African Congress held in 1900, 1921, 1923, 1927, and 1945. African Americans began to identify with Africa as the origin of civilization and a source of racial pride and economic and political power. Pan-Africanism began to address issues outside the borders of the United States. The Pan-African Congress fostered the idea that "various groups of Africans, quite separate in origin, became so united in experience and so exposed to the impact of new cultures that they began to think of Africa as one idea and one land."[18] Minister Louis Farrakhan was influenced by Dr. DuBois at a very early age. He says, "When I was just learning to read my mother gave me the Crisis Magazine. The magazine of the N.A.A.C.P., in which the writings of W.E.B. Dubois were. This inspired my early development in Black consciousness."[19]

The Nation of Islam under Elijah Muhammad was an early advocate of international cooperation to change the problems of Blacks in the United States, i.e., the nation-within-a-nation. Minister Louis Farrakhan no doubt has been influenced by his mentor. Through extensive studies and world travels, he has developed a definite Pan-African perspective. He has "reached out" to Africans beyond the borders of the

United States to include the Caribbean, Mexico, and Africa. Minister Louis Farrakhan established mosques in Africa and the Caribbean. Minister Akbar Muhammad was the Nation of Islam's international representative in Ghana and served as the host of the 1994 Saviour's Day in Accra. The president of Ghana, Jerry John Rawlings, Dr. Kenneth Kaunda, and Minister Louis Farrakhan led the opening ceremonies. There were cultural, economic, health, education, and religious workshops. Topics such as the changing roles of the African woman, religion in Africa, and health issues facing the black world were discussed. Minister Louis Farrakhan's keynote address was entitled *Fulfilling the Vision of the Honorable Elijah Muhammad*. Minister Louis Farrakhan has often worked with Hispanics, Native Americans, radical whites, and Third World leaders throughout the world. Clearly, Minister Louis Farrakhan's international outreach and Pan-African perspective is consistent with the original doctrine and practice of the Honorable Elijah Muhammad. In a global economy and a changing economic/political world climate it was essential and politically astute for Minister Louis Farrakhan to make international linkages with people of color. Minister Louis Farrakhan explains the need to continue the Pan-African legacy of early leaders:

> I am proud to say that six years before the close of this century, in the spirit of Marcus Garvey, in the spirit of W.E.B. Dubois, and in the spirit of the Honorable Elijah Muhammad. We the Nation of Islam, shall return to the mother continent to the sacred ground of Accra, Ghana. Ghana's national flag has a five pointed black star that reflects the influence of Marcus Garvey on Dr. Kwame N'Krumah. It was the Honorable Marcus Garvey who started the black star line that he hoped would ultimately not only return some of us to Africa, but involve us in international trade.[20]

Marcus Garvey
The Universal Negro Improvement Association
1914–1930

Certainly it would be impossible to discuss the Honorable Elijah Muhammad and Minister Louis Farrakhan's black nationalist ideas without discussing the views of Marcus Mosiah Garvey. Garvey's influence on nationalist thought prior to and after the Great Depression (1914–1930) was remarkable. Race pride and African nationalism were inextricably woven together in the Garvey philosophy, and in the program of the Universal Negro Improvement Association (UNIA). Elijah Muhammad lived during the Garvey era and many ex-Garveyites joined the Nation of Islam and founded such organizations as the Rastafarian Movement.

Minister Louis Farrakhan explains Marcus Garvey's influence on his childhood socialization.

> My father was also a follower of the Honorable Marcus Garvey. My mother was also on the fringe of his teachings and I was certainly affected by what he and my father taught. My uncle was also a follower of the Honorable Marcus Garvey. My mother permitted me to visit my uncle in New York City. I saw a picture of a Black man prominently displayed on his wall. My uncle told me that he was a man that came to unite Black people. My uncle told me that he was dead and the tears rolled down my cheeks. I was 11 years old.[21]

Garvey's Universal Negro Improvement Association was founded in Jamaica in 1914 to work for "the general uplift of the Negro people of the world." The motto of the UNIA was, "one God, one aim, one destiny!" A young Marcus Garvey was influenced by African nationalist Duse Muhammad Ali. Duse was born in Alexandria, Egypt, November 21, 1866. He started a publication in 1912, the *African Times and Orient Review*. When Garvey arrived in London in 1912, he became an "astute student of Duse and a tireless worker for the journal. Garvey's slogan, Africa for Africans, at home and abroad, was indicative of race pride and dignity he received from Duse.[22] Garvey immigrated to the United States and made Harlem his home base for a worldwide black nationalist/separatist Movement. Garvey's influence was a direct result of both his charisma and having a dynamic organization. Garvey did not expect to leave America immediately; he had a plan based on the "rules of modern economics." He says, "We cannot all go back to Africa in a day or year, even twenty years. It must take time under the rules of modern economics, to entirely and largely depopulate a country of people who had been its residents for centuries, but we feel that with help for fifty years the problem could be solved."[23]

Marcus Garvey's UNIA glorified everything black. He established an African Orthodox Church where Jesus was black and African Americans were the chosen people. For women, there was the Black Cross Nurse Organization. For men, there was the African Legion with the dark blue uniforms and red trousers. A new African American flag struck the nationalist vein of black Americans. It was red (for the blood of the race), black (for the color of the race), and green (for the hope of the race) embodied in a free independent land.

The UNIA instituted an economic program which established a chain of grocery stores, restaurants, factories, and publishing houses. Through the Black Factories Corporation, Garvey sought to develop business and job opportunities for African Americans.

The UNIA also owned and operated a newspaper, The *Negro World*, which was established in January 1918. Within the space of a few months the *Negro World* became one of the leading Black weeklies and as such it proved to be a most effective instrument for the promotion of Garvey's program. The circulation of the *Negro World* was estimated as 2,000,000 readers by June 1919. The paper was distributed all over the world, and certain sections were printed in Spanish and French to benefit West Indian and Central American Blacks.

UNIA's economic and self-help program included the Black Star Line Steamship Company, which would connect black people of the world through commercial and industrial intercourse. The UNIA sold stock in the company to any black person interested in supporting the enterprise. The Black Star Line purchased three ships—*Yarmouth, Kanawha,* and *Shadyside.*

Garvey's movement had its most powerful influence between 1920 and 1921. In 1920 the UNIA held an international convention representing "the Negroes of the World." The convention drew 25,000 people to Madison Square Garden. During the convention Garvey was declared provisional president of the African Republic.

Elijah Muhammad's son, Imam Warith Deen Muhammad, explains Garvey's influence during an interview with the author. He says, "not only the Honorable Elijah Muhammad, but his teacher who was a foreigner and not an American, Fard Muhammad" (was also influenced by Garvey). His teachings were obviously influenced by Garvey. The emphasis was on identity, black identity, and economic development."[24]

Marcus Garvey's influences on the Honorable Elijah Muhammad and the Nation of Islam are as follows:

1. Black Factories Corporation—black business
2. Back to Africa culturally while developing a nation-within-a-nation in the United States
3. Race pride and African consciousness
4. Black nationalist credo—red for the blood of the race, black for the color of the race, and green for an independent homeland

Elijah Muhammad and Economic Development

The primary Garvey concept adhered to by the Honorable Elijah Muhammad, and sustained by Minister Louis Farrakhan, was the Black Factories Corporation. Garvey used a lot of the ideas of early nationalist leaders, but his economic and commercial ideas were influenced by Booker T. Washington. Garvey admired Washington's Tuskegee Institute and felt that economic cooperation and a bootstrap work ethic were essential for African American liberation.

The "Economic Blueprint" for freedom devised by the Honorable Elijah Muhammad was very similar to the Garvey Black Factories Corporation ideas. Under the Honorable Elijah Muhammad, the Nation of Islam established many businesses, restaurants, and cleaners; and sold bean pies, whiting fish, *Muhammad Speaks*, and *Final Call* under Minister Louis Farrakhan. In 1994, the top ten cities in the *Final Call* sales which average one million dollars per month were Chicago, Newark, New York, Detroit, Los Angeles, Baltimore, Washington, D.C., Philadelphia, Houston, Atlanta, Cleveland, and Dallas. The Nation of Islam has also purchased several tractor trailers to transport the *Final Call* and other products across the country. The vehicles are called the Leotis Fleet. It is named after Leotis X Beasley, who established a national trucking system and also drove trucks for the Nation of Islam. Minister Louis Farrakhan can be seen on ninety-five television stations throughout the country and can be heard on forty-three radio stations throughout the United States. Farms and apartment buildings are all economic development initiatives started by the Honorable Elijah Muhammad. Minister Louis Farrakhan continues to establish businesses in the black community. The businesses of the Nation of Islam provide revenue for the organization, employ members and nonmembers, and provide inspiration for African Americans to buy "Black" and support black business. Minister Louis Farrakhan has also created "power" cosmetic products and solicited and received funds from Housing and Urban Development (HUD) to provide security for some of the worst housing projects in urban America. The motto of the NOI Security Agency, Inc. is, "the force with proven results."

Presently, Minister Louis Farrakhan continues the Honorable Elijah Muhammad's economic development program with the *Three-Year Economic Development Program.* This program is designed to purchase farmland (over 5,000 acres). The organization plans to develop dairies, canneries, chicken farms, and crop production on the land. The economic enterprise also includes urban development in over 120 cities, beginning in Chicago. The motivation behind the economic development program is economic (jobs, economic stability), security (community safety), and self-esteem (beautify and dignify the community). In a *Final Call* article (1994) entitled *A Program for Self-Development,* the Honorable Elijah Muhammad exclaims, "We must stop relying upon the White man to care for us. We must become an independent people." The following is a twelve-point plan devised by the Honorable Elijah Muhammad.

1. Separate yourselves from the slavemaster.
2. Pool your resources, education, and qualification for independence.

3. Stop forcing yourselves into places where you are not wanted.
4. Make your own neighborhood a decent place to live.
5. Rid yourselves of the lust of wine and drink and learn to love self and your kind before loving others.
6. Unite to create a future for yourself.
7. Build your own homes, schools, hospitals, and factories.
8. Do not seek to mix your blood through racial integration.
9. Stop buying expensive cars, fine clothes, and shoes before being able to live in a fine home.
10. Spend your money among yourselves.
11. Build an economic system among yourselves.
12. Protect your women.[25]

Noble Drew Ali, Master Fard Muhammad,
and
The Yacub Theory, 1914–1930

Minister Louis Farrakhan's ideology and belief system is a direct extension of the ideas initiated by the founding fathers of separatism and nationalism in the United States. Minister Louis Farrakhan's adherence to Africa as the "mother of civilization" is not only historically correct, but consistent with the legacy of the movement. In 1994, Minister Louis Farrakhan realized that Back to Africa is not a realistic goal; therefore, Minister Louis Farrakhan began to rely on the social and psychological benefits of an Afro-centric perspective to enhance self-esteem, and pride in self and the race for followers of his nationalist movement. The belief in Islam for members of the Nation of Islam was influenced by early nationalists like Wilmont Blyden. Master Fard Muhammad, the founder of the Nation of Islam, felt Islam was "the natural religion for Black people." The Honorable Elijah Muhammad, during the first resurrection, realized that he required a unique blend of Islam and Christianity to "fish" the seas of urban America (especially during the Depression) for fresh converts.

When Elijah Muhammad assumed leadership of the Nation of Islam in 1930, he deemed Master Fard Muhammad as "God in Person" or Allah, and Elijah became the prophet of Allah. Master Fard Muhammad believed that European names denied African Americans a black identity and identification with the mother land, Africa. Master Fard Muhammad taught that the proper identity was Muslim, Islam, and Africa. Therefore, the names Muhammad and X were used. The combination of Islam and Christianity were great bait for the Nation of Islam to "fish" for new converts. Remember, the Honorable Elijah Muhammad was the son of a Baptist preacher and was very knowledgeable of the Bible. Both

Garvey and Drew Ali felt that the black man's God must be black. Marcus Garvey and Noble Drew Ali wanted to liberate black people from worshipping white images of God and religious prophets. Garvey: "By way of saying that the Messiah was Black, Drew Ali was saying that Islam was the Black man's true religion. Fard synthesized these two positions and raised them to the highest level."[26]

The Yacub Theory was created by Master Fard Muhammad. Master Fard Muhammad was influenced by Marcus Garvey, Noble Drew Ali, and the Moorish Science Temple to provide a black political perspective for followers to correlate personal and racial injustice to institutional inequality. Therefore, heaven and hell were on earth, and correspondingly the devil (white man), and God in person (Master Fard Muhammad) were also living beings. Hell for followers of the "nation" was man-made, and men could change these conditions through organizing as a nation-within-a-nation.

Dr. Abdul Alim Muhammad has a different interpretation of the Yacub Theory. He says,

> He, Yacub, was a great scientist. He separated that secondary nature out, into a separate biological form that we identify as caucasian. Yacub said alongside your divine nature is another nature in opposition to the first one. So the Mahdi, Master Fard Muhammad, is present having mastered the two natures that are in people. One is mastered to destroy it. The other masters to nurture it to perfection. That's what the Nation of Islam is. That's where Yacub's history falls into it.[27]

The "white man is the devil theme" is a direct influence of Noble Drew Ali, who started the Moorish Science Temple in Newark, New Jersey. In 1914, Noble Drew Ali's philosophy was published in his sixty-four-page Holy Quran, a pamphlet consisting of principles from the Islamic Quran, the Christian Bible, some of Marcus Garvey's African nationalist ideas, and Drew Ali's own historical interpretations. The Holy Quran is regarded as a book to be read only by his followers. Imam Warith Deen Muhammad explains Noble Drew Ali's influence on the Yacub Theory: "Master Fard Muhammad studied Noble Drew Ali's approach to introduce the Quran to the Black community. Professor Fard introduced the whole text of the Quran, in the very inception of the Nation of Islam. To introduce it, he had to put it in the package of Drew Ali."[28] Noble Drew Ali interpreted the Bible to identify white people as the oppressors of the chosen people, blacks. Imam Warith Deen Muhammad details Drew Ali's interpretation of the scriptures:

> Noble Drew Ali felt the caucasians were the embodiment of evil. Master Fard Muhammad used the ideology of Noble Drew Ali. Drew Ali associated White people with the embodiment of evil in scripture, which is Satan.[29]

Elijah Muhammad and the Nation of Islam
1930–1975

The Honorable Elijah Muhammad carried the African nationalist banner for forty-five years. From 1930 until his death in 1975, Elijah Muhammad was a dedicated servant of Allah. Minister Louis Farrakhan saw the Honorable Elijah Muhammad's death as an opportunity for the "real Muslims to stand and be recognized and provide us with an opportunity to actually see who the true Black Muslims are. Many of us had been pretending all along."[30] Furthermore, the Honorable Elijah Muhammad was the single greatest influence on the black nationalist thought of Malcolm X and Minister Louis Farrakhan. Shortly after the death of the Honorable Elijah Muhammad, Minister Louis Farrakhan reinforced his commitment to Muhammad's teachings. In a speech at the Institute for Positive Education on November 15, 1977, Minister Louis Farrakhan exclaimed,

> The position that I take is the position that the Honorable Elijah Muhammad stood upon and that is that America has not been the friend of Black people, and is not now doing justice by Black people. The Honorable Elijah Muhammad took the position that America was spiritually and morally more wicked than ancient Sodom and Gomorrah. More imperialistic in her dealing with other nations than ancient Rome. More wicked in her enslavement of the Black man than Egypt was with Israel.[31]

Minister Louis Farrakhan adopted the Honorable Elijah Muhammad's ideology and program, because he felt that the ideology was inclusive and was a functional socioeconomic plan for all black people, not just Muslims. Minister Louis Farrakhan believed that the Honorable Elijah Muhammad's program was "wide enough, broad enough, and strong enough for every Black man, woman, and child to stand on its base without feeling threatened in the least in their own ideological development."[32] Minister Louis Farrakhan has resurrected the Nation of Islam and continues the ideology of Elijah Muhammad as the representative of the Honorable Elijah Muhammad.

The Honorable Elijah Muhammad as an advocate for African American nationalism and separatism exceeded the accomplishments of those nationalists who proceeded him. Unlike Cuffee, Delaney, and Blyden, the Honorable Elijah Muhammad remained in the United States and for forty-five years worked for a "nation-within-a-nation," while simultaneously demanding "equal justice under the laws of the United States and equal employment opportunities."

Furthermore, the Honorable Elijah Muhammad's tenure of forty-five years as the leader of a separatist organization was longer than any leader who proceeded him, and that includes Cuffee, Garnet, Delaney, Blyden,

Noble Drew Ali, Marcus Garvey, and Malcolm X. His longevity was remarkable considering that his ideology, theology, and strategy were
threatening enough to warrant constant surveillance by the FBI and other
law enforcement agencies throughout the country. Elijah Muhammad's
contribution to African American nationalism is as follows:

1. An independent nation within the United States for African
   Americans as an option to segregation, racism, and political
   oppression.
2. An inner-city school system to educate African American youth
   and The University of Islam.
3. A prison ministry for incarcerated African Americans.
4. A strong centralized system of mosque organizations throughout the United States, Africa, and the Caribbean.
5. Recruitment and indoctrination of future generations of African
   American leaders, i.e., Malcolm X, Muhammad Ali, Dr. Abdul
   Alim Muhammad, Silas Muhammad, the Five Percenters, and
   Minister Louis Farrakhan.
6. *Muhammad Speaks* newspapers and warehouse.
7. Operation of a seafood import business for whiting, Hagg fish,
   and salaam sardines.
8. Development of business enterprises for employment, apartment units, supermarkets, bakeries, cleaners, salaam restaurants,
   and health care clinics.
9. Introduced Islam to African Americans as an alternative to
   Christianity.
10. Importance of adapting Islamic names and replacing the slave
    names with an X and Muhammad.
11. Encouraged the study of the Quran and learning Arabic.

Minister Louis Farrakhan Succeeds Malcolm X as National Spokesman for the Nation of Islam

On March 8, 1964, Malcolm X announced he was leaving the Nation of
Islam. Elijah Muhammad promoted Minister Louis Farrakhan to succeed
Malcolm X. Minister Louis Farrakhan was originally named Louis Walcott, then Louis X, and finally Minister Louis Farrakhan. He attended high
school and prep school in Boston, Massachusetts. Louis Walcott attended
Winston-Salem State Teachers College in North Carolina. The young
Walcott acquired the artistic skills of creative writer, poet, playwright, and
violinist. Young Walcott also had an excellent singing voice. He married
his childhood sweetheart in September of 1953 during his junior year in
college. In February of 1955, Louis Walcott accepted the teachings of the

Honorable Elijah Muhammad and became a member of the Nation of Islam. Minister Louis Farrakhan explains how he became a follower of the Honorable Elijah Muhammad after his uncle, a former Garveyite, joined the Nation of Islam: "My uncle later became a follower of the Honorable Elijah Muhammad and constantly sent some of the Muslim brothers to get my brother and me to join the mosque in Boston. On February 26, 1955, I became a follower of the Honorable Elijah Muhammad."[33] On the request of Minister Malcolm X, Louis X, as he was known then, moved to Boston. In 1956, Louis X became the Minister of Temple No. 11 in Boston. In May of 1965, three months after the assassination of Malcolm X, the Honorable Elijah Muhammad appointed Louis X minister of Temple No. 7 in New York City. This was a very significant, strategic, yet politically volatile and dangerous career move. Temple No. 7 was the temple that Malcolm X led. Minister Malcolm spent several years on the streets of Harlem and throughout New York City "fishing" for new recruits for the Nation of Islam. Minister Louis X had to overcome these allegiances to Minister Malcolm X and confront and dispel the allegations that the Nation of Islam was involved in the assassination of Malcolm X. Minister Louis Farrakhan, in an interview in *Black Books Bulletin* in 1978, explained the circumstances surrounding the assassination of Malcolm X:

> Malcolm, as you know was Elijah Muhammad's national representative and spokesman. He was articulate, popular, and his popularity created jealousy and envy among some top officials within the movement, which resulted in severe problems for him. Malcolm saw in the Honorable Elijah Muhammad what from his perspective, was serious contradictions and Malcolm left the Nation or was put out.[34]

Minister Louis Farrakhan felt that Malcolm may have provoked threats on his life once he defected by "slinging mud" at the Honorable Elijah Muhammad. Minister Louis Farrakhan explains the incendiary atmosphere after his defection:

> Malcolm in his anger and bitterness, however, made what in my judgement, was a tragic mistake which was to sling mud at his former teacher. This lit the fuse in the highly incendiary atmosphere creating the conditions which allowed Malcolm to be assassinated.[35]

There is no doubt that Malcolm's ideological growth, organizational ability, and perspective was fed, nurtured, and cultivated by the Honorable Elijah Muhammad and the Nation of Islam. Malcolm came to the "Lost-Found Nation" with charisma and an iron will; however, the organizational structure, financial stability, and African separatist ideology of the Nation of Islam provided Malcolm X with a platform and a vehicle to address social, economic, and political problems which oppressed

African Americans. Malcolm's "works lack an overarching theory, and in fact, he became a famous organizer not in a system devised by himself, but by the Honorable Elijah Muhammad."[36]

Minister Louis Farrakhan, National Representative of the Honorable Elijah Muhammad, 1977

When the Honorable Elijah Muhammad died in 1975, his son Imam Warith Deen Muhammad assumed leadership and immediately began to dismantle the largest, oldest, most powerful, and influential black nationalist organizations in the United States. Minister Louis Farrakhan left the World Community of Al-Islam in the West (WCIW) in 1977. There were fears that there might be similar violence which followed the split between Malcolm X and the Honorable Elijah Muhammad. When he resurrected the Nation of Islam in 1977, Minister Louis Farrakhan explains the differences between his departure from the WCIW in 1977 and Malcolm X's departure from the Nation of Islam in 1964. Minister Louis Farrakhan explains:

> I am not bitter with W. D. Muhammad or members of the W.C.I.W. In my returning to the message and program of the Honorable Elijah Muhammad, and Malcolm going completely away from his teachings and programs, lies the internal difference between us.[37]

Minister Louis Farrakhan left the WCIW because he felt that the Honorable Elijah Muhammad's program was the best solution for socioeconomic problems in the African American community. Specifically, there were seven reasons why he decided to resurrect the program of the Honorable Elijah Muhammad in 1977. They are as follows:

1. The loss of gains made by the great black leaders of the past.
2. The turn of America from benign neglect to a malignant neglect of the real problems facing black people in America—jobs, police brutality, housing, welfare, etc.
3. The rise of a Nazi, Ku Klux Klan fascist mentality in white America.
4. The pull back from affirmative action by the private and public sector of the American economy.
5. The moral and spiritual degeneracy of the black community; the increase of drugs and prostitution.
6. The murder and robbery of our elderly; the disrespect for our women.

7. The decline of moral strength and morale within the Muslim community; the loss of discipline.[38]

Minister Louis Farrakhan's resurrection of the Nation of Islam continues an African Nationalist legacy that is over 179 years old. The African nationalist ideology has been a consistent theme throughout the black political struggles in the United States. Imam Warith Deen Muhammad has essentially fallen from the African nationalist ideological tree. The American Muslim Mission, formerly WCIW, does not represent the ideas of the Honorable Elijah Muhammad or the founding fathers of this race's conscious ideology. Minister Louis Farrakhan, however, continues a legacy of African nationalist thought, which calls for black Americans to "rise up you mighty race." Minister Louis Farrakhan has picked up the baton from the Honorable Elijah Muhammad and continues his legacy as his spiritual son. The following chapter will discuss the Nation of Islam in the 1970s after the excommunication of Minister Louis Farrakhan.

Notes

1. Author's note: W. D. Muhammad's name change (from Wallace to Warith) is a part of his personal spiritual growth and reflects ideological changes in the organization.

2. James E. Turner, "Blyden, Black Nationalism and Emigration Schemes," *Black Books Bulletin,* vol. 6, no. 1, Spring 1978, p. 20.

3. Adib Rashad, *The History of Islam and Black Nationalism in the America's* (Beltsville, Maryland: Writers Inc., 1991), p. 79.

4. Louis Farrakhan, "Are Black Leaders and Organizations Really Ours," *The Final Call,* vol. 13, no. 24, September 14, 1994.

5. Interview, Dr. Abdul Alim Muhammad, Abundant Life Clinic, Washington, D.C., September 9, 1994.

6. H. L. Aubrey, Ph.D. ASA, Abdul Alim Muhammad, M.D., Barbara Justice, M.D., "The Efficacy of Multiple Sub-Type Low Dose Orally Absorbed Alpha-Interferon Therapy in Patients with HIV-Infection: A Clinical Retrospective Analysis" [abstract], October 26, 1992.

7. Minister Louis Farrakhan, "Fulfilling the Vision," *The Final Call,* vol. 13, no. 25, September 28, 1994.

8. John Hope Franklin, *From Slavery to Freedom* (New York: Vantage Press, 1969), p. 238.

9. Raymond Hall, ed., *Black Separatism and Social Reality: Rhetoric and Reason* (New York: Pergamon Press, Inc. 1977), p. 2.

10. Rashad, *History of Islam and Black Nationalism,* p. 46.

11. John T. McCartney, *Black Power Ideologies: An Essay in African American Political Thought* (Philadelphia: Temple University Press, 1992), p. 7.

12. McCartney, *Black Power Ideologies,* p. 7.

13. Ibid., p. 22.

14. Hollis Lynch, *Edward Wilmont Blyden* (London: Oxford Press, 1967), p. 25.

15. Rashad, *History of Islam and Black Nationalism,* p. 52.

16. Lynch, *Blyden,* pp. 23–24.

17. Kala Adelaja, "Sources in African Political Thought" - Part I, *Presence Africaine,* 70, 2nd quarter, 1969, p. 10.

18. W.E.B. Dubois, *The World and Africa* (New York: The Viking Press, 1947), p. 7.

19. Minister Louis Farrakhan, "Fulfilling the Vision," p. 21.

20. Ibid.

21. Ibid.

22. Rashad, *History of Islam and Black Nationalism,* p. 58.

23. Amy Garvey, *Philosophy and Opinions of Marcus Garvey,* (New York: Atheneum Press), 1969. p. 122.

24. Interview, Imam Warith Deen Muhammad, Chicago, Illinois, 1979.

25. The Honorable Elijah Muhammad, "A Program for Self-Development," *The Final Call,* vol. 13, no. 24, September 14, 1994, p. 19.

26. Rashad, *History of Islam and Black Nationalism,* p. 70.

27. Interview, Dr. Abdul Alim Muhammad.

28. Interview, Imam Warith Deen Muhammad.

29. Ibid.

30. Minister Louis Farrakhan, "BBB Interviews Minister Abdul Farrakhan." *Black Books Bulletin,* November 1978, p. 44.

31. Ibid., p. 71.

32. Ibid.

33. Minister Louis Farrakhan, "Fulfilling the Vision," p. 21.

34. Minister Louis Farrakhan, "BBB Interviews," p. 71.

35. Ibid.

36. McCartney, *Black Power Ideologies,* p. 185.

37. Minister Louis Farrakhan, "BBB Interviews," p. 71.

38. *New York Amsterdam News,* vol. 69, no. 2, January 14, 1978.

Chapter 8

A Historical and Philosophical Analysis on the Ideological Dispute between Imam Warith Deen Muhammad and Minister Louis Farrakhan, 1974–1980

"The next serious dispute came between Malcolm X and his mentor and teacher, the Honorable Elijah Muhammad. This dispute was historically significant in that it set a precedence that struck at the very fabric of (so-called) Orthodox Islam and Islamic Nationalism. This precedence has resulted in the disputations division between blacks who are Muslims (so called orthodox) as opposed to blacks who are Black Muslim Nationalist."[1]
—Adib M.Rashad

It was inevitable that Minister Louis Farrakhan and Imam Warith Deen Muhammad would come into conflict over the ideology, theology, and direction of the Nation of Islam. Imam Warith D. Muhammad was in constant conflict with his father, the Honorable Elijah Muhammad, over the philosophy (self-help), theology (Islamic nationalism), and ideology (black separatism) of the Nation of Islam during the turbulent 1960s. Imam W. D. Muhammad was a student of Orthodox Islam and a confidant of Malcolm X. He often communicated with Malcolm X and discussed the unorthodox approach of his father's Nation of Islam. Imam W. D. Muhammad explains his excommunication and his relationship with Malcolm X:

> I was the first to be excommunicated. I was charged with trying to influence Malcolm's theological thinking. I was also charged with giving him personal, private knowledge of the Honorable Elijah Muhammad's living, which was a lie. I told him at the time I was falsely accused and I would like to face the accusers. The Honorable Elijah Muhammad told me, "Malcolm X is not facing his accusers either. We are talking to you separately." So he talked to me separately and he made his decision right there. His decision was to excommunicate me.[2]

Once Malcolm X made the Hajj to Mecca and ate and slept with "blue eyed devils" he was convinced that Islam had changed their hearts and minds. Malcolm X believed Islam would achieve the same in the United States. Imam W. D. Muhammad refused to accept the God image (God in Person) of Master Fard Muhammad. The designation of the Honorable Elijah Muhammad as the prophet of Allah was also a point of contention for Imam W. D. Muhammad. According to Imam W. D. Muhammad, the Honorable Elijah Muhammad was a messenger and not a prophet in the true Biblical and Quranic sense:

> The Honorable Elijah Muhammad on many occasions said, "I am not a prophet." The Honorable Elijah Muhammad didn't speak in the same theological spirit as the Bible and the Quran. I think he was saying he didn't get a revelation like Moses or Christ or like Muhammad and the other great prophets. He was saying "a man came to me with solutions for your health problems, social problems, and I bring you the message he gave me."[3]

Imam W. D. Muhammad was excommunicated by the Honorable Elijah Muhammad over similar ideological and theological disputes. Ultimately, Imam W. D. Muhammad followed the same "orthodox" path of El-Hajj Malik El-Shabazz (Malcolm X), and Minister Louis Farrakhan followed the teachings of the Honorable Elijah Muhammad (Black Muslim nationalism). The major difference was that Minister Louis Farrakhan and Imam W. D. Muhammad were able to spiritually separate and eventually divorce without bloodshed and violence. For the nonviolent divorce, both men should be commended for their courage, wisdom, and restraint.

Imam Warith D. Muhammad "took the Nation of Islam on a path that reflected his spiritual character and his spiritual experiences. He was never a devoted teacher of nationalism of any kind. Therefore, his approach to the Nation of Islam should be understood within the context of his spiritual experiences."[4]

Imam W. D. Muhammad's Ideological Conflict with the Honorable Elijah Muhammad

For several years members of the Nation of Islam were aware of Imam W. D. Muhammad's ideological and theological differences with the Honorable Elijah Muhammad. The frequent excommunications (at least three or four times) and ideological conflicts were a prelude to the changes to come; therefore, no one intimate with the functions of the organization was surprised by the "man chosen for the mission" and his changes.

In 1970 Imam W. D. Muhammad was accepted back into the Nation of Islam for the final time. In 1974, he was accepted back into the ministerial ranks of the Nation of Islam and immediately began this theological revision and ideological duels with his father. He was given the freedom to teach and preach as he saw fit. He would often test the support of his father by, in his words, "saying things I knew were different from some of the things the people had been taught under the leadership of the Honorable Elijah Muhammad."[5]

Approximately one year prior to his death the Honorable Elijah Muhammad, according to Imam W. D. Muhammad, accepted the revisions in theology and ideology from his son. Imam W. D. Muhammad describes a meeting between he and his father in 1974 as follows:

> One time a tape was brought to the Honorable Elijah Muhammad by officers of the FOI [Fruit of Islam], who were like the police in the Nation of Islam, checking everything. He hadn't heard it himself. He called me over and played it while I was present. . . . He jumped up out of his seat and applauded and said, "My son's got it!" That's what he told the officers sitting around the table and his wife. He said, "My son can go anywhere on earth and preach."[6]

So, according to Imam W. D. Muhammad, shortly before his passing the Honorable Elijah Muhammad himself accepted the changes and gave his son his blessing to change the organization as he saw fit; however, even though the leadership was aware of the changes, not everyone was ready or able to comprehend and accept the massive restructuring and dismantling of the most powerful and oldest black nationalist organization in the United States. Initially, Minister Louis Farrakhan supported Imam W. D. Muhammad and out of a spirit of unity he resisted the temptation to contradict the new leader.

In a public address at Virginia Union University in Richmond, Virginia, on February 4, 1976, Minister Louis Farrakhan had this to say about the transition of power from the Honorable Elijah Muhammad to Imam W. D. Muhammad:

> Out of the dark shadows emerged the Honorable W. D. Muhammad. The son of the Honorable Master Elijah Muhammad. The world was shocked! The son of the Honorable Elijah Muhammad, who was he? The public had no knowledge of W. D. Muhammad. But many of us in the leadership knew that this was the one who was supposed to work behind the father and bring to fruition that which the father designed. There was no squabble for leadership, no fighting, no bickering, no arguing, but a smooth transition of power.[7]

Imam W. D. Muhammad Unveils the Nation's Secrets

The organization had been very secretive of its finances, membership, and other facets of the Nation of Islam. For many years, when asked about the most intimate details, Muslims would always respond, "Those who know, don't say. Those who say, don't know!" In June of 1975, Imam W. D. Muhammad made a public disclosure of the Nation of Islam's financial affairs. The major source of income was a $22-million fish import business. The Nation of Islam under the Honorable Elijah Muhammad's tenure also purchased $6.2 million in farmland and employed 1,000 people on a payroll of $1.3 million and paid $1 million corporate taxes. The total assets were approximately $46 million.

Roy Wilkins, executive director of the NAACP and a staunch advocate of integration, praised the new direction of the Nation of Islam. In a *New York Post* article on June 28, 1975, entitled, "The Muslims," he exclaimed:

> The new leader of the Black Muslims revealed a new interpretation of their religion which may have more effect, psychologically, than any balance in the bank. Today's Muslims do not exclude people merely because they are white. It was only a few years ago that the term white devil was applied by Black Muslims to all whites. This is the latest in the discovery that a man is not evil or good simply because he is white, brown, yellow, red or black.[8]

It's Boogie Time in the Nation
September 1, 1975

The changes in the Nation of Islam were immediate, radical, and earth-shaking. On September 1, 1975, fight promoter Don King gave a party in the Chicago headquarters for the manager of heavyweight champion Muhammad Ali, Herbert Muhammad (son of the Honorable Elijah Muhammad). Ali had become a two-time heavyweight champion with a "rope-a-dope" knockout of George Foreman in November of 1974. The guests included Ron "Superfly" O'Neal, Andy Williams, Howard Cosell, and even talk show host Phil Donahue. A September 1, 1975, *New York Times* article described the gathering thusly: "There was singing, dancing, cigarette smoking, some profanity, and dresses that were short and low cut, all once decreed taboo by the Honorable Elijah Muhammad."[9] There were performances by Clifton Davis and Della Reese. Stevie Wonder sang "Superstition" and the sensuous Lola Falana did a "disco dance." One party goer shouted, "It's boogie time in the Nation."

The Nation of Islam under the Honorable Elijah Muhammad served a valuable function for Afro-centric blacks who wanted a strong black nationalist organization to join. One observer put it into perspective when he said, "if the Nation [of Islam] becomes another civil rights organization or something akin to the National Business League, it will be unfortunate."[10] There were a number of politicians in attendance—democrats, republicans, and independents. The Reverend Jesse Jackson, then president of Operation People United to Save Humanity, said, "This is truly an historical event."

Don King's gala was in appreciation of Muhammad Ali and Herbert Muhammad. It also was a coming-out party for the new Nation of Islam under the Imam W. D. Muhammad. Somewhere in the crowd of party goers was Minister Louis Farrakhan probably shaking his head in disbelief, clutching the star and crescent and remembering the red, black, and green legacy of the Honorable Elijah Muhammad. However, he still supported Imam W. D. Muhammad. He said, "No ill winds will ruffle the shades of this divine nation. No one among us is high enough to tie the shoes laces of Wallace."[11]

During the transition, Minister Louis Farrakhan's title was the National Representative of Chief Minister W. D. Muhammad, Supreme Minister of the Nation of Islam. Minister Louis Farrakhan was the minister of Mosque No. 7 in New York City and developed a strong following. Imam W. D. Muhammad transferred Minister Louis Farrakhan to Chicago. Many perceived this move as a demotion and an attempt to control and rein in the charismatic Minister Louis Farrakhan. During the early stages of the transition Minister Louis Farrakhan changed his name to Abdul Haleem Farrakhan and continued his support of Imam W. D. Muhammad.

Malcolm X. Shabazz Temple No. 7, New York City
1976

Imam W. D. Muhammad continued to reshape the Nation of Islam and on February 2, 1976, he decided to honor El-Hajj Malik El-Shabazz (Malcolm X) for his contribution to the Nation of Islam. Mosque No. 7 in Harlem, New York, was renamed in honor of Malcolm X. Imam Wallace D. Muhammad explained why he restored Minister Malcolm to a position of honor in the Nation of Islam:

> I couldn't accept that Minister Malcolm be written off. He established himself. He was the greatest minister the Nation of Islam ever had, except for the Honorable Elijah Muhammad. I can't say he was greater than the Honorable Elijah Muhammad. He was, in my opinion and many other ministers, the most faithful minister to the Honorable Elijah Muhammad in the whole history of the Nation of Islam.[12]

This proclamation by Imam W. D. Muhammad and obvious admiration of Malcolm X was another change that was sweet and sour for the rank and file. The sweet was his restoring Malcolm X Shabazz to an honorable status. The sour was proclaiming Minister Malcolm as the "greatest minister" and the most "faithful" to the Honorable Elijah

Muhammad. Minister Malcolm X, once he began to accept a more traditional interpretation of Islam and question the ideology, programs, and teachings of the Honorable Elijah Muhammad, was no longer "faithful." As a matter of fact, Minister Louis Farrakhan accused Malcolm X of "slinging mud" at his teacher the Honorable Elijah Muhammad during Malcolm's reassessment of the Nation of Islam's ideology, theology, and programs.

Furthermore, Minister Louis Farrakhan had replaced Malcolm X as minister of the New York Mosque and served "faithfully" for ten years until Imam W. D. Muhammad relocated him to Chicago. It was a cruel irony for Minister Louis Farrakhan to hear Imam W. D. Muhammad praise Malcolm X and rename the mosque after him after Minister Louis Farrakhan had toiled in the fields of Harlem to resurrect the mosque after Malcolm's assassination. Minister Louis Farrakhan perceived Malcolm as being impatient for the changes that Imam W. D. Muhammad ultimately made. Minister Louis Farrakhan felt Malcolm made a mistake when he says, "Malcolm X knew where the Nation of Islam should go and would ultimately go, but as a leader he lacked the patience to wait for the development of the minds of the followers toward that direction."[13] To his credit Minister Louis Farrakhan continued to support the changes. He said that "Malcolm's place in the history of Islam is assured. It forces the community to deal with it and think about it, and assess this man unemotionally. It stimulates growth and development."[14]

Saviour's Day, 1976

Saviour's Day, February 29, 1976, marked the end of one year under the leadership of Imam W. D. Muhammad. The Saviour's Day is an annual tribute to the founder Master Fard Muhammad. Members of the Nation of Islam believe that Master Fard Muhammad is still alive, which would make him 117 years old as of 1994. During the 1976 Saviour's Day, Imam W. D. Muhammad revealed severe "cash flow problems" dating back to 1967. These problems left the Nation of Islam $4.5 million in debt. Imam W. D. Muhammad explained the debt: "We are grateful that we have been able to trace the problem as quickly as we have and then act to develop programs to correct this problem, which has been festering unnoticed for ten years."[15]

Imam W. D. Muhammad believed that the accumulating debt was a failure to develop "an accounting system to monitor income and expenditures effectively."[16] The debt reached a peak of $9.5 million in 1973. The largest liability was a $3 million loan to purchase Mosque No. 2 in Chicago. W. D. Muhammad devised an 18-month plan to reorganize and prioritize business opportunity and to streamline its payroll. Imam W. D.

Muhammad also revealed that the Nation of Islam had state and federal tax problems. The NOI owed the federal government several million dollars in back taxes and owed money to Social Security, and to the Department of Labor for workmen's compensation and minimum wage laws.

The southern farmland was not monitored by the organization and many of the farms were not profitable. One Muslim official exclaimed, "It turned out that our farms were not making money for us, but the people managing them made enough money to buy farms nearby that were doing well."[17] Imam W. D. Muhammad began to sell the various business enterprises and offered Muslims the first opportunity to purchase the stores and shops. The Nation of Islam also worked with the Small Business Administration to arrange loans for the new owners.

The foundation of the Honorable Elijah Muhammad's self-help program was slowly being dismantled, sold off, and abandoned. The Nation of Islam under Imam W. D. Muhammad was relinquishing the self-help philosophy for purely "spiritual" endeavors. The Nation of Islam was becoming purely a nation of fellowship and not business. Furthermore, former Muslim officials who were loyal to the Honorable Elijah Muhammad like Abbas Rassould and Raymond Sharieff were either ousted or demoted, and replaced with new unknown members loyal to Imam W. D. Muhammad.

Minister Louis Farrakhan Excommunicated from the World Community of Al-Islam in the West (WCIW), 1977

"For many of you who do not understand the phenomena of change; to many of you who think that we should keep it [the Nation of Islam] the way the Honorable Elijah Muhammad had it. And don't do anything with it, because it was alright then. You just don't understand."[18] These words were spoken by Minister Louis Farrakhan to the author and a group of college students and community residents at Virginia Union University during a public address in 1976. In retrospective hindsight, Minister Louis Farrakhan was speaking with a heavy heart. There is no way to determine exactly when he decided to detour from the ideological path of Imam Warith Deen Muhammad; however, as of 1977, one year after the public address at Virginia Union University, Minister Louis Farrakhan left the WCIW to resurrect the Nation of Islam as the national representative of the Honorable Elijah Muhammad. By 1978, the former "Black Muslims" were divided into separate ideological directions: W. D. Muhammad's WCIW; Minister Farrakhan's NOI; and a small faction of true believers following the NOI headed by a former official under Elijah Muhammad, Silas Muhammad. Silas Muhammad's national headquarters is in Atlanta, Georgia.

Excommunication has played a significant role in the Nation of Islam. Each excommunication of renowned leaders has led to turmoil and change. The Honorable Elijah Muhammad excommunicated Imam W. D. Muhammad and Malcolm X for disagreement over the ideology and theology of the Nation of Islam. Minister Malcolm X eventually left the Nation of Islam and started the Organization of African American Unity and Muslim Mosque, Inc. Imam Warith D. Muhammad was accepted back into the Nation of Islam after frequent excommunications. He remained in the Nation, assumed control and the power to exercise his authority as the chief minister. Imam Warith D. Muhammad transformed the Nation of Islam to the World Community of Al-Islam in the West (1970s), the American Muslim Mission (1980s), and eventually the Muslim Mission (1990s). Each change was an effort to make the organization and its members adhere to strict, traditional Islamic principles and to exclude race, nationalism, and the racial images of God and prophets from theology and worship.

Clearly, Minister Louis Farrakhan disagreed with the numerous changes and began to reassess the Honorable Elijah Muhammad's program. His reassessment led Minister Louis Farrakhan to believe that the ideological path taken by Imam Warith D. Muhammad was the fork in the road between the two leaders.

Once he was excommunicated, Minister Abdul Haleem Farrakhan changed his name to Minister Louis Farrakhan. On November 15, 1977, at the Institute of Positive Education, Minister Louis Farrakhan in one of his first public addresses explains his excommunication from the WCIW:

> The effects of the changes within the World Community of Al Islam, in addition to the information I gained about our people in my travels abroad caused me to reassess the Honorable Elijah Muhammad. His teachings and programs for Black people. My articulation of this caused Imam W. D. Muhammad to announce to the entire Muslim body that I was no longer a person with whom the Muslims (W.C.I.W.) should associate, listen to or even be given the Muslim greeting. I naturally took this to mean that I was ex-communicated from the World Community of Islam.[19]

Minister Louis Farrakhan's belief in the teachings of the Honorable Elijah Muhammad cast him as the "spiritual son," while the "biological son" Imam Warith Deen Muhammad totally disagreed with his father's teachings. Imam Warith Deen Muhammad believed that both men, Minister Louis Farrakhan and the Honorable Elijah Muhammad, were out of touch with the Islamic world.

On March 24, 1978, in Chicago, Imam Warith D. Muhammad responded to Minister Louis Farrakhan's resurrection of the Nation of Islam:

As I have told you, if the information I'm getting is correct, Minister Louis Farrakhan is asking people to go back to the same things exactly that were being taught in 1974. I am told that he is teaching the same kind of Black consciousness. If that is so, then he's not teaching Al-Islam. Wherever you go, Muslims believe as we believe here in Chicago and throughout this community. We believe as Muslims believe all over the Muslim world.[20]

In the above reference, 1974 is the year before the death of the Honorable Elijah Muhammad. According to Imam Warith Deen Muhammad, Master Fard Muhammad planned a "stream of gradualism" to first introduce Islam to the African American community. W. D. Muhammad believed that the first "stream" was the "Black Muslim" phase under the Honorable Elijah Muhammad and eventually the "plan" was for the Nation to be gradually transformed into a traditional, orthodox Islamic community.

As far as Imam Warith Deen Muhammad is concerned, he is carrying out the plans of Master Fard Muhammad and the Honorable Elijah Muhammad. Imam W. D. Muhammad claims he has "statements" and talked to Master Fard Muhammad in person and was told that this transformation was the "original plan." If, however, that was the original plan, why did the Honorable Elijah Muhammad excommunicate Imam W. D. Muhammad several times for straying from the black nationalist doctrine of the Nation of Islam?

Imam Warith Deen Muhammad explains how Minister Louis Farrakhan has broken from the original program:

If his [Minister Louis Farrakhan] is not that [Orthodox Islam] then he has broken from the program, the plan, the scheme of the Nation of Islam, as we were called and has not understood and accepted the psychology and gradualism for the total religious transformation of the Lost Found Nation of Islam in America.[21]

One of the central differences between Minister Louis Farrakhan and Imam W. D. Muhammad is that Minister Louis Farrakhan believed that "God's will, which is at the core of his [the Honorable Elijah Muhammad's] ministry was to give life to the spiritually dead Black man in America and the world."[22]

Whereas Minister Louis Farrakhan believed that the Nation of Islam should spiritually, politically, and economically uplift African Americans, Imam W. D. Muhammad wanted to spiritually uplift all people regardless of race. Furthermore, the WCIW was not in the "self-help business," but the Nation of Islam under Minister Louis Farrakhan followed the self-help philosophy of the Honorable Elijah Muhammad. The Nation of Islam also had a responsibility to prevent and intervene to solve social problems in the black community.

Minister Louis Farrakhan believed that the uplift message was essential, because in every country he visited, "where there is a plurality of races, the Black man, everywhere is on the bottom. He's on the bottom in Christianity; he's on the bottom in Islam; he's on the bottom in Capitalism; he's on the bottom in Socialism, and under Communism, America and the world."[23] Minister Louis Farrakhan explains the need for the mission of the Honorable Elijah Muhammad to solve social problems:

> The effect of the mission of the Honorable Elijah Muhammad directed the energies of the Muslim community toward the eradication of drunkenness, dope addiction, prostitution, and crime. Those energies were also directed toward strengthening the family life.[24]

The "Nation" under the Honorable Elijah Muhammad also utilized the "talented tenth" theory devised by Dr. W.E.B. DuBois wherein the black professional class had an obligation to help "uplift the race." Minister Louis Farrakhan explains, "The mission of Muhammad stimulated the intellectual and professional class toward general uplift of our people."[25]

Imam W. D. Muhammad believed that Minister Louis Farrakhan's plan for economic development, social problem solving, and spiritual uplift were doomed by the black nationalist philosophy he practiced and preached. Imam W. D. Muhammad believed that the black nationalist's philosophy of his father as practiced by Minister Louis Farrakhan gave Americans an excuse to deny his followers opportunities. Members of the Nation of Islam, according to Imam W.D. Muhammad, are perceived as un-American and don't uphold the democratic process. Imam W. D. Muhammad says of Minister Louis Farrakhan's black nationalist philosophy, "As soon as Minister Louis Farrakhan gets branded as a Black supremacist, as a Black Nationalist, right away his immediate followers and all those influenced by him will be ostracised."[26]

Furthermore, Imam W. D. Muhammad felt that his plan for economic development was more realistic than Minister Louis Farrakhan's. He "threw down" the gauntlet and issued a challenge to Minister Louis Farrakhan. In a March 24, 1978, Jumah prayer service he exclaimed:

> Minister Louis Farrakhan wants economic success. He wants business growth. He wants the development of the African communities. I want the same, but I want it with Al-Islam. *If any of you talk to him, I hope you go back and tell him this is a challenge I'm making to him right now.* I'm challenging him to produce more businesses with his philosophy than I produce with Al-Islam, with the Holy Quran.[27]

William Kunstler Reopens the Malcolm X Murder Trial

In 1978, while Minister Louis Farrakhan and Imam W. D. Muhammad were engaging in their verbal and philosophical battle, the casualty of a previous battle was being reexamined. The Malcolm X murder trial was reopened in the New York State Supreme Court. William Kunstler was representing Talmadge Hayer, Thomas 15X Johnson, and Norman 3X Butler. These three men were convicted of shooting and killing Malcolm X Shabazz in the Audubon Ballroom on February 21, 1965. Kunstler submitted an affidavit signed by Hayer who admitted his part in the murder, but absolved Thomas 15X Johnson and Norman 3X Butler.

According to the Kunstler affidavit, "four torpedoes" from New Jersey were ordered to shoot Malcolm. "The affidavit gives their names and addresses and also describes the guns that were used in the Sunday afternoon attack, which came just as Malcolm had greeted a large audience."[28] Kunstler also charged that the Federal Bureau of Investigation (FBI) knew "all along that there were four men involved in the killing and that two of the men convicted were innocent."[29] The FBI refused to turn over their findings in the case to the court.

Racial Images of God

According to Minister Louis Farrakhan, the African American community was in need of an awakening. The awakening occurs when African Americans reject the Caucasian way of civilization and build a new civilization which would "pull apart and destroy the falling force of Caucasian civilization." The awakening according to Minister Louis Farrakhan would require the following four ingredients:

1. Research Black history and build on efforts of former and present Black historians.
2. Be reached by a particular knowledge of self to be in tune with the creative force that gave civilization to the world.
3. Focus on the internal enemy (weakness) so external enemy can't manipulate Blacks against each other.
4. Develop independent scholarship and analytical thought in religion, politics, education, science, and economics.[30]

In 1978, Imam W. D. Muhammad began to rigorously attack all racial images of God through the Committee to Remove All Images of the Divine (CRAID). Imam Warith D. Muhammad explains the social psychological imperative of this campaign:

As long as Caucasian people think that their physical white image is in the world as the image of God, and as long as non-Caucasian people see and know that the Caucasian image is in the world as the physical image of God, there will be no real coming together and no peaceful meeting of the minds of Caucasians.The strongest wedge between non-Caucasians and Caucasians is a Caucasian image of God on the cross.[31]

Imam Wallace D. Muhammad believes that racial conflict could be resolved if God images and prophets had no color or race. The present system of placing racial identity on images of God adds to racial conflict and restricts efforts toward integration and equal opportunity in America. However, Minister Louis Farrakhan is in complete disagreement with Imam W. D. Muhammad. Since there is de facto segregation, and since America is divided into two worlds, one black and one white, separate and unequal, black separation could be used as an asset to uplift the race. Minister Louis Farrakhan reiterates this perspective:

Color is a reality in the world. There will come a time when men will not judge men by color, but since that is not the reality at present; since we live in a society that has put us in this position, because of our color, then we ought to maximize what God has given us and lift ourselves up from under the foot of this oppressor and this oppression.[32]

Minister Louis Farrakhan and Imam W. D. Muhammad continued their ideological conflict throughout the 1970s into the 1980s. Unlike the conflict between Malcolm X and the Honorable Elijah Muhammad, however, the Minister Louis Farrakhan/Imam W. D. Muhammad conflict was not a violent one.

Both men were very cautious not to say anything provocative that might ignite a flame of revolt between the NOI and WCIW members. As a matter of fact, Imam W. D. Muhammad issued a warning and a challenge to the enemies of himself and Minister Louis Farrakhan; in a public address he exclaimed:

This leadership is going to provide more jobs. This leadership is going to have more businesses. This leadership is going to have more human dignity at home and abroad. That's my challenge. This is not a challenge to him [Minister Louis Farrakhan] as my enemy. This is my challenge to him as my friend. I want to show my friend I have a better way than he does. Now here's my word to my enemy and for Minister Louis Farrakhan's enemy:

You bastard! You will never pull me out in the street to do one ounce of harm to Minister Louis Farrakhan! You go to hell, you bastard![33]

The Nation of Islam and the NAACP
1979–1980

The problems Dr. Ben Chavis, Executive Director of the NAACP encountered working with Minister Louis Farrakhan and the Nation of Islam in 1994 were not precedent-setting. During the fall, September of 1979, the Los Angeles branch of the NAACP and the NOI joined forces to "work towards strengthening the Black community." The event was considered a "family reunion." Los Angeles chapter president Paul Hudson invited Dr. Maleek Rashadin, the western regional representative for Minister Louis Farrakhan, to speak to a meeting of members of the NAACP. Dr. Rashadin explained the philosophy of the Honorable Elijah Muhammad.

The two groups felt that they had been "bitten by the same dog," and vowed to work together. Mr. Hudson recognized and acknowledged the Christian church as the "backbone" of the NAACP. However, the two organizations wanted to work through ideological differences to achieve black unity. Mr. Hudson blamed the rift between the NAACP and the NOI on the media for allowing the two groups to be pitted against each other. Furthermore, Mr. Hudson pointed out that Minister Louis Farrakhan was influenced by reading articles written by Dr. W.E.B. DuBois published in the *Crisis* magazine.

Mr. Hudson also endorsed the accomplishments of the Honorable Elijah Muhammad: specifically, nation building and black economic development. He went on to say that "in the 1980s we expect the two champion organizations for Black dignity to stand side-by-side and shoulder-to-shoulder to meet the challenges."[34]

In 1979, Minister Farrakhan began publishing the *Final Call* newspaper. It would eventually serve as a valuable resource for community outreach and a source of revenue for NOI. The embryonic stages of the philosophical and ideological split revealed numerous differences in theology as well. Entering into the 1980s, both organizations continued to build, grow, develop, and move further away from each other. Chapter 9 will discuss the progress, changes, and significant events of the Nation of Islam under Minister Louis Farrakhan from 1980 to 1990.

Notes

1. Adib Rashad. *The History of Islam and Black Nationalism in the America's* (Beltsville, Maryland: Writers Inc., 1991), p. 74.

2. Interview, Imam Wallace D. Muhammad, Chicago, Illinois, July 25, 1979.

3. Ibid.

4. Rashad, *History of Islam and Black Nationalism,* p. 74.

5. Interview, Imam Wallace D. Muhammad.

6. Ibid.

7. Public Address, Minister Abdul Haleem Farrakhan, Virginia Union University, Richmond, Virginia, February 4, 1976.

8. Roy Wilkins, "The Muslims," *New York Post,* June 28, 1975.

9. "Interracial Fete Symbolizes Changes in Black Muslims," *New York Times,* September 1, 1975.

10. Ibid.

11. "Black Muslims Will End Longtime Ban on Whites," *New York Times,* June 17, 1975.

12. Interview, W. D. Muhammad.

13. "Black Muslim Harlem Temple Renamed in Honor of Malcolm X," *New York Times,* February 2, 1976.

14. Ibid.

15. "Muslims Reveal Debt," *Newsday,* March 12, 1976.

16. Ibid.

17. "Muslims to Sell Holdings; Losses and Taxes Cited," *New York Times,* August 8, 1976.

18. Public Address, Minister Abdul Haleem Farrakhan.

19. BBB Interviews Minister Farrakhan," *Black Books Bulletin,* The Institute of Positive Education, vol. 6, no. 1, Chicago: Spring, 1978, p. 42.

20. "Imam Wallace D. Muhammad's Appeal to Minister Farrakhan" *Bilalian News,* April 28, 1978.

21. Ibid.

22. *New York Amsterdam News,* vol. 69, no. 2, Saturday, January 14, 1978.

23. "BBB Interviews," p. 42.

24. *New York Amsterdam News,* vol. 69, no. 2, Saturday, January 14, 1978.

25. Ibid.

26. *Bilalian News,* "Imam Wallace D. Muhammad's Appeal to Minister Farrakan." April 28, 1978, p. 22.

27. Ibid.

28. "Malcolm X Killer Talks; Names 4," *New York Amsterdam News,* vol. 69, no. 17, April 29, 1978.

29. Ibid.

30. "First World Interviews Minister Farrakhan," *First World,* Spring 1978, pp. 11–13.

31. "Year of Progress for W.C.I.W. Under Imam Muhammad's Leadership," *Bilalian News,* January 20, 1978, p. 4.

32. *Black Books Bulletin,* Spring 1978, p. 43.

33. *Bilalian News,* April 28, 1978, p. 22.

34. "N.A.A.C.P., Nation of Islam Unite for Black Survival: Could Impact Nation," *Los Angeles Sentinel,* September 20, 1979.

Chapter 9

The Growth, Development, and Change of the American Muslim Mission and the Nation of Islam, 1980–1990

"The Nation of Islam was more or less a social reformation. Something that was very much needed at that time (1930–1975) under the leadership of the Honorable Elijah Muhammad the tone of society was more or less in demand of social reformation. Although we used the name Islam, it was basically a label. Now under the leadership of the Honorable Imam. Warith Deen Muhammad, the transition to (A.M.M.) follows Islam according to the Holy Quran and the Sunni (The Ways of prophet Muhammad) 1400 years ago."[1]

—Imam Saadig Saafir
American Muslim Mission, Los Angeles, California, 1980

During the spring of 1980, Imam Warith Deen Muhammad changed the name of the former Nation of Islam from the World Community of Al-Islam in the West (WCIW) to the American Muslim Mission (AMM). In a span of five years Imam Warith Deen Muhammad had essentially dismantled his father's Nation of Islam. Whatever it means, "one thing is certain: it will be a long time before the likes of the empire his father built is seen again."[2]

Shortly after assuming leadership in 1975, Imam W. D. Muhammad began to unveil the "Nation's secrets." He began dismantling the organization, economic enterprises, ideology, and theology, "myths and fairy tales." Membership in the once all-black Nation of Islam opened its membership to all people. Imam W. D. Muhammad sold many of the commercial holdings and he insisted that his followers adhere to the universal tenets of Islam in order to be in harmony with so-called Orthodox Muslim ideas and beliefs. Imam W. D. Muhammad's changes were a reflection of his study of Orthodox Islam, his unique personality, leadership style, and the belief that the "Black Muslims" were a phase in the ultimate transformation to the American Muslim Mission.

Initially, after he was excommunicated, Minister Louis Farrakhan had to rely entirely on his own charisma through public addresses and fund-raisers to provide economic stability to resurrect the Lost-Found Nation of Islam. The social and economic conditions of the 1960s had been conducive to the rise of nationalism in the African American community. There was a relative decline toward nationalist perspectives, in the

115

1970s. In the 1980s, however, the right-wing, conservative policies of the Reagan/Bush administration, along with the economic depression suffered in the African American community, produced a socioeconomic atmosphere conducive for the growth and spread of black nationalism. The economic recession of 1981 was a major economic depression in the African American community.

Lawrence H. Mamiya, in his article *From Black Muslim to Bilalian,* explains how the 1980s provided fertile ground for the ideas and ideals of Minister Louis Farrakhan and the Nation of Islam:

> For the decade of the 1980's the prospects for continued growth of Far-rakhan's Black Muslim Movement looked very good because the economic and racial conditions have worsened. With the Black unemployment rate more than double that of whites, and the unemployment rate of Black teenagers at more than 50% nationwide, and the gains of the 1960's slipping away, Minister Louis Farrakhan is finding large responsive audiences for Muslim soldiers in the Final Call to Black Islam.[3]

The cutbacks on social programs, the neglect, and obvious disdain by the Reagan/Bush administration concerning urban problems signalled an abandoning of the African American community. There was a coming together of many forces including the rise of the Religious Right, the Ku Klux Klan, and other right-wing organizations, combined with inflation and recession, and high rates of unemployment. These conditions created "anger and resentment that will give birth to the new generation of Black Muslims in America."[4]

The socioeconomic inequality and institutionalized racism led Minister Louis Farrakhan to believe that racism will destroy the country. Minister Louis Farrakhan explains in his book, *A Torchlight for America*:

> We live in one country with two realities, separate and unequal; one black, one white; one predator, one prey; one skilled, one non-skilled; one slave-master, one slave. Classism, racism, and sexism; are used to keep the people divided, and these three evils threaten to sink and destroy the entire country.[5]

Followers of the American Muslim Mission believed that the Nation of Islam was "indoctrinated by racism" and did not "fit the times." "Times and people have changed," they said. For them, the "race game" was over. They accepted a universal brotherhood based on one humanity. Saadiq Saafir explains, "Now we are going to help people whether they are Christians or Jews. No matter what their beliefs are. Recognizing first that we are all part of one humanity."[6] For followers of the American Muslim Mission, they are Black Muslims no longer. W. D. Muhammad says, "There will be no such category as a White Muslim or a Black Muslim. All will be Muslims; All children of God."[7]

Entering the 1980s, there was a general perception that there were class distinctions between the followers of both groups. Imam W. D. Muhammad's American Muslim Mission "has retained a largely middle class membership, while Farrakhan's resurrected Nation of Islam is seeking to find its mass base again in its lower class origins."[8] The Nation of Islam has also expanded its membership base during the transition. Many middle-class professionals are hired to work as doctors and nurses in health clinics. The Nation of Islam also employs degreed professionals in teaching and management positions in their schools and businesses. The class distinction and mission of each organization is exemplified in a quote from a new convert to Minister Louis Farrakhan's NOI. Brother Eddie X explains why he was attracted to the Nation:

> What attracted me to Minister Louis Farrakhan was his deep concern for the despised and rejected of American Society. I don't see Wallace's group as being concerned with the outcastes [sic]. They seem to me to be Arabicizied [sic] intellectuals sprouting Arabic phrases at you.[9]

Imam Wallace D. Muhammad's Orthodox approach and the financial empire he acquired gave him a tremendous advantage over Minister Louis Farrakhan (in 1977) and opportunity to spread Orthodox Islam. One former member of the Nation of Islam described Imam W. D. Muhammad's financial dismantling of the Nation of Islam's business empire as an "economic coup."

To provide more democratic governance, Imam W. D. Muhammad established a council of Imams in 1980. The council enabled the AMM to institutionalize the leadership and not rely on the charismatic personality of a single leader. Former heavyweight champion Muhammad Ali chose to follow Imam W. D. Muhammad. A member of the Nation of Islam, Kariem Aziz, said that the former champ was "a victim of madness in the white man's world." Aziz blames Ali's physical problems with his return to the ring and his departure from the NOI: "If he had remained faithful to the Nation of Islam, Ali would never have entered the ring again."[10] During the early 1980s Minister Louis Farrakhan still believed in a separate state. He perceived, however, the separate state as a form of reparations for slavery. Minister Louis Farrakhan explains in a 1980 interview, "Anything is possible. Blacks are owed this land as reparation for centuries of slave labor."[11]

The 1980s saw the Nation of Islam under Minister Louis Farrakhan grow in size, power, and visibility, while the AMM under Imam W. D. Muhammad was almost invisible in the day-to-day struggles of the African American community. A 1982 *New York Times* article reveals the difference in influence: "Minister Louis Farrakhan's efforts have met with growing success, even as membership of the American Muslim Mission has dwindled."[12]

The forty-five years of visibility, self-help, and outreach of the Nation of Islam under the Honorable Elijah Muhammad was instrumental in the organization's gaining significant inroads into the African American culture and collective psyche. Whether you believed in their ideology or not, most members of the African American community from coast-to-coast were impacted by the clean-shaven, bow tie-wearing, confident, fearless men of the Nation of Islam. Dorothy Gilliam sums up the feelings of many when she declares:

> I always remembered how polite the young men were when they knocked on my door, selling fish, carrot cakes, and bean pies. And if Muslims were seen as super righteous and stuffy by some, to others they were pillars of the community. I remember that when I had to go into tough neighborhoods, I always felt a little safer to see some Muslims standing on the corner.[13]

The Estate of the Honorable Elijah Muhammad, 1982

Herbert Muhammad wore several hats while he was a member of the Nation of Islam. The "hats" included: manager of Muhammad Ali; son of the Honorable Elijah Muhammad; and administrator of the estate of the Honorable Elijah Muhammad. It was Herbert Muhammad's role as an engineer of the "economic coup" that became a problem for him and his brother Imam W. D. Muhammad. It was during the week of February 21, 1982, when Herbert Muhammad was "ordered replaced as administrator of the estate by a judge who also ruled that $46 million had incorrectly been transferred to the World Community of Al Islam in the West."[14] Herbert Muhammad was replaced by a court-ordered administrator. Probate Judge Henry Budzinski made his ruling after receiving a petition for recovery by Attorney Rufus Cook. The Honorable Elijah Muhammad had not left a will, therefore his twenty-one children were engaged in a legal struggle for their share of his estate against the former Nation of Islam. Attorney Cook represented five of the Honorable Elijah Muhammad's children. Attorney Cook was intending that the money should be put back into the Honorable Elijah Muhammad's personal estate. For seven years there was a legal battle for the Honorable Elijah Muhammad's estimated $25 million estate. The $25 million included $3.2 million held in a "poor fund" account at the First Pacific Bank of Chicago. The legal struggle was over how much of the Honorable Elijah Muhammad's estate belonged to his heirs and how much belonged to the American Muslim Mission. Along with the cash, there were millions of dollars more in land left in the estate. Judge Budzinski ordered the First Pacific Bank of Chicago to return the money from the American Muslim

Mission's account to the estate for distribution among the Honorable Elijah Muhammad's heirs. Herbert Muhammad estimated his father's personal fortune was $363,000, and that excluded relatives' homes, a $300,000 Learjet, and Muslim commercial holdings. The heirs' lawyers, Mr. Cook, and the original filer of the petition, Attorney Julian Wilkins, described Mr. Herbert Muhammad's estimate of his father's wealth as "ridiculously small." Herbert's brother, Imam W. D. Muhammad argued that "Elijah Muhammad kept his personal property separate from that of the religious organization."[15]

Judge Budzinski ruled that the heirs had no rights to the relatives' homes. However, Judge Budzinski directed Imam W. D. Muhammad to return "four oriental rugs, four brass cups, and a ring that he took when his father died."[16]

Run Jesse Run: Minister Louis Farrakhan Registers to Vote, February 24, 1984

"If we ask the Christian community, how do you spell relief? you would say Jesus. If we asked the Muslims, how do you spell relief? They would say Allah. If we want relief from the crooked, corrupt rule of the Democratic party, which favors the front runner, I think I spell it, Jesse. How do you spell relief if you want to keep from being locked out of White American society? Jesse, one more time, Jesse. Brothers and sisters let us receive the next President of these United States, the Rev. Jesse Louis Jackson."[17]

—Minister Louis Farrakhan
February 25, 1984,
Saviour's Day Convention

During the 1984 Savior's Day Convention, Minister Louis Farrakhan introduced Rev. Jesse Jackson to the audience. It was the beginning of the "run Jesse run" odyssey for Minister Louis Farrakhan and the Nation of Islam. Minister Louis Farrakhan also accompanied Rev. Jackson to Washington, D.C. to launch his 1984 campaign in the nation's capital. The host of the evening was Mayor Marion Barry, who supported Rev. Jackson's run for the highest office in the land. Minister Louis Farrakhan had known Rev. Jackson since the 1960s. In 1972, the Nation of Islam's mosque was attacked by the New York police department. Rev. Jackson came to the Nation's defense. When the Honorable Elijah Muhammad died in 1975, Rev. Jesse Jackson eulogized him and gave Minister Louis Farrakhan advice not to "come out" against the old man (Elijah Muhammad), like his son W. D. Muhammad had.

Their personal friendship grew over the years. There was a unique contrast between a Muslim minister, Louis Farrakhan, a Black separatist dedicated to the teachings of the Honorable Elijah Muhammad, and Rev.

Jesse Jackson, a Baptist preacher, staunch integrationist and true believer in the ideals and ideas of the Rev. Dr. Martin Luther King. Rev. Jackson led many voter registration drives throughout the United States, particularly in the South during the 1960s and 1970s. Minister Louis Farrakhan registered to vote for the first time to endorse Rev. Jesse Jackson as president. There was a potent coalition between Farrakhan and Jackson:

> Between two of the smartest and most charismatic figures of the African American Community had ever produced Jackson with his ability to focus on jobs and business opportunities for the Black middle class and the Muslim's unique ability to attract radical grass roots activists and to reform drug addicts and prisoners such as Malcolm X.[18]

Minister Louis Farrakhan was one of Jackson's early supporters in running for the presidency. Early in 1983 Minister Louis Farrakhan "wrote Jackson a letter urging him to seek the country's top office and offering his support."[19] Prior to Rev. Jackson being considered a serious candidate, he received no Secret Service protection. Minister Louis Farrakhan directed his "Fruit of Islam" to protect Rev. Jackson on the campaign trail. In each city in which Jackson arrived to speak, he was greeted, escorted, and protected by disciplined cadres of bow tie-wearing black men. When candidate Jackson was finally given Secret Service protection by the U.S. government, the agents would complain that they "couldn't get close to him for the crowd of Muslims around him."

Minister Louis Farrakhan played a significant and vital role in enabling Jesse Jackson to secure the release of Navy Lt. Robert Goodman. Minister Louis Farrakhan accompanied Rev. Jackson to Syria. Surely, this would be a test for the ideas of the Honorable Elijah Muhammad. The so-called contrast between Orthodox Islam and the Nation of Islam could derail negotiations, put Lieutenant Goodman's life in further danger, and embarrass the United States and the entire African American community. The charismatic Minister Louis Farrakhan impressed Syria's heads of state, Imams, Muslim scholars, and true believers with his knowledge of Islam and ability to speak perfect Arabic. He led the Jumah prayer service with all the grace and eloquence of Bilal himself. So much for those who said the international community of Islam would not accept the ideology of the Lost-Found Nation of Islam in America. To support candidate Jesse Jackson, "Minister Louis Farrakhan broke with the Nation of Islam's tradition of not participating in electoral politics and registered to vote for the first time."[20]

The Jackson campaign was given a boost by pollster George Gallup, Jr., who in 1984 revealed that Rev. Jackson was the third most admired person by the people of the United States. His popularity was only less than that of former president Ronald Reagan and Pope John Paul II.

Minister Louis Farrakhan continued his support of the Jackson candidacy. He also in the following year 1985, turned his wrath on the mayor of Philadelphia, Wilson Goode, for his mishandling of the "Move" [a Black Nationalist Organization] social movement, and the police confrontation. Instead of mediation, negotiation, and traditional police firearm practices, Mayor Goode and the police chief decided to drop a bomb on the homes of the Move members. The home was in a black neighborhood consisting of row houses and it ignited and destroyed hundreds of homes throughout the community, displacing thousands of families. Minister Louis Farrakhan called Mayor Goode a "Mad Bomber":

> A mad bomber in Philadelphia—a power crazy mayor—and a police chief dropped a bomb on Black people with men, women and children inside the home, killing all of them. And the Mayor had the gall to come before the people and say he would do it over and over again. The Black people of America are tired of Black leaders selling us out after we put them in office; working for our enemies, rather than working for ourselves."[21]

Minister Louis Farrakhan continued to work to help Rev. Jackson; however,they were caught in an ideological no man's land in American politics. Jesse Jackson was perceived as a radical, left-wing Christian liberal. The coalition with Minister Louis Farrakhan was an ideological Molotov cocktail ready to explode and destroy the Jackson presidential campaign. The conflict with the Jewish community began long before Minister Louis Farrakhan agreed to work on the Jackson campaign. [The Jewish community perceived Farrakhan as anti-semetic and racist.] The primary example in the 1970s, was the Supreme Court's decision on so-called reverse discrimination cases like Allen Bakke who wanted to be admitted to the University of California Medical School. Blacks and Jews drew a "line-in-the-sand" and opposed each other on affirmative action and reverse discrimination cases. Rev. Jackson further alienated the Jewish community when he visited the Middle East in September of 1979. During his visit Yasser Arafat and Rev. Jesse Jackson "embraced" and Jackson suggested that the Palestinian Liberation Organization be included in all peace negotiations.

In November of 1979, United States ambassador Andrew Young resigned after it was discovered he secretly met with a PLO United Nations observer, Zehedi Labib Terzi. African American leaders "blamed Jews for Ambassador Andrew Young's departure from the Carter administration."[22]

The social and historical circumstances in the 1960s and 1970s leading up to the 1984 Jackson presidential campaign, made the Jackson/Farrakhan coalition a political liability, and ultimately candidate Jackson was forced to dissociate himself from Minister Louis Farrakhan. There were seven significant events and dates which cumulatively contributed to the Farrakhan/Jackson breakup:

1. January 25, 1984, a Black reporter, Milton Coleman of the *Washington Post,* claimed that while traveling with the Jackson campaign during an informal and casual conversation, candidate Jackson referred to Jews as "Hymies" and the Big Apple (New York City) as "Hymie town."
2. February 13, 1984, Milton Coleman's story is published in the *Washington Post.* It became a controversial story and cast Jackson in the light of an anti-Semite.
3. February 25, 1984, during the Saviour's Day speech when he introduced Rev. Jesse Jackson for the presidency, Minister Louis Farrakhan made the following comments:

   > We are not making idle threats. We warn you in his name, leave this servant [Jackson] of Almighty God alone. If you want to defeat him, defeat him at the polls. We can stand to lose an election, but we cannot stand to lose our brother.[23]

Members of the Jewish community and some black elected officials perceived these comments as a threat to those who opposed Rev. Jackson's candidacy. There was pressure on Jackson to break up his coalition with Minister Louis Farrakhan and the Nation of Islam.

4. February 27, 1984, Rev. Jesse Jackson admitted his "Hymie town" remarks and then apologized:

   > However innocent and unintentional, the comment was insensitive and wrong. I am to blame and for that I am deeply distressed. I categorically deny that this in any way reflects my basic attitude towards Jews or Israel.[24]

5. March 11, 1984, Minister Louis Farrakhan is accused of threatening the *Washington Post* reporter Milton Coleman's life. United States Attorney for the Northern District of Chicago, Don K. Webb, felt Minister Louis Farrakhan may have violated a federal law. The law prohibits person to person threats over interstate communications. The investigation was stopped when Webb admitted he had insufficient evidence to convict Minister Louis Farrakhan for criminal wrongdoing.
6. June 26, 1984, *Chicago Sun Times* reporter Don Hayner claimed in a public address that Minister Louis Farrakhan, in a national broadcast, referred to the creation of Israel as "an outlaw act."
7. June 28, 1984, Rev. Jesse L. Jackson, candidate for the presidency of the United States severs his coalition with Minister Louis Farrakhan and the Nation of Islam. Rev. Jackson referred to Minister

Louis Farrakhan's remarks and behavior as "reprehensible and morally indefensible."

The breakup between Minister Louis Farrakhan and Rev. Jesse Jackson in 1984 endures even ten years later in 1994. They rarely talk formally or informally and during public appearances like the 1994 NAACP Black Leadership Summit in Baltimore, Maryland, called by Dr. Benjamin Chavis, Farrakhan and Jackson were never photographed standing "close" or next to each other. Minister Louis Farrakhan knew what his mission was in helping candidate Jackson. It was to "help raise the dead":

> There's one other Black man in America that has the power to raise the dead and that is myself. But you don't know Farrakhan. You're not ready for Farrakhan, but God is ready. So God gives you one that you like. That's closer to you. To start you jumping out of your grave. My job takes off where Jesse's leaves off.[25]

This quote by Minister Louis Farrakhan in reference to his venture into "mainstream" American politics is an echo of Malcolm X's ballot or the bullet. Social change will either come from voting and the ballot box or it will come in the streets as exhibited in the Rodney King riots of 1992. The ballot or the bullet? The ballot box or the streets?

Imam W. D. Muhammad and Minister Louis Farrakhan Agree to Resolve Differences, 1985

For several years after Minister Louis Farrakhan's excommunication, the relationship between the AMM and the NOI remained distant and strained. The two leaders, Farrakhan and W. D. Muhammad, settled on a verbal agreement. Imam W. D. Muhammad agreed that he would not defame his father, but that he should be left free to criticize the Nation of Islam's beliefs. "I, Minister Louis Farrakhan, have kept my part of that accord and I intend to keep it."[26] Minister Louis Farrakhan believed that the verbal agreement was necessary so as not to inflame the followers of both the AMM and NOI which would cause conflict. Minister Louis Farrakhan explains:

> I disagreed with the Imam. and I left and I did what I had to do. But I would not throw any mud on Imam. Wallace D. Muhammad. For to do so would be to inflame his followers. And to inflame his followers would mean a clash between Muslims. And so, because of that history, I would not walk into that trap.[27]

The "history" Minister Louis Farrakhan is referring to is the previous struggle between the Honorable Elijah Muhammad and Malcolm X. Obviously, both leaders learned from the tragic mistakes of the past and vowed not to repeat the same mistakes. During the mid-1980s, Minister Louis Farrakhan expressed a desire to improve relationships between other groups like Christians and Jews. Former members of the Nation of Islam were not surprised with Minister Louis Farrakhan's conciliatory tone. They "cited shifts in his teaching on such matters as the sects' founding and timing of religious observations to coincide with Islamic practices, like his changing the observance of Ramadan, a month-long fast that the Nation of Islam celebrated in December and changed to February to coincide with the Orthodox Muslim calendar."[28] Imam W. D. Muhammad was eager for a peace treaty as well. He said "There's always a desire on this side and I'm sure on the other side too for a desirable atmosphere. I think the media plays up problems for us and blows them out of proportion."[29]

The American Muslim Mission was disbanded by 1985. Imam W. D. Muhammad dissolved the organization and advised his followers, "You should put down the term [American Muslims] and never pick up any term again that lumps you all together in one community. You should be members of a Muslim community that's international."[30] The Imam W. D. Muhammad also continued to sell several properties owned by the former American Muslim Mission. The decision to dissolve the AMM enabled two hundred mosques to become autonomous and independent to unite with "Islamic groups of all races and ethnic origins."

During the same period that the AMM was going out of business, the NOI was increasing its business empire. Minister Louis Farrakhan announced that he was given a $5 million dollar interest free loan from Libyan leader Moammar Khadafy to promote black business in America. The NOI used the money to develop its "People Organized and Working for Economic Rebirth" (POWER). POWER's purpose was to develop and produce a line of soaps, personal care products, and detergent.

Nation of Islam's Program for
Crime Prevention and Community Safety
"The Dope Busters," 1988

"Ridding Mayfair Mansions in Washington, D.C., of dope traffic and rehabilitating the addicts is a success story of the Nation of Islam at no cost to the country. We have a 'dope busters' program that has been very successful and is applauded by the communities in which the 'dope busters' or Nation of Islam security are present. How is it that with nothing we can do what the government has not been able to do with $12 billion."[31]

—Minister Louis Farrakhan

Residents of the Mayfair Mansions and Paradise Manor public housing units remember life before the "dope busters." They also remember how gradually the dope dealers took over the community. They methodically chased children off the playgrounds and away from the courtyard to isolate the area for their drug business. The dealers began to hang out in entrances of the apartment units, harassing residents and soliciting customers. Fights and gun battles erupted over drug profits. Residents repeatedly dialed 911 and requested assistance to no avail. The police seemed unable to assist the residents. However, several tenants of the Mayfair Mansions noticed how drug dealers would scatter and move away when members of the Nation of Islam came into the community to sell the *Final Call,* bean pies, and POWER products. The manager of the Mayfair Mansions, Mr. Glenn French, made overtures to the Muslims to come into the units and assist them to eradicate the drug problem in their community.

National spokesman for the Nation of Islam, Dr. Abdul Alim Muhammad, answered the call of the residents and agreed to patrol the complex. In an interview in the Paradise Manor units with the author, Dr. Abdul Alim Muhammad explains how they cleaned up the apartment complex:

> The moral force and power that is generated by the teachings of the Honorable Elijah Muhammad and his training and discipline given to us according to the instructions of Master Fard Muhammad, gives us power in the world to reform our people. We take people that would ordinarily to control them you would ordinarily have to beat them; lock them up or shoot them or whatever. We can win with just a word, control and reform them. We would have total success in that, if we were not opposed so vehemently by outside forces who still control life in the ghetto.[32]

The members of the Nation of Islam, armed with flashlights, walkie-talkies, and patrolling in small groups, cleaned up the Mayfair Mansions complex. Similar patrols were initiated in New York City with great success. Within a matter of weeks, the units were cleared of the drug dealers and the problems associated with the drug underground economy. Local residents like Charlie Riddick, a resident in Bedford-Stuyvesant for fifteen years, exclaimed, "People who are doing wrong know the Muslims mean business. They are doing a hell of a job."[33] Eleven-year-old Jerry Lamont Bush, a resident of Mayfair says, "We love it around here now."[34] Even local police had to acknowledge the good work of the "dope busters." New York City police officer Sergio Rivera says, "Without those Muslim guys, this street would be a mob of dealers. You could not walk here two months ago with all the people drinking and smoking that stuff."[35] Washington D.C. mayor Marion Barry praised the Nation of Islam and called for citizens to "rise up against drug dealers and form patrols." D.C. city councilman H. R. Crawford (D-Ward-7) interrupted a city council meeting and exclaimed to Dr. Abdul Alim Muhammad who was in attendance, "I can't shower you with sufficient accolades. You have succeeded where others have failed."[36] The entire Washington D.C., City Council voted a resolution praising the Nation of Islam for their work in cleaning up the apartment complex. One local resident said, "What those people did [Nation of Islam] is more than the Police or F.B.I. have done."[37]

The Nation of Islam also began to address the youth gang problem in the major urban areas. During October of 1989, Minister Louis Farrakhan invited nine hundred gang members to the Bonaventure Hotel in downtown Los Angeles. Nearly six thousand people, including the Bloods and the Crips, packed the hall to hear Minister Louis Farrakhan's "Stop the Killing" speech. The crowd filled three ballrooms and many had to hear Minister Louis Farrakhan over closed-circuit television. One gang member in attendance said, "It can be about gangs about blacks anything he's got to say I want to hear."[38] Another twenty-year-old member of the Bloods said, "Farrakhan's very name commands respect, and if the minister's words could change the attitude of just one of my homeboys, it could be a good start."[39]

Leading into the decade of the 1990s and finishing the decade of the 1980s, showed that the two organizations the AMM (now dissolved) and the NOI have taken drastically different directions. Imam W. D. Muhammad dissolved the American Muslim Mission and resigned himself to the spiritual needs of all people. However, Minister Louis Farrakhan continued to utilize the Nation of Islam to address social problems in the African American community, such as its economics, education, family stability, gang violence, drug addition, and community safety.

The Farrakhan train began to pick up speed in the 1980s thanks to the right-wing, conservative push of the Reagan/Bush administration. Leading into the new decade of the 1990s it appears the train cannot be stopped. Minister Louis Farrakhan has grown in stature, prestige, power, and influence. Minister Louis Farrakhan compares himself and his message to Jesus:

> You read the book and you know what Jesus said, and you hear what I'm saying and it's parallel, and the reaction against me is the same as you read would come against Jesus. They were afraid because the multitudes came out to hear him. There is no Black leader on the scene today who commands 10 and 20,000 Black people to come out and listen to him and he's not a politician, and he's not a musician. The multitudes are coming and they're saying, "He must be stopped now." Stop me now? For what and with what? No, no, no, no![40]

The following chapter will discuss the growth and development of the Nation of Islam from 1990 to 1994; from the halls of the United States Congress to the Black Star Square in Accra, Ghana.

Notes

1. "Muslims Emerge as Community Force," *Los Angeles Sentinel,* October 2, 1980, p. A-14.

2. Dorothy Gilliam, "Winds of Change for Muslims," *The Washington Post,* (month unknown) 1985.

3. Lawrence H. Mamiya, "From Black Muslim to Bilalian." *Journal for the Scientific Study of Religion,* June 1982, p. 11.

4. Ibid.

5. Louis Farrakhan. *A Torchlight for America.* Chicago: FCN Publishing Company, 1993, p. 35.

6. "Muslims Emerge as Community Force," p. 14.

7. Mamiya, "From Black Muslim to Bilalian," p. 9.

8. Ibid., p. 7.

9. Ibid., p. 10.

10. "Muslims Ask Return of Separatism," *New York Daily News,* October, 1982.

11. Mamiya, "From Black Muslim to Bilalian," p. 5.

12. Nathaniel Sheppard, Jr., "Nationalist Faction of Black Muslim Movement Gains Strength," *New York Times,* March 8, 1982.

13. Gilliam, "Winds of Change for Muslims."

14. "An Heir's Error," *New York Times,* February 21, 1982.

15. "Transfer of Funds to Muslims Voided," *New York Times,* February 18, 1982.

16. Ibid.

17. George Curry, "Farrakhan, Jesse and the Jews," *Emerge,* July/August 1994, p. 30.

18. Ibid., p. 31.

19. Ibid.

20. Ibid.

21. Ibid., p. 34.

22. Ibid., p. 35.

23. Ibid., p. 30.

24. Ibid., p. 37.

25. Ibid., p. 39.

26. Tony Brown, *American Muslim Journal,* May 3, 1985, p. 6.

27. Ibid.

28. Lena Williams, "Move to Heal Black Muslim Rift Appears to be Under Way Amid Pressures," *New York Times,* November 19, 1986, p. 6.

29. Ibid.

30. Majorie Hyer, *Washington Post,* May 9, 1985.

31. Farrakhan, *Torchlight for America,* p. 12.

32. Interview, Dr. Abdul Alim Muhammad, Washington, D.C., September 9, 1994.

33. "Armed in Faith, Muslims Wage War in Brooklyn," *Washington Post,* April 26, 1988, p. 4.

34. William K. Stevens, "Muslims Keep Lid on Drugs in Capital," *Washington Post,* April 26, 1988.

35. "Armed in Faith," p. 4.

36. Sara Horwitz and Michael Abramowitz, "Muslims in Mayfair Mansions Drug Patrols," *Washington Post,* April 21, 1988.

37. Nathan McCall, "Vote Calls, D.C. Council into Conflict," *Washington Post,* December 11, 1989.

38. Charisse Jones, "Gang Youth Get Farrakhan Peace Message," *Los Angeles Times,* October 9, 1989.

39. Joseph D. Eure and Richard M. Jerome, ed., *Back Where We Belong, Selected Speeches by Minister Louis Farrakhan* (Philadelphia: International Press, 1989), p. 126.

40. George Curry, "Farrakhan, Jesse and the Jews," *Emerge,* July/August 1994, p. 30.

Chapter 10

The Nation of Islam from the Halls of the U.S. Congress to the Black Star Square in Accra, Ghana, 1990–1994

> "Louis Farrakhan is not an enemy of America, not an enemy of Jews, not an enemy of white people. I have a profound message. A message that can, I believe correct some very, very serious problems in this nation. The most serious of which is the worsening condition of 30 million Black people in this country who have become the Achilles heel of this nation."[1]
>
> —Minister Louis Farrakhan

Entering the decade of the 1990s, the Nation of Islam continued to adhere to its original mission to "uplift the so-called Negro in North America." The self-help philosophy continued to be the cornerstone for economic development. The red, black, and green African nationalist ideals continued to gather recruits, income, power, and influence.

During the decade of the 1990s the Nation of Islam began to expand its influence like some giant black nationalist octopus, spreading its arms and intervening to correct all forms of social problems. Many Muslims feel they have such an intimacy with the black community that they have become a barometer to measure the pulse and mood of the African American community. Abdul Wazi Muhammad, the minister of the Muslims' Los Angeles Mosque says, "We are a barometer of the conditions and feel of the Black community. If you really want to know how Black people feel, then watch the Muslims."[2]

The Nation of Islam also continued to work in the public health arena in the 1990s. The Abundant Life Clinic under the leadership of Dr. Abdul Alim Muhammad continued treating patients with AIDS and other diseases with alternative medical treatment. The AIDS treatment was essential for the Nation of Islam to stay abreast and try to solve many problems crippling the black community.

The fight against AIDS was essential, because Minister Farrakhan believes that AIDS is killing us at a larger or greater rate than any other ethnic or racial group everywhere in the world.[3]

The Nation of Islam continued to clean up the drug-infested public housing units. The NOI Security Services received several local, state, and federal (HUD) government grants. Some of the grants were as much as $50,000 per month.

129

The Prison Ministry and the Struggle for Freedom of Religion

According to the Bureau of Justice statistics, in 1994 there were more than one million (1,012,851) prisoners in local, federal, and state prisons in the United States. Black men incarceration rate is 1,432 per 100,000 citizens (whites 116 per 100,000). Elijah Muhammad first established the Nation of Islam prison ministry in 1942. Elijah Muhammad and his son Emmanuel served four years (1942–1946) in federal prison for refusing to register for the draft during the Second World War. The NOI established prison ministries throughout the country for incarcerated African American men and women. The prison ministries were a catalyst for the Nation of Islam to fight for freedom of religion in the nation's prisons. "Congress should make no law respecting an establishment of religion or prohibiting the free exercise thereof." Three cases established the rights of members of the Nation of Islam to practice their religion in prison. They are Sewell v. Pegelow, Banks v. Hariener, and Knuckles vs. Prasse. Harry E. Allen and Clifford E. Simonsen in their book, *Corrections in America,* dedicated a chapter to "Prisoners Rights In Confinement." Allen and Simonsen explain the impact of the Nation of Islam on acquiring religious rights for inmates:

> These three cases dealt with the right of Black Muslim inmates to freedom of religion. In Knuckles vs. Prasse, the Court of Appeals held that prison officials were not required to make available to prisoners Black Muslim publications that urged defiance of prison authorities and thus threatened prison security, unless properly interpreted by a trained Muslim minister. In the Sewell decision, a clear instance of discrimination against a Black Muslim prisoner was brought before the Court of Appeals, which dismissed the case on the grounds that it properly came under the jurisdiction of the district court. In Banks vs. Hariener, responding to a petition under the civil rights acts by Black Muslim prisoners, the district court held that the antipathy of inmates and staff occasioned by the Black Muslim's belief in black supremacy was alone not sufficient to justify suppression of the practice of the Black Muslim religion.[4]

The prison administrators originally feared the Nation of Islam. The Muslim population is now viewed as a "source of stability among inmates." These three cases enabled the prison administration to realize that "the Black Muslim faith did constitute an established religion and that the Muslims were therefore entitled to follow the practices that the religion prescribed. The resolution of the Black Muslim issue means that the standards applied there can be applied to any duly recognized religion."[5] Minister Farrakhan feels the Nation of Islam's prison ministries are a vital program to rehabilitate the offenders.

Minister Farrakhan thinks the prisons are filled with incarcerated Malcolm X's. He perceives the inmate population as victims of institutional racism: "You are not criminals; you are the victims of criminals." Minister Farrakhan says:

> Since the prisons are full, you really don't rehabilitate prisoners; You loved Malcolm X, so you say. Well look at Malcolm; he was a thief, a hustler, a pimp, abuser of drugs, a seller of drugs, a bank robber. Would you love him in that condition? But we reclaimed him. We did; And the brilliance of that man is the same brilliance that's hiding in prisons all over America. Malcolm was not the exception. Malcolm is the rule. There are many brilliant Black people. All they need is a chance.[6]

The spiritual and moral uplift message was delivered in urban arenas all over the cities of the United States. The prison outreach programs have served to rehabilitate and recruit ex-offenders to become members of the Nation of Islam.

Dr. Abdul Alim Muhammad:
A Candidate for the United States Congress, 1990

In the 1990s the Nation of Islam continues to venture into mainstream politics. Minister Farrakhan spoke to 10,000 people in the Washington, D.C., Convention Center and used the occasion to register people to vote. The Nation of Islam continued to build alliances with activists within the Democratic Party and with non-Muslim clergy.

In the year 1990, three Muslims ran for political office in the nation's capital. Shawn X Brakeen ran for a seat on the school board. George X ran for election as a Washington, D.C., delegate. Dr. Abdul Alim Muhammad challenged the well-known congressman Steny Hoyer, the incumbent in Maryland's Fifth District. Congressman Hoyer was the chairman of the powerful House Democratic Caucus and has been a shining star in Prince George's County politics for twenty years.

Dr. Abdul Alim Muhammad received 21% of the vote to 79% for Congressman Hoyer. In an interview with the author Dr. Muhammad explained his candidacy for elected office:

> You are looking at a man who ran for Congress in Prince George's County four years ago. We were sick and tired of the Black population of Prince George's County, which is the majority and the most prosperous Black population in the country, sitting around and letting white folks run everything. So we entered the race to kick down the door and wake everybody up and say, look what in the hell are you doing? Why don't you stand up and run your own affairs. I'm not a politician, but we got involved to show them what could be done.[7]

Dr. Abdul Alim Muhammad was born in 1949 in York, Pennsylvania. He attended public schools in York. Dr. Muhammad's father was a postal worker and when Dr. Muhammad was in elementary school, his father moved the family to an all-white Pennsylvania suburb. Dr. Muhammad remembers the day his family moved into the white community. He says, "I'll never forget it, the day the moving vans came down the street. All of the whites were in their yards and they blocked the street and told the movers, you've got to take these niggers back."[8]

The neighbors issued a threat to his father that they would hurt his children. Dr. Muhammad's father exclaimed, "If something happens to my children, then something might happen to your children."[9] The young Muhammad was deeply influenced by his father's courageous stand in the face of a community of white racists. It forever changed his life and motivated him not to tolerate injustice. Dr. Muhammad explains the traits he learned from his father: "He just could not tolerate injustice and he would not tolerate injustice. That's another way I take after him. I hate to see people mistreated and abused."[10]

The young Muhammad attended Antioch College in Yellow Springs, Ohio. He earned a bachelor's degree in biology and a medical degree from Case Western Reserve University in Cleveland. On Labor Day weekend of 1968, he accepted the teachings of the Honorable Elijah Muhammad. He explains why he joined the Nation:

> I joined the Nation of Islam because I felt that the Honorable Elijah Muhammad's teaching was exactly what we needed as a people to rise from the condition we have been left in as a result of being enslaved and oppressed for nearly four centuries at that time.[11]

In 1973, Dr. Muhammad became a minister of the Nation of Islam. He was trained as a surgeon and briefly worked as a surgeon in 1982 at Howard University Hospital and Washington Hospital Center. When the "Nation of Islam duties began to consume most of his time, he halted his surgical practice."[12]

In 1985, Dr. Muhammad cofounded the Abundant Life Clinic and the Paradise Manor Drug Rehabilitation Center in Paradise Manor public housing complex in Washington, D.C. In 1988, Minister Louis Farrakhan selected Dr. Muhammad to become the national spokesman for the Nation of Islam.

The Nation of Islam Impacts Mainstream Organizations

The Nation of Islam is also working with non-Muslim religious organizations. In Los Angeles in April of 1990, 125 members of the "First

A.M.E. Church, the oldest and most influential black congregation in the city, traveled to a nearby mosque to worship with so-called Black Muslims from the notorious Nation of Islam."[13] The following week members from the Nation of Islam attended services at Pastor Cecil Murray's A.M.E. Church.

Pastor Murray explained the purpose of the Muslim/Christian interaction. "The purpose was not to argue about dogma and doctrine, but to ask what we can do jointly to help take our community back from drugs and crime."[14] Clearly, the efforts by the Nation of Islam to solve the drug and crime problem is being noticed by all segments of the African American community.

The Nation of Islam has moved from the fringe of traditional Black moderate leadership and established a welcomed presence in the African American community. The community leadership influence is reiterated by Khallid Abdul Muhammad, special assistant to Minister Farrakhan. Khallid Muhammad explains that these coalitions "put us into a position where Black people are now turning to us for leadership."[15]

The Nation of Islam in the 1990s is addressing problems traditional black leadership ignores, fears, or fails to address. During the 1960s, Malcolm X realized that the problem of millions of African Americans was not a civil rights problem anymore, but a problem of human rights. Clearly, the Nation of Islam under Minister Farrakhan has moved beyond the "civil rights" approach to address human rights issues like disease, nutrition, gang violence, health care, homicide, housing, and shelter in the African American community.

Many leaders feel that the eradication of black youth gang violence is a "man thing" and black men should stand and deliver. Joseph H. Duff, the president of the Los Angeles branch of the NAACP watched in amazement as a thousand black men, many former gang members, heard Minister Farrakhan speak and joined the ranks of the Nation of Islam. Mr. Duff exclaims, "The problem of confronting gang violence and drugs is the responsibility of the Black male. And Muslims have always been a symbol of strong black manhood."[16]

In January of 1989, the Los Angeles police and county sheriffs shot and killed a 27-year-old member of the Nation of Islam. The local "N.A.A.C.P. and other mainstream Black organizations rallied to support the group, something that had rarely happened in the past."[17]

The Nation of Islam is being recognized by police departments as a positive force for social change. The Los Angeles Police Department and County Sheriffs have created films on the Nation of Islam to educate the officers on the Muslim community.

Commander William Rathburn of the Los Angeles Police Department's South Bureau attributes a portion of the 17% decrease in gang-related crime and violence to the contribution of the Nation of Islam.

"We don't attribute all of that to the Nation of Islam. But I would not say they're not responsible for some of it," says Rathburn.[18] Reluctantly, many men in blue of the Los Angeles police are admitting to the positive influence the Nation has in the black community. A black deputy, Jim Cleaver, says, "I am not a borderline Muslim and I am not about to become a Muslim. I just respect what they do!"[19]

"A White Man's Heaven is a Black Man's Hell"
The Nation of Islam Charms the Hip Hop Generation

> "I was the only white person at the luncheonette and was treated as if I were the invisible man. No one spoke to me. No one acknowledged me. I got the message, but just in case I hadn't, one of the customers played the same record over and over on the juke box. A white man's heaven is a black man's hell. I went up to the juke box to read the name of the singer. It was Louis Farrakhan!"[20]
>
> —Nat Hentoff

The Nation of Islam was beginning to charm "popular" culture. Creative artists in urban contemporary music, film, and the arts are incorporating the Nation's leaders, symbols, and ideology in their art. Filmmaker Spike Lee's epic three-hour movie *Malcolm X* provided a positive and dramatic portrayal of the Nation of Islam. Spike Lee spotlighted Minister Farrakhan in his movies *School Daze,* and *Do the Right Thing.* Jermaine Jackson (of the Jackson Five) stood on stage in Ghana during the 1994 Saviour's Day and raised Minister Farrakhan's hand in triumph. The "A Man," Arsenio Hall, sat on his couch and welcomed Minister Farrakhan to his show.

Rap artists like Public Enemy, Big Daddy Kane, Professor Griff, Kenney X, K.R.S. One, Egyptian Tut, and former Nigga with an Attitude (N.W.A.), Ice Cube, have used Nation of Islam symbols and characters in their music and videos. Many rap artists have stood on stage and dedicated their music awards to Minister Louis Farrakhan and the Nation of Islam. Clearly, a new generation of African American youth is hearing the Final Call. Nation of Islam student associations are springing up all over college campuses. Bow tie-wearing Muslim students are becoming a part of the student culture with a message for the black man and woman in America. Minister Farrakhan, Dr. Abdul Alim Muhammad, and Khallid Muhammad, among others, are frequent speakers on college campuses throughout the country.

The Nation of Islam's influence on artists of the hip hop generation is reminiscent of Marcus Garvey's UNIA's influence on the artists of the Harlem Renaissance. Writers of the Renaissance exhibited an enormous amount of "negritude" and African consciousness in their work as a result of Garvey's influence. Presently, the members of the hip hop generation are picking up on the vibes of Minister Louis Farrakhan and the Nation of Islam.

Early in the 1960s Nat Hentoff was introduced to Minister Farrakhan through his music. He describes the voice of the "charmer," one of the names Minister Farrakhan was known as during his years as a professional calypso singer. In his teens, Minister Farrakhan "won first prize on the Ted Mack Amateur Hour. In high school he played violin for the Boston Civic Symphony."[21]

Nat Hentoff describes Minister Farrakhan's vocal stylings on the record "A white man's heaven is a black man's hell" in the following manner:

> I would have gone back to reading the Times except for the voice on the record. A light, resilient tenor whose phrasing was as buoying as an ocean breeze. He was singing in a calypso time, and the high spirits of that way of moving through space contrasted ominously with the bittersweet of the lyrics. It was like a sunny threnody over the corpse of one's worst enemy.[22]

Minister Farrakhan's early training as a singer and violinist has served him well. His ability to vocally maneuver through the political mine fields of Syria with the Jumah Prayer impressed Syrian heads of state. During the 1990s, Minister Farrakhan performed publicly (for the first time in forty years as a violinist) several times. August 7, 1991, Minister Farrakhan "blew some minds" at the 72nd National Association of Negro Musicians Convention (NANMC) at the Bismarck Hotel.

The people at the convention expected to hear a program by a "Who's Who of black classical artists." The crowd had no idea that the man "best known as a fiery advocate of black self-help would show up with his Guadagnini violin and the message that music brings colors together, nations, and human beings."[23]

Minister Farrakhan gave a ten-minute speech on culture and music and played two tunes. Ms. Sylvia Olden Lee accompanied him on the piano. Minister Farrakhan "charmed" the audience with a meditation from the opera "Thais," by Jules Massenet. Minister Farrakhan called the piece a favorite, "because there is no discord." His second selection was "Caardas" by Vittorio Monti, an Italian violinist and composer."[24]

The 74-year-old Ms. Sylvia Olden Lee performed at the dedication of the Nation of Islam's Mosque in Chicago in 1989. Ms. Lee suggested the organizers of the NANMC invite Minister Farrakhan as a "classical artist" to perform at the convention. Ms. Lee expressed the feelings of many in the audience when she said, "His performance has dispelled the public myth about his character and added a new dimension to him as a person."[25]

Helen Dilworth, a classical soprano at the convention, upon hearing
Minister Farrakhan's violin performance, was certainly "charmed. He
played the strings in my heart. Minister Farrakhan's performance made
people put aside their agendas and we were all one," she said.[26] Two
years later in 1993 in a Winston-Salem, North Carolina, musical conference, Minister Farrakhan sent a conciliatory message to the Jewish community. He played a Mendelssohn violin concerto at a musical conference. Mendelssohn was Jewish; Minister Farrakhan felt that people
could get to know him through his music and that music often leads "to
understanding that the spoken word cannot achieve."

The Status of Women in the Nation of Islam
A Case Study: Minister Ava Muhammad

The Nation of Islam has also elevated the status of women in the organization. It has slowly eroded the super masculine and often chauvinis-
tic perspective of Islam to a more egalitarian approach to men and
women in interpersonal relations and the workplace. Presently, women
hold ranks of minister, such as Ava Muhammad. Minister Ava Muhammad is also an attorney and does work with the Nation of Islam's legal
department. Dr. Abdul Halim Muhammad explains the status of women
in the Nation of Islam:

> The provisional constitution of the Nation of Islam holds that no woman
> should be prevented from rising as high as her talent would permit. The
> Honorable Elijah Muhammad once said, that when "you teach a man, you
> teach an individual. When you teach a woman, you teach a nation." We feel
> that we can't really make progress unless we bring about reform in the sta-
> tus of women.[27]

Attorney Ava Muhammad, on September 19, 1994, led a team of at-
torneys into the New York State Supreme Court "to fight attempts by the
New York Post to examine Minister Louis Farrakhan and probe internal
records of the Nation of Islam in a $4.4 billion libel suit filed against the
tabloid on March 15, 1994."[28]

The lawsuit was over a column the New York Post writer Jack Newfield
wrote. In the article Newfield alleged that Minister Farrakhan played a role
in the death of Malcolm X. Attorney Ava Muhammad, a former New York
City prosecutor, repudiates the Post's story in the strongest terms:

> This claim is damaging to the character and reputation of Minister Farrakhan.
> But even more important than that is this suit we are seeking to protect the
> 40 plus million descendants of slaves in America, whose hope for liberation
> and upliftment depends upon the ability of Minister Farrakhan and the

Nation of Islam to engage in the mission of redemption and resurrection of our people unhindered and unimpeded by the enemies of our liberation.[29]

A former member of Malcolm X's organization of Afro-American Unity, Dr. James Smalls, agrees with Attorney Ava Muhammad. Dr. Smalls was a professor in the Black Studies Department at City University of New York. Dr. Smalls was also an Imam for Malcolm X's Muslim Mosque Inc. Dr. Smalls doubts that Minister Farrakhan had anything to do with the assassination of Malcolm X. He feels that the resurrection of Malcolm X's memory is an attempt to divide and conquer:

> They are trying to resurrect Malcolm and use him against the Minister [Farrakhan]. These are the same people that killed Malcolm and defamed him in newspapers. I think most people realize that Minister Farrakhan didn't have nothing to do with the death of Malcolm X.[30]

Saviour's Day 1992/1993

The Malcolm X assassination accusations were serious enough for Minister Farrakhan to dedicate the 1993 Saviour's Day to the controversy. On Sunday, February 21, 1993, at the University of Illinois in Chicago, Minister Farrakhan addressed the assassination questions in a speech entitled "The Honorable Elijah Muhammad and Malcolm X, 27 Years Later, What Really Happened."

During the 1992 Saviour's Day on October 18, 1992, Minister Farrakhan announced before 55,000 people in Atlanta's Georgia Dome that the 1994 Saviour's Day would be held in Accra, Ghana. Minister Farrakhan assigned International Representative Akbar Muhammad to organize the event. The first International Saviour's Day would be cohosted by the president of Ghana, Jerry John Rawlings. The Saviour's Day would be viewed via satellite in public sites in 23 cities in the United States, the United Kingdom, and the Caribbean.

The Nation of Islam and The Congressional Black Caucus "The Sacred Covenant" 1993

In 1993, during the swearing-in ceremonies of the 103rd Congress of the United States, the Nation of Islam was invited to participate in the ceremonies. Dr. Abdul Alim Muhammad was sponsored by the Congressional Black Caucus to address an ecumenical prayer service. The new black members of Congress were sworn in by Judge Leon Heggenbotham, Chief Judge Emeritus, U.S. Court of Appeals, Third District.

Shortly after the swearing-in ceremonies in September of 1993, the Congressional Black Caucus entered into a "sacred covenant" with the Nation of Islam. The two organizations would work together on issues like substance abuse and crime in urban communities. Maryland Democratic congressman Kweisi Mfume was the chairman of the Black Caucus. Congressman Mfume pledged his support for the sacred covenant and praised the Nation of Islam:

> We know full well the tremendous things the Nation of Islam has been able to do to bring safety to public housing projects. To create a climate of self-esteem among young people, to stop the killing, the violence, pain, and to work toward economic development.[31]

The sacred covenant between the Black Caucus and the Nation of Islam was an attempt to combine resources to address social and economic problems in the black community. The covenant was tested almost immediately. On November 29, 1993, Khalid Abdul Muhammad, an aide to Minister Farrakhan, gave a speech at Kean College in Union, New Jersey. During the speech Khallid Muhammad allegedly called Jews the "blood suckers" of the African American community; called Pope John Paul II a "no good cracker," and urged Africans in South Africa to "kill all whites."

Khallid Muhammad's speech was immediately condemned by many black leaders like Jesse Jackson, Dr. Benjamin F. Chavis (NAACP executive director), and William Gray III (president of the United Negro College Fund). Representative John Lewis, the black congressional democrat from Georgia, called Khallid Muhammad's speech "an obscene and ugly attack on decency."[32]

Kweisi Mfume, Congressional Black Caucus chairman, asked that Minister Farrakhan "clarify" his position on the speech. Congressman Mfume also wanted to know if Khallid Muhammad's remarks represented those of the Nation of Islam. When Minister Farrakhan did not immediately disavow himself from Khallid Muhammad's remarks, the "sacred covenant" was in jeopardy.

Minister Farrakhan's immediate response was that people were using Khallid Muhammad's words to "divide the house." Eventually, on February 7, 1994, Minister Farrakhan chastised Khallid Muhammad and condemned his speech for "tone but not content." Minister Farrakhan also suspended Mr. Muhammad from his duties as senior aide.

On Wednesday, February 3, 1994, the Congressional Black Caucus renounced its "sacred covenant" to work with the Nation of Islam. Congressman Kweisi Mfume "labeled evil and vicious the remarks made by Dr. Khallid Abdul Muhammad on November 29th at Kean College in New Jersey. Nowhere in American life can we give sanctuary to such garbage."[33]

Khallid Abdul Muhammad

Khallid Abdul Muhammad often goes by the name Dr. Khallid Muhammad. In 1980, Dr. Muhammad was appointed minister of Temple No. 7 on 125th Street and Fifth Avenue, in Harlem, New York. Eventually, he became the national assistant to Minister Louis Farrakhan. The Kean College speech was one of many for Khallid Muhammad. He was a popular speaker on the college circuit.

On May 29, 1994, Khallid Abdul Muhammad spoke at the University of California, Riverside. When the speech was over, Khallid Muhammad gathered outside the gymnasium to speak informally to about 150 people. A former member of the Nation of Islam and a minister of the Seattle mosque named James Edward Bess opened fire on Dr. Muhammad with a 9-millimeter handgun, shooting him in both legs. The Fruit of Islam who served as bodyguards along with angry members of the crowd nearly beat Mr. Bess to death.

The police rescued Mr. Bess and rushed him to Riverside Community Hospital. Mr. Bess sustained head injuries and lost several teeth. He was transferred from a hospital room to a jail cell on June 1, 1994, and has pleaded not guilty to charges of premeditated attempted murder and assault with a firearm.

Besides Dr. Muhammad, two of his bodyguards, Caliph Sadig and Varno Puckett, and a bystander, Terrel P. Stait, were shot. All received minor wounds and fully recovered.

Minister Louis Farrakhan
"Gets Busy" on the Arsenio Hall T.V. Show
February 25, 1994

On February 25, 1994, African American comedian/actor and television talk show host Arsenio Hall welcomed Minister Farrakhan on his television show. Mr. Hall's purpose for having Minister Farrakhan on his show was to "strive for peace and harmony in America." Arsenio says, "I feel a strong responsibility to not only use my late night arena for entertainment, but also as a vehicle to open dialogue as we strive for peace and harmony in America."[34]

Arsenio Hall's television show changed the face of late-night television. Mr. Hall was the first black person to have a talk show on a major national television network. The show lasted for five years. Arsenio Hall invited presidential candidate Bill Clinton to "wear some shades" and play his saxophone with Hall's band, "The Posse." Mr. Hall introduced the hip hop generation to the American public and many rap artists and controversial guests sat and talked on the couch with the "A Man."

None of Mr. Hall's guests, however, were more controversial than Minister Louis Farrakhan. Mr. Hall asked questions of Minister Farrakhan from "who killed Malcolm X," to "the conflict with Jewish groups," to "drug abuse" and "black-on-black crime."

Minister Farrakhan was very critical of those who condemned Arsenio Hall for having him on his television show. Minister Farrakhan exclaimed:

> You brought me here to your show and what happened Arsenio? You incited so much rage; so much venom, so much hatred, that now they don't want your show to show in the marketplace that it has shown. They threatened you that they will take you off of the air and ruin your career. As long as you don't mistreat us, you don't have to fear anything from us.[35]

While Minister Farrakhan was in Hollywood taping the Arsenio Hall Show he addressed a gathering of influential Hollywood celebrities. In attendance were actors Charles "Roc" Dutton and Wesley Snipes. The Arsenio Hall Show was one of many television shows Minister Farrakhan attended. He also appeared on Phil Donahue, Nightline, Black Entertainment Television (BET), CBS Nightly News, and 20/20.

Shortly after Minister Farrakhan appeared on his show, the Arsenio Hall Show was cancelled due to low ratings. Many people believed that Mr. Hall's endorsement of Minister Farrakhan's appearance against the wishes of the "powers of the Hollywood industry" put his late-night television career in danger. There was no great opposition to Minister Farrakhan's appearance on Nightline, Phil Donahue, 20/20, or CBS Nightly News; however, "it was because Arsenio moved ahead in defiance of industry opposition. Arsenio was put to a 'boy' test and came out a 'man,' so they tilted the support scales against the show."[36]

The Arsenio Hall Show was already in limbo "because Arsenio's contract had not been signed and there was conflict over some CBS affiliates bumping Arsenio for Letterman."[37] Whatever the reason for Arsenio Hall's show's cancellation, I witnessed the "A Man" grow from entertainer to ambassador.

He helped calm the streets after the "Rodney King" riots. He was active in the civic affairs of Los Angeles and as a concerned citizen of the world. Mr. Hall, along with the help of his church, worked to purchase vacant homes formerly used as crack houses and renovated the homes for community programs.

Mr. Hall was visibly nervous the night Minister Farrakhan appeared on his show. I am reminded of what my father told me about the difference between the coward and a hero. Dad said, "The hero in a war is afraid like the coward, but the hero goes to war anyway." That night before a national television audience, the "A Man" stood tall and, "I for one am with him on that tip. F____ Hollywood, power to Arsenio."[38]

Dr. Ben Chavis and Minister Louis Farrakhan
The NAACP Black Leadership Summit, 1994

"His call for the Black Summit back in February 1994 and the acceptance of that call by Ben Chavis and the NAACP and nearly all other black organizations, including the Congressional Black Caucus. That is going to prove itself to be the single most important thing he's [Minister Farrakhan's] done. The Honorable Elijah Muhammad called for a National Black Front, I believe, in 1964. We now see a different kind of leadership and, even though there's turmoil in the NAACP, the principle of unity has been accepted by all."[39]

Dr. Abdul Alim Muhammad
National Spokesman for Minister Louis Farrakhan
September 9, 1994

This quote by Dr. Abdul Alim Muhammad was given during an interview with the author on September 9, 1994. It was in response to my question concerning the significant achievements of the Nation of Islam since Minister Farrakhan's departure from the WCIW in 1977. Moderate leaders of the African American community continued to "flirt" with the Nation of Islam. Dr. Ben Chavis's overtures to Minister Farrakhan put him at odds with the tradition, ideology, and legacy of the NAACP.

Dr. Ben Chavis was forty-five years old when he became executive director of the NAACP in April of 1993. Dr. Chavis's election "by the N.A.A.C.P.'s 64-member board of directors represented a generational change for the 85 year old civil rights organization, the nation's oldest."[40]

Dr. Chavis was aware of the NAACP's traditional liberal white and Jewish allies as well as the black middle-class constituency of the NAACP. Dr. Chavis immediately began to detour from the party line of the NAACP by calling gang summits, showing concern for the plight of the black underclass and reaching out to alienated youth; meeting with radical African Americans and Minister Louis Farrakhan.

During the leadership summit, Dr. Chavis said, "Those who try to drive a wedge between me and Minister Farrakhan are really worried that blacks will gain control of our communities."[41] The Executive Board of the NAACP should not have been surprised by Dr. Chavis's leadership, style, and philosophy. Dr. Chavis had always been left-of-center ideologically and even somewhat radical.

Dr. Chavis had spent four years in a North Carolina prison. He was a 23-year-old minister who was convicted of conspiracy to firebomb a white-owned grocery store in Wilmington, North Carolina. His conviction was later overturned. Dr. Chavis became known as one of the "Wilmington 10" and Amnesty International deemed him as a political prisoner.

Dr. Chavis was executive director of the United Church of Christ's Commission for Racial Justice before he led the NAACP. Dr. Chavis's history was one of radical, confrontational, take-to-the-streets politics; therefore, the executive board should not have been surprised when Dr. Ben Chavis extended the olive branch of peace to Minister Louis Farrakhan and the Nation of Islam.

Dr. Chavis was trying to diversify the mission of the NAACP by reaching out to the Nation of Islam, gang members, and low-income blacks. Dr. Chavis reiterates this point:

> The N.A.A.C.P. is the only national organization other than the black church that has the capacity to broadly represent the diversity within African American people. The question is, can you have that kind of diversity in one organization? For me, the answer is yes. In fact, I think it is necessary.[42]

On June 12 through 14, Dr. Ben Chavis and the NAACP hosted a Black summit in Baltimore, Maryland. The idea of a summit grew out of a unity forum that was convened and chaired by Representative Kweisi Mfume (D-MD). The forum was held "at the Congressional Black Caucus weekend on September of 1993. At that meeting, Representative Mfume declared a sacred covenant between the Congressional Black Caucus, the Rainbow Coalition, the N.A.A.C.P., and the Nation of Islam."[43]

More than eighty African American leaders attended the summit. Leaders from a wide spectrum of views in the African American community, Kweisi Mfume, Jesse Jackson, Lenora Fulani of the new Alliance Party, Conrad Warrill, chairman of the National Black United Front (NBUF), Kurk Schmoke, the mayor of Baltimore, Rev. Dr. Frank M. Reid III (pastor of Bethel A.M.E. Church), and Minister Louis Farrakhan were among others in attendance.

The summit was called to address problems confronting the black community such as economic development, delinquency, and youth and spiritual renewal. The summit had immediate results for Minister Farrakhan and Rev. Jesse Jackson. They had "a strained relationship since 1984, were chatting amiably at one lunch break and at other times during the summit they went into a back room to confer privately."[44] Minister Farrakhan believed the summit was vital for African Americans to develop a political and economic agenda for the future. Minister Farrakhan had this to say about the summit:

> I came away from the summit more convinced than ever that this is the time for the unity of our leadership and people. It is incumbent upon all of us in leadership to make whatever sacrifice necessary to insure that what we started in Baltimore is an ongoing process that will not end until and unless

all of our people are free from fear and want a life under conditions of prosperity and security.[45]

By all accounts the three-day Black Leadership Summit was a resounding success. The troubles, however, for Dr. Ben Chavis were exaggerated by the summit. On August 20, 1994, "by a voice vote, the NAACP board fired Dr. Ben Chavis as its seventh executive director since the NAACP was founded in 1909. A quick show of hands confirmed his fate."[46] Dr. Chavis's fall from grace was an accumulation of political, legal, and financial mistakes.

They are as follows:

1. Dr. Chavis held a secret meeting of black nationalists in Detroit without informing the NAACP board.
2. Dr. Chavis lobbied for the North American Free Trade Agreement in disregard of the NAACP's position against the NAFTA.
3. The accumulation of financial debt during Dr. Chavis's tenure.
4. Apparent false claims of large increases in the NAACP membership.
5. Reaching out to non-NAACP constituent segments of the African American community.
6. The intimate relationship with Minister Louis Farrakhan and the Nation of Islam.
7. An out-of-court settlement to pay Ms. Mary Stansel, a Chavis transition team member who sued him. Ms. Stansel sued for job discrimination and sexual harassment. The terms of the settlement were, "the N.A.A.C.P. would pay Ms. Stansel $35,000 immediately, $15,000 within 15 days, and $5,400 a month for up to six months or until Dr. Chavis helped her received a suitable job offer for $80,000 a year in the Washington area. If she got no such offer, the N.A.A.C.P. would pay her $250,000 over 12 months."[47]

Dr. Chavis reached this settlement without consent or knowledge of the NAACP board, and he insisted it was within his authority as the executive director to do so. The board members felt they had no financial or legal obligation to pay Ms. Stansel; therefore, Mr. Chavis was responsible for the debt.

On August 22, 1994, the new NAACP administration was introduced. Dr. William F. Gibson became chairman of the board of directors. Mr. Earl Shinhoster, former NAACP field director, assumed the role of interim administrator. Mr. Ben Andrews became vice-chair of the NAACP board. Fred Rasheed was installed as NAACP director of economic development and both were assigned to assist Mr. Shinhoster.

Minister Louis Farrakhan's "I Make Men" Lecture Tour of 1994

On June 27, 1994, the author attended a speech by Minister Louis Farrakhan. It was one of Minister Farrakhan's many stops on his "I Make Men" lecture tour throughout urban America during the months leading up to the Saviour's Day in Accra, Ghana. I parked my car about two blocks from the Baltimore Arena. As I walked toward the entrance of the arena, I saw three distinct rows of people blocking my way to the entrance. The first row was a line of white and Jewish protestors. They held placards that said, "Farrakhanism equals Anti-Semitism."

I penetrated the first row of protestors and was welcomed by a large group of African American women. They were shielding the black men from the white and Jewish protestors. The women held signs proclaiming, "Rise up black man!," "The sisters are with you, brothers," and "Minister Farrakhan makes men!" As I passed the lines of black women they shouted, "Go black man, Go black man, We believe in you, brother." I finally made it to the third row of people which was a line of the Fruit of Islam, searching each individual as they entered the arena. I walked up the steps and there were lines of black, bow tie-wearing men selling goods and saving souls; "Torchlight, my brother," "Final Call, Black man," they shouted.

I took my seat in the upper deck of the Baltimore Arena next to a young black man about nineteen years old. He had his son who appeared to be about four years old with him and we were joined by over ten thousand other black men that night. Minister Farrakhan spoke for over two hours on a multiple range of topics from domestic violence to economic and spiritual development. Minister Farrakhan referred to his For Men Only lecture as, "Let Us Make Men." Mr. Jamil Muhammad, the Baltimore minister of Muhammad's Mosque No. 6, said of the event, "Never before has a meeting like this been held in the history of the City of Baltimore."[48]

When Mr. Jamil Muhammad asked for donations, men, young and old, dug down deep in their pockets and contributed. Minister Farrakhan received several standing ovations that evening. Everyone jumped to their feet when Minister Farrakhan told the white community, "God did not make us to serve you, God made us to serve him." The crowd continued to applaud, then Farrakhan roared,"The black man is the original man. Each one of you is a God," he said. Thousands of black men jumped from their seats, many shouting, "Teach Brother Minister!" "Take us home!"

Minister Farrakhan attacked black-on-black crime. He accused black men of "assisting the enemy" by "killing, maiming and destroying yourself." Minister Farrakhan encouraged the men to become producers and captains of industry by using the African American community buying power of $300 billion a year to create businesses and employ the jobless.

During this presentation Minister Farrakhan mentioned he was organizing a million man march on Washington, D.C. in October of 1995.

This scene was repeated in many cities throughout the United States. In New York City, February 1994, twelve thousand black men packed the 369th Street Armory. A line of "black men standing five abreast stretched more than five blocks."[49] Four thousand men had to be turned away that night. Minister Farrakhan told the cheering crowd, "I came here tonight to have a brother/fatherly chat with the men. This society has been so destructive to the black male."[50]

On March 21, 1994, in Washington D.C., the nation's capital, nine thousand black men showed up at the D.C. Armory for his "Men Only" lecture. D.C. councilman Harry Thomas, boxing promoter Rock Newman, and African American Catholic Congregation Bishop George Stallings were in attendance. One attendee, Melvin Fisher, a twenty-five-year-old D.C. resident, after hearing Minister Farrakhan speak, exclaimed, "I'm going home tonight, get my act together, and get back on my own two feet. I'm not living right. Minister Farrakhan touched a lot of things I'm still out here doing. It's time for me to make a change."[51]

On March 9, 1994, Minister Farrakhan traveled to Boston. Two thousand men braved a snowstorm to hear him speak. On April 11, 1994, in Houston, Texas (on April 25th 15,000 men were in attendance in Dallas), some 35,000 black men attended a "Men Only Meeting" at Pleasant Grove Missionary Baptist Church. The church auditorium quickly overflowed the 13,000 capacity." City officials reported that 35,000 people showed up and the line to get in stretched for six miles."[52] Minister Farrakhan told the Houston crowd that the black man's greatest need is "for knowledge of himself and God's purpose for his life."

A curious trend began to develop at each city along the Men Only Tour. In every city black women turned out in mass to support the men. In Houston black women marched, gave black power salutes, and held signs saying, "Unity, Black men, get it together."

In Atlanta, Georgia, on May 23, 1994, 16,000 men jammed the Omni Arena to hear Minister Farrakhan exclaim, "God's desire is to save the black man. God wants to come into the house (minds). Let him in."[53] In one of Minister Farrakhan's last appearances on the "Men Only Tour" before the first International Saviour's Day in Ghana, 10,000 black men showed up at the Philadelphia Civic Center.

In the politically correct 1990s you would think Minister Farrakhan would come under some heavy criticism from women's groups. Well, you're right! Black women all over the country were angry and outraged. They wanted Minister Farrakhan to have a "For Women Only Tour." Tiffany Hamill led a drive in Baltimore for a Women Only Meeting. She collected over 6,000 signatures from black women. In regards to the "separation of the sexes" in the Men Only tour, Ms. Hamill says:

We don't feel it's sexist or discriminatory that the black man has his unique
set of problems. The black woman has hers and we need separate environ-
ments to deal with those problems. The petitions helped us explain Men
Only Meetings to other women. White women groups don't represent black
women.[54]

At the request of African American women throughout the United
States, Minister Farrakhan held a For Black Women Only lecture on
June 25, 1994. In Atlanta, Georgia, 12,000 black women packed the
World Congress Center to hear Minister Farrakhan's speech entitled
"The black woman is sacred." Minister Farrakhan approached the mi-
crophone with trepidation. He began to speak and said, "I have been
stressed for two days [thinking about talking to you]. This has never hap-
pened to me before."[55] Minister Farrakhan told the Atlanta For Women
Only crowd:

Who are you black woman? What makes you so special? Sisters, you have
carried us not only in your womb, but you have carried us on your backs
for over 400 years. Now Allah has come to relieve you of that burden and
make a man for you that you will be proud to honor and respect.[56]

The women accepted Minister Farrakhan and erupted in wild applause
several times. Members of the Muslim Girls in Training Class in Atlanta
sang a song to commemorate the evening. They sang, "What you gonna
do? What you gonna do? Keep your mind moving! Our nation can rise
no higher than its women! We're movin' on, keepin' strong. Don't you
let them lead you wrong! It's a sistah thang!"[57] Black men paraded outside the World Congress Center in support of black women. It was "pay
back time for the sistah's." One man held up a sign that captured the moment. It read, "The black woman is second to none!"

Entering into the year 2000, Minister Louis Farrakhan is the only
black man in America with the charisma to draw 15,000 people on less
than a week's notice! Many of the urban information outlets for the "Nation" are by leaflets, posters, and "word of mouth." Through this type of
grass roots mass communication, the Nation of Islam is able to fill arenas all over the country. The 1994 "I Build Men Lecture Tour" proved
beyond a doubt that Minister Louis Farrakhan's popularity, influence,
and power is growing.

Saviour's Day—Accra, Ghana—October 9, 1994

"Marcus Mosiah Garvey preached it. Dr. W.E.B. Dubois organized for it.
The Honorable Elijah Muhammad gave it spiritual direction. Osageyfo
(leader) Dr. Kwame Nkrumah died in exile because of it. And others to

various degree put their shoulders to the milestone to make it reality. On October 9th at Independence Square the Honorable Minister Louis Farrakhan fulfilled the dream of these great visionairies, who undoubtedly smiled as the leaders of the Nation of Islam and his excellency President Jerry John Rawlings embraced before a crowd of 30,000 including 2,000 blacks from America who made the 'pilgrimage' to celebrate the Nation of Islam's first International Saviors Day."[58]

—James Muhammad (Editor in chief of the *Final Call*)

The crowning achievement of the decade was the October 6 through 9, 1994, International Saviour's Day in Accra, Ghana. It was truly an historic event. The Pan-African ideals of Cuffee, Blyden, Delaney, Garvey, Noble Drew Ali, Master Fard Muhammad, DuBois, and the Honorable Elijah Muhammad were reborn on the sacred ground of mother Africa. Africans and African Americans united in racial solidarity. The Saviour's Day Convention was attended by 30,000 people in Ghana's Black Star Square (named after Marcus Garvey's Black Star Line). Saviour's Day opened October 6 with the "pageantry of a victory celebration. African drums and horns sounded the arrival of President Rawlings and Minister Louis Farrakhan to the International Conference Center. Dancers brought smiles to the faces of delegates, smiles that would last the entire day."[59] President Rawlings welcomed both Africans and African Americans with a passionate 90-minute address and described the gathering as a "prayer meeting and a pilgrimage." President Rawlings and many Ghanians have been admirers of the work of the Nation of Islam. President Rawlings exclaimed:

This is not Medina or Mecca, but you are coming home. Ghanians have watched with admiration the way the Nation of Islam brought a moral revolution, a reawakening of family and community values and pride to some of the most socially deprived areas of the United States.[60]

Also, on October 6, there was a fashion show hosted by designer Kadijah Farrakhan (wife of Minister Farrakhan). On October 7, delegates gathered at the Lombardi Beach Hotel to celebrate the 97th birthday of the Honorable Elijah Muhammad. Dr. David DuBois, son of Dr. W.E.B. DuBois, gave the keynote address. Dr. DuBois praised the Nation of Islam for holding Saviour's Day in Ghana. He compared Minister Farrakhan to his father. Dr. DuBois said, "Charges of hate mongering and anti-Semitism being hurled at Minister Farrakhan are the same as the charges of communism directed at W.E.B. DuBois 45 years ago, and for the same reasons. In an attempt to silence the truths that Minister Farrakhan and the Nation of Islam expose."[61]

On October 6, 7, and 8 there were several workshops. The following is a list of workshops and the guest speakers:

October 6–8—Accra International Conference Center

Workshop	*Special Guests*
Religion in Africa: Mutual Respect for One Another	Min. Akbar Muhammad, Ghana Representative, Nation of Islam
The Changing Role of the African Woman	Dr. Muhammed Ibn Chambas, Deputy Minister, Foreign Affairs Ghana
Health Issues Facing the Black World	Dr. Ben Chavis—USA Gamal Nkrumah—Egypt
Talk Radio: Its Impact on America and Potential for Africa	Amb. Asiel Ben Israel—Israel Dr. Sonia Sanchez—USA
Toward Understanding Africans in the Diaspora	Rev. Lewis James—A.M.E. Church—USA
Economic Development: The Business Connection	Sis. Tynnetta Muhammad—Mexico
Education and Culture	Dr. Etienne Massac—USA Dr. Alim Muhammad—USA Dr. Na'im Akbar—USA Kwame Ture—USA Dr. David DuBois, Egypt Dr. Muhammad Ben Abdallah—Ghana Chuck D—USA Haki Madhuti—USA

There was also an address by His Excellency, Dr. Kenneth Kaunda of Zambia. Rahbee Ben Ammi also spoke. He is the spiritual leader of the Original Hebrew Israelite Nation. On October 8 there was a concert featuring Jermaine Jackson, Public Enemy, Black Girl, Akilah, Sister Maria Farrakhan, Kenny X, and Egyptian Tut.

Minister Louis Farrakhan's 1994 Saviour's Day Address "Fulfilling the Vision of the Honorable Elijah Muhammad"

Minister Farrakhan spoke in the Black Star square before an audience of 30,000 people. He greeted President Rawlings, who sat in the front row 40 yards from the stage, with members of the Ghanian government and several tribal chiefs. There were three opening prayers in Christian, Muslim, and Hebrew. Minister Farrakhan began his address by explaining the vision of the Honorable Elijah Muhammad:

> Our fulfilling the vision is deeper than Garvey. It's deeper than Kwame Nkrumah. The vision is a divine vision Elijah Muhammad received from God. Our fulfilling the vision goes back to God himself. And what he has caused to be spoken by the mouth of his prophets concerning yesterday, today, and tomorrow.[62]

Minister Farrakhan believes that scholars have tried to write his mentor the Honorable Elijah Muhammad "out of history." By fulfilling the Honorable Elijah Muhammad's vision, however, his legacy lives on:

> I thank God for my teacher, the Honorable Elijah Muhammad. Who gave me a word to speak that will liberate the minds of our people. Such a great leader, such a great teacher, that the enemy wanted to write him out of history. But as long as we live, we will carry his idea and his vision.[63]

Elijah Muhammad's vision was fulfilled in Accra, Ghana. The Nation of Islam planted the vision in the motherland. The International Saviour's Day was an important step to implement the idea of Pan-Africanism. Minister Farrakhan reiterates this in his address:

> As long as we live the idea of Pan-Africanism will live so that all over the earth, wherever we are found, we must link up and never allow the old vision of the old world order to break us down ever again.[64]

After Minister Farrakhan's address, President Rawlings was invited to the stage. President Rawlings said of Farrakhan's address, "The beauty of Minister Farrakhan is he brings you news. It may be good, it may be bad, but what's important is that he's giving you the truth."[65]

The Saviour's Day was concluded by pouring of libations. Jermaine Jackson performed one final song for the audience. At the airport before his departure, Minister Farrakhan "pledged to the people of Ghana that the Nation of Islam will establish a mosque and school in Nema. He said, Nema residents are the jewels of Ghana."[66]

Minister Farrakhan boarded the plane to leave Accra, Ghana, the site of the 1994 Saviour's Day. The Nation of Islam had just taken another giant step into the future of African and African American history. The Saviour's Day also elevated the status of Minister Farrakhan. He was received by a head of state in Ghana, President Rawlings. One of the delegates fixed Minister Farrakhan's place in history. He said: "History will say that the Honorable Elijah Muhammad talked about Africa and building a bridge. Minister Farrakhan has picked up the baton and fulfilled that vision and he was received by the head of state who opened the convention and closed it. That's significant."[67]

In 1995, the black nationalist ideology, which began with Cuffee in 1815, is alive and beating in the heart, mind, and soul of Minister Louis Farrakhan. He continues to be that voice from the past, who keeps reminding black Americans that they are African people. Up you mighty race! Hear the final call! The Nation of Islam, under the leadership of Minister Farrakhan, is continuing the legacy and vision of the Honorable Elijah Muhammad. The "old man" must be proud!

Notes

1. *Washington Post,* March 1, 1990.
2. "Doing the Right Thing," *Time* April 16, 1990.
3. *Washington Post,* March 1, 1990.
4. Harry E. Allen, and Clifford E. Simonsen, *Corrections in America,* (New York: Macmillan, 1992), p. 291.
5. Ibid., p. 281.
6. *Washington Post,* March 1, 1990.
7. Interview, Dr. Abdul Alim Muhammad, Washington, D.C., September 9, 1994.
8. *Washington Post,* September 22, 1990.
9. Ibid.
10. Ibid.
11. Interview, Dr. Abdul Alim Muhammad.
12. "Facing the Farrakhan Factor," *Washington Post,* November 4, 1990, p. c-5.
13. *Time,* April 16, 1990.
14. Ibid.
15. Ibid.
16. Ibid.
17. Ibid.
18. Ibid.
19. Ibid.
20. Nat Hentoff, "How Minister Farrakhan Became a Part of My Life," *New York Voice,* April 30, 1991, p. 22.
21. "Farrakhan Plays for Harmony" *Chicago Sun Times,* August 8, 1991.
22. Hentoff, "How Minister Farrakhan Became a Part of My Life," p. 22.
23. "Farrakhan Plays for Harmony," *Chicago Sun Times,* August 8, 1991.
24. Ibid.
25. Ibid.

26. Ibid.

27. Interview, Dr. Abdul Alim Muhammad.

28. *Final Call,* October 19, 1994, p. 3.

29. *Final Call,* March 30, 1994.

30. Ibid.

31. Ibid.

32. *Washington Post,* January 29, 1994.

33. *Los Angeles Times,* February 31, 1994.

34. "Farrakhan to Get Busy on Arsenio Hall Show," New York *Newsday,* February 8, 1994.

35. Arsenio Hall T.V. Show, February 25, 1994.

36. Anthony 2X, "Arsenio Hall Standing Up as a Black Man in Hollywood," *Final Call,* July 6, 1994.

37. Ibid.

38. Ibid.

39. Interview, Dr. Abdul Alim Muhammad.

40. *Baltimore Sun,* June 13, 1994.

41. Ibid.

42. *Baltimore Sun,* April 11, 1994.

43. *Final Call,* March 16, 1994, p. 23.

44. *Emerge,* September 1994.

45. *Final Call,* July 6, 1994.

46. *Baltimore Sun,* August 22, 1994.

47. Ibid.

48. *Baltimore Afro-American,* July 2, 1994.

49. *Final Call,* February 16, 1994.

50. Ibid.

51. Ibid.

52. *Final Call,* April 3, 1994.

53. *Final Call,* April 27, 1994.

54. *Final Call,* June 8, 1994.

55. *Final Call,* July 20, 1994.

56. Ibid.

57. Ibid.

58. Ibid.

59. *Final Call,* November 2, 1994.

60. Ibid.

61. Ibid.

62. Ibid.

63. Ibid.

64. Ibid.

65. Ibid.

66. Ibid.

67. Ibid.

Afterword

On July 25, 1979, in Chicago, Illinois, I interviewed Imam W. D. Muhammad. It was two years after the excommunication of Minister Louis Farrakhan. The "Farrakhan phenomenon" had not caught hold to the national consciousness at that time. In the afterword of the first edition I concluded that

> whether the W.C.I.W. will prosper or not is too early to predict. History will record their achievements and generations yet to be born will judge their contributions. However, there are two factors that cannot be debated: It is no longer a black separatist movement nor are its members black Muslims. The World Community of Al-Islam in the West is comprised of Muslims who believe in Islam. *The Transition from Black Muslims to Muslims is complete.*

The second edition has provided me an opportunity to update the manuscript and document changes, transformations, and even resurrections. After a thorough analysis of the data for the second edition, I realized it would be appropriate and scientifically sound to rename the title of the book. The first edition was entitled. *From Black Muslims to Muslims: The Transition from Separatism to Islam, 1930–1980.* The first edition covered the origin, development, and change of the Nation of Islam from 1930 to 1980. From 1975 until 1980 Imam W. D. Muhammad began to dismantle and dissolve his father's "nation."

Therefore, the first edition covered the transition from black nationalism under the leadership of the Honorable Elijah Muhammad to the "orthodoxing," early dissolution and non-Afrocentric/anti-nation building perspective of Imam W. D. Muhammad. The second edition details the resurrection, transformation, and change of the Nation of Islam from 1980 to 1995. In fifteen years the organization originally known as the Lost-Found Nation of Islam has undergone radical changes.

In the second edition, I included the term "resurrection." Clearly, in 1979 no one could have predicted the enormous charismatic power of Minister Louis Farrakhan. If Minister Farrakhan would have remained a loyal follower of Imam W. D. Muhammad the Nation of Islam would have died a quiet death. There would still be a few true believers scattered throughout the black community. In 1977, however, it was judgement day for Minister Farrakhan; he left the WCIW. Minister Farrakhan adopted the ideas of the Honorable Elijah Muhammad; he became the spiritual son. In his role as spiritual son of the Honorable Elijah Muhammad, Minister Louis Farrakhan brought back to life the Lost-Found

Nation of Islam in America. In this historical period of its growth, the organization was truly *lost* under the leadership of the biological son, Imam W. D. Muhammad. Minister Louis Farrakhan, the spiritual son, *found* the Nation in his heart, mind, and soul, and began to "raise from the dead" and revive the 200-year-old African nationalist legacy practiced by his spiritual father the Honorable Elijah Muhammad.

The sociological study of the Nation of Islam provided a valuable opportunity to study the role of charismatic leaders and social change. The classical Weberian principles of charismatic power and authority can be examined in the life and times of Minister Louis Farrakhan and the Nation of Islam. During the "early years" (1977–1980) of the resurrection, Minister Farrakhan was left with only his charisma, a vision, and an idea. The social and economic conditions of the 1980s during Reaganomics created class, gender, and racial conflicts throughout the country. The hostile political, economic, and social climate made it conducive for the African American community to be receptive to Minister Farrakhan's ideas, and the ideology of the Nation of Islam. Minister Farrakhan's impressive oratorical ability to convey his vision of a better life for African Americans enables the Nation of Islam to receive millions of dollars in revenue and to remain financially stable and politically independent.

In the fifteen years since the first edition we have witnessed the Nation of Islam expand its influence into mainstream political organizations like the NAACP and the Congressional Black Caucus, black musicians, artists (rap and otherwise), black college students, and youth at risk (gang members). The 1994 Saviour's Day in Accra, Ghana, was a significant achievement for the Nation of Islam. The organization is beginning to exert its influence internationally. The positive interaction between Minister Farrakhan and Ghanian president Jerry John Rawlings opens the political doors for trade, import, export business, loans, and numerous economic development initiatives for the Nation of Islam.

Heading into the year 2000 and beyond, the Nation of Islam's future seems bright. The oppressive social and economic conditions suffered by the African American community continues to produce social problems in need of a cure.

African American leaders from Paul Cuffee (1815) to Minister Louis Farrakhan (1995) have used various forms of African nationalist ideologies as a remedy for the socioeconomic ailments of the African American community. The ailments blacks suffer in America have changed since early leaders like Cuffee, Garnet, Blyden, Garvey, and even Dr. W. E. B. DuBois tried to "uplift the race."

Clearly, the Nation of Islam has answered the call and is addressing some of the most significant and disabling social problems of our time. The organization continues to address domestic violence, gang violence, public housing issues, AIDS, and health care/medical research, prisoners' rights, community safety and security, women's rights, and black-on-black crime.

There are enough social and economic problems to keep the members of the Nation "gettin busy" for a long time. The resurrected Nation of Islam is alive and well and living in the heart of the African American community.

I'm going into the heart of the community and buy a bean pie and a *Final Call* newspaper from Brother Muhammad. I'm going home to review the tape of the 1994 International Saviour's Day from Accra, Ghana. I can start to feel the idea for a third edition growing in my soul.

As the second edition of this book was going to press, Minister Farrakhan organized "Million Man March" on October 16, 1995. The co-organizer was former NAACP official Ben Chavis. The black men, women, and children who marched wanted to demonstrate a commitment to self-reliance, family responsibility, and to have a day of atonement. Estimates of the crowd ranged from 800 thousand to over one million. The participants formed the largest demonstration in the history of the nation's capital. This march demonstrated the growing influence of Minister Farrakhan and the Nation of Islam.

Appendix A

Interview with Imam
Wallace D. Muhammad

The Chief Minister of the World Community of Al-Islam in the West, Imam Wallace D. Muhammad, was interviewed by the author in Chicago on July 25, 1979.

CEM: Was the Nation of Islam (NOI) a social movement organization or a religion?

WDM: It was a religion and a social movement organization. In fact, the religion as it was introduced to the Nation of Islam was more a social reform philosophy than Orthodox Islam.

CEM: How would you define the World Community of Al-Islam in the West?

WDM: A combination of both, but in line with the Koranic teachings. The old organization teachings were not in line with the Koranic teachings.

CEM: Were social and economic conditions during the thirties instrumental in the development of the ideology?

WDM: They certainly were. I think the present community thinking in the World Community of Al-Islam in the West is a result of the earlier teachings. We find many Islamic organizations but I don't believe there is one to be found like ours. I don't know of a single Islamic organization in America or outside that is really like ours. We put emphasis on the application of religion in one's daily life and involvement in the outer community. In the East, Muslims do apply their religion to their daily lives because that's what it's for. But few of them who live in America practice their religion that way.

As you know, we are addressing community issues and are trying to find some common ground for Muslims and non-Muslims. The old Nation of Islam was designed to fight problems peculiar to black people — social problems, lack of economic development among poor blacks, and alcoholism. In those days, dope addiction wasn't much of a problem. Alcoholism was treated. The earlier teachings were designed to give us a socialism ideology. In fact, it did introduce a socialist philosophy. That's why it was feared in the earlier days, the early thirties.

The members were locked up in Chicago and Detroit in the middle thirties. The original teacher who introduced the NOI was ordered out of Detroit. Then he came to Chicago in 1934—within months [he] was asked to leave Chicago. He left the movement. The pressure on the Nation of Islam during its early development was out of fear of a kind of Communist philosophy being introduced in the guise of religion.

CEM: Was Marcus Garvey's Black Factories Corporation influential in the Honorable Elijah Muhammad's creation of the business enterprises?

WDM: Not only the Honorable Elijah Muhammad, but his teacher who was a foreigner and not an American, Fard Muhammad [was also influenced by Garvey]. His teachings were obviously influenced by Garvey and Noble Drew Ali, who started the Moorish America movement. I say that because the dress he originally gave the male members of the Fruit of Islam is the same dress the Drew Ali people had. The garbs the women wore were like the garbs the Marcus Garvey women wore. The emphasis on identity, black identity, and economic development—I am sure that was influenced by the Garvey teachings.

CEM: Was Wallace Fard Muhammad ever a member of the Moorish Science Temple, or did he just study the teachings of Noble Drew Ali?

WDM: I don't believe he was ever a member. He was really a very wise man in Islamic teachings and comparative religion, very wise in understanding the symbolisms in religion. I think what he did was to look for a way to introduce the Koran in the black community. He studied Noble Drew Ali's approach. I believe he felt that Drew Ali had that as a part of his own plan. His own plan was to introduce the Koran but he didn't; he produced a small booklet that he called "Koran," but it had no resemblance to the Koran at all.

Professor Fard introduced the whole text of the Koran—the complete text as it is known all over the world—to the Nation of Islam. To introduce it he had to put it in the package of Drew Ali. The teachings he gave us were similar to what Drew Ali gave his people. He taught us we were black Asiatics and descendants of a great Islamic Kingdom; Drew Ali taught his people the same. He taught us the Caucasians were devils and Drew Ali taught his people the same. A lot of his people don't know this. He identified white people with the embodiment of evil in scripture, which is Satan. But he was more elusive than Fard Muhammad was. Drew Ali said white people were the rider of the horse—he took that out of the Bible to identify the white man as the pale horse, whose rider is death. He didn't say devil, but the angel of death riding a pale horse is disguised as the devil. Fard Muhammad, because of his comparative religious studies, was able to pick up what the average follower [of] Drew Ali couldn't pick up—Caucasian race is the embodiment of evil. Fard Muhammad came out in plain language and said they are devils.

CEM: What is the status of the numerous business enterprises since your administration? Does the World Community of Al-Islam in the West still run and control the enterprises?

WDM: Well, no. I couldn't say we do. We leave it to individuals and corporations that are formed within WCIW and some without. We have a property manager now—Brother Omar. He manages properties and he is independent. If we have a complaint, it's like the tenant giving the landlord a complaint. He has a free hand to manage the income, monies, and everything. We just look for him to show a profit. If he shows a profit we want our share. He runs the management of the real estate. What used to be Salaam Restaurant is now in the hands of Brother Omar. The farms that used to be operated by members in the community are now leased out to others, to outsiders.

CEM: You have established Masjids in several Caribbean locations, Barbados, Bermuda, Jamaica, Nassau-Bahamas, St. Thomas and St. Croix, Virgin Islands. Why have you established Masjids in the Caribbean and what role do you see the West Indians playing in the struggle for human rights?

WDM: I have a personal interest in the Caribbean, but it was not my personal interest that brought about the establishment of Masjids in the Caribbean. They were actually established under the Honorable Elijah Muhammad. What we did was try to improve the membership and propagation work.

CEM: Could you tell me something about Fard Muhammad's background and why he disappeared so mysteriously?

WDM: I believe he was a genius of theology, with reference to its symbolic nature. The really interesting thing about Fard Muhammad—which Elijah Muhammad himself recognized—is that this man was introducing himself as a Christ figure to displace the "old" Christ that Christianity gave black people. That is what caused him to disappear so mysteriously; he wanted to create mystery about himself.

A number of things he did . . . [were] mere cheap magic or premature witch doctor's tricks. The Honorable Elijah Muhammad used to talk about how he took a strand of his hair out of his head and told some of the members to take a strand of hair from their heads. They would all put the hairs in one pile and Fard Muhammad would take a strand from his head and lift them all up. The Honorable Elijah Muhammad, being the son of a

Baptist preacher who had preached for fifty years, made the connection right away, "Lift me up and I will draw all men unto me!"
They tell me Fard Muhammad would come one day and his hair
would be completely gray and he would appear the next time
and—no gray hair. He purposely tried to draw their attention.

CEM: You have stated that you were chosen for the mission to lead.
Why were you selected to replace the Honorable Elijah
Muhammad and not other members of your family and/or other
members of the organization?

WDM: The power of mystery. The other children were already born
when Fard Muhammad came. I was the only child born during
his stay with us. I was chosen because a new baby, new birth—
they wanted a Christ figure, someone with a mystery about
[him]. Here was this newborn baby predicted by Fard Muhammad to be a male and it so happened the guess was right. I say
a "guess" not to laugh at our religion. I say "guess" because
that's the language the Honorable Elijah Muhammad used.

I hope I represent the Honorable Elijah Muhammad. To me the
Honorable Elijah Muhammad was a man like I try to be. That
is, a wise leader for his people. He was a man that laughed and
joked, but he was very serious, even his jokes were serious,
even his jokes were a teaching. I have admired his wisdom and
I try to follow it.

CEM: You have decentralized the organization; where is the central
leadership of the organization now?

WDM: The central leadership is still in myself, but it's not an absolute
leadership. The power is shared with a council of Imams and
about seventeen advisors to that council. Many others not
named [are] in the body of advisors. We try to share the leadership. The Imam's meeting going on right now is supervised
by Brother Imam Fatah; he has a free hand to do that. The business, real estate, and other capital holdings throughout the
country—we look to the people who are over those regions to
make the best decisions for the interest of community.

CEM: Detroit is presently the Midwest regional headquarters?

WDM: Yes it is. Dr. G. Haleen Shabazz is the Imam over the Midwest
region.

CEM: What is the status of Muhammad Ali in the organization now?

WDM: Actually, his membership, in my opinion, is an honorary one.

CEM: What does that mean?

WDM: That means we hardly ever seem him, but we still honor his
membership.

CEM: Why did Louis Farrakhan leave the World Community of Al-
Islam in the West and what is he doing now?

WDM: To my knowledge, he is preaching a kind of moderate form of the very early teachings. I'd say he has gone back in time; he has gone back further than the Honorable Elijah Muhammad himself was at the time of his death. To try to introduce again, black nationalist philosophy, I think he is trying to stay abreast politically with the black movement.

In my opinion, he is doing a disservice to himself. He has ability, intelligence to deal with the African problem in the context of man's problems on earth. That's the only way to deal with it, in my opinion.

CEM: You originally had a national decision-making board. Has that been disbanded in favor of the Council?

WDM: We had a decision-making board. The name itself created a problem—the name of the board. I was the chief administrator over the board. The old habit of passing the buck gave that structure too many problems. The council of Imams didn't replace that body but we have found leadership to satisfy us. Whereas, with the decision-making board we did not have the leadership to satisfy us.

CEM: Malcolm X Shabazz was suspended from the nation of Islam in 1964. The same year you and your brother Akbar left the movement. Was there any relationship between the two events?

WDM: Yes. When Minister Malcolm was suspended I was already excommunicated. I was the first to be excommunicated. Then Minister Malcolm received the suspension. When Minister Malcolm received the suspension, it was news right away, but because of my low profile and almost insignificant position in the Nation of Islam at that time, the news of my suspension did not hit the press like Malcolm's suspension did.

I was charged with trying to influence Malcolm's theological thinking. I was also charged with giving him personal, private knowledge of the Honorable Elijah Muhammad's living, which was a lie. I told him at the time I was falsely accused and I would like to face the accusers. The Honorable Elijah Muhammad told me, "Malcolm X is not facing his accusers either. We're talking to you separately." So he talked to me separately and he made his decision right there. His decision was to excommunicate me.

CEM: How did you influence Malcolm X's theological thinking?

WDM: I have no knowledge of any effort on my part to influence his theological thinking. That was the accusation made. Malcolm X . . . said I had been an influence in his life. He didn't put it that way but in effect that's what he said. I had been an influence on second to the Honorable Elijah Muhammad.

CEM: What year were you excommunicated?

WDM: The first time must have been late 1964.

CEM: You say the first time; you were excommunicated twice?

WDM: No. Many times—at least three or four times and always for the
        same charge that I was not accepting the God-image given to
        Fard Muhammad.

CEM: What was the longest period you were suspended and what did
        you do during your suspension?

WDM: The longest period of my suspension was between the years
        1964 and 1969. During that time I was stripped of all minister's
        privileges. In 1966, early 1967 all support—even family rela-
        tions were denied me. I couldn't even socialize with family
        members. During this period I had several jobs. First, I bought
        a carpet and furniture cleaning machine and started cleaning
        carpet and furniture just on my own. It was very hard. I didn't
        have enough money to run an office. I couldn't advertise; I just
        had to go from customer to customer. I did manage to live and
        finally I got a good welding job and things improved for me.

CEM: You were admitted back into the organization in 1969?

WDM: No. I don't believe it was '69. In '69 things began to warm up.
        In 1970 I was admitted back. Once right after Malcolm's as-
        sassination I was admitted back, but that didn't last very long.
        I was right back out. I was admitted back in 1970 again. I stay
        in the good graces of Elijah Muhammad until now.

CEM: When did the changes start to take place in the organization? I
        am sure it didn't occur in 1975. Did you start discussing the
        transformation long before then?

WDM: No. Not long before then. I would say nine months to a year. It
        was in 1974 that the Honorable Elijah Muhammad accepted me
        back into the ministry. I started teaching here in Chicago. The
        Honorable Elijah Muhammad gave me complete freedom to
        teach here in Chicago with Imam Shaw. At one point he told me
        to assume authority of the Mosque here in Chicago. From that
        point on I was free to propagate and preach as my own wisdom
        dictated. I say that because I would actually test the support for
        me from the Honorable Elijah Muhammad. Nobody else was
        restricting my movement; I answered only to the Honorable
        Elijah Muhammad. I would say things I know were different
        from some of the things the people had been taught under the
        leadership of Elijah Muhammad. I would use my own discre-
        tion. I would test what the Honorable Elijah Muhammad would
        accept. He never ever called me in and said what I was teach-
        ing was causing problems [or to] slow up or go in another di-
        rection. He was satisfied with it.

One time a tape was brought to the Honorable Elijah Muhammad by officers of the FOI [Fruit of Islam], who were like the police in the Nation of Islam, checking everything. He hadn't heard it himself. He called me over and played it while I was present. . . . He jumped up out of his seat and applauded and said, "My son's got it!" That's what he told the officers sitting around the table and his wife. He said, "My son can go anywhere on earth and preach."

CEM: The Pillars of Islam include testimony, prayer, fasting, alms, and pilgrimage to Mecca. Did the Nation of Islam follow these principles and does the World Community of Al-Islam in the West follow them?

WDM: We follow them. The Nation of Islam accepted those principles. They were vaguely taught; they weren't clearly taught. Fasting was taught. We fasted during December; we didn't fast during the proper month. The Honorable Elijah Muhammad didn't bother with that. He picked December. He explains the reasons for picking December, because during that time you are normally converted to Christian life. You have a tendency to go out and waste your money and get into the Christmas season. So we used his month because it's good protection for us. He introduced December as the month of Ramadan, which is unorthodox Islam. During the last four or five years of his life, he began to observe the month of Ramadan in the Islamic calendar.

CEM: Under Elijah Muhammad, members were discouraged from serving in the armed services, voting, or supporting political candidates. Why? And have you changed this?

WDM: Minister Malcolm, in his attack on the conservative leadership when he was suspended, described the Nation of Islam as a straitjacket religion. I don't take too well to that kind of criticism, but I think Malcolm X had discovered something. He was very emphatic and clear in what he had to say. He didn't beat around the bush. The Honorable Elijah Muhammad admitted he was containing our minds to remake our minds. He said, "If I let you go out into the world, you will never become the people Allah wants you to be." He designed the teachings to contain the thinking of his followers. While he was containing their thinking, it was almost as if he had their brains on a lab table. He was treating social diseases, operating on their minds. This kind of containment of the thinking of the people didn't allow the Honorable Elijah Muhammad to introduce new concepts to his people. The concepts remained mystical, and even fictional . . . many concepts of the religion as the birth of God. The Christians don't have a concept like that. They say the birth of Jesus but not the birth of God.

CEM: Three of the basic principles of the Nation of Islam were Master Fard Muhammad is God, the white man is the devil, and Elijah Muhammad is the prophet of God. Has this changed since your administration?

WDM: Certainly, the Honorable Elijah Muhammad, the way he discussed his own messianic prophet image, made it possible for us to reestablish the Honorable Elijah Muhammad as a minister. In the early days, and this is on record, he was called first minister of the Nation of Islam. That's why when I assumed the position of leadership, I took on the name of Chief Minister which means first minister.

The Honorable Elijah Muhammad on many occasions said, "I am not a prophet. I am like the mailman. The mailman has a letter for you. That's your letter; he has to give it to you." He had a message to give. The Honorable Elijah Muhammad didn't speak in the same theological spirit as the Bible and Koran speak in. He talked of himself as a messenger of God. He played down that supernatural experience. The Honorable Elijah Muhammad said, "I am not a prophet but I am a messenger of God." I think what he was trying to say was [he] didn't get a revelation like Moses or Christ or like Muhammad and the other great prophets. [He] got a message in the ordinary sense. Like you get a letter from your friend or boss.

The Honorable Elijah Muhammad didn't fix his image in the minds of his people in such a scriptural way that it couldn't be undone. What I have done is simply talk on the double meaning of Elijah Muhammad's teachings. Elijah Muhammad was a student of the Bible; his father was a Baptist minister. That's why Fard Muhammad chose him, because he was so learned in the Bible. The people were already Bible-oriented. There were other reasons, too, I guess. The Bible called the preacher a messenger of God. Honorable Elijah Muhammad was speaking in a common language, the daily spoken language and Bible references. He was not speaking from Koranic context. He was saying, "A man came to me with solutions for your health problems, social problems, and I bring you the message he gave to me."

CEM: What is the status of women in the organization since your administration?

WDM: We have tried to reexamine the role of women in Al-Islam. What I've done is study the treatment of women during the early rise of Islam under prophet Muhammad himself and the early rulers to succeed prophet Muhammad. I have come to the conclusion that prophet Muhammad and the Koran saw the women in a different way than most Muslims see the women.

They have rights to equal education. This was done during the lifetime of prophet Muhammad. During his lifetime, women were given the right to engage in business to compete with men and to hire men. The rights of women to equal education were protected by Islam during the days of prophet Muhammad.

I have looked at the role of women in that light—in the light of what prophet Muhammad did, to give more freedom, more equality to women. I have come to the conclusion that actually in our religion, we cannot make any distinction between man and woman in terms of intelligence, spirituality, or nature. Morally and intellectually speaking, women are equal with men and they are not to be treated any differently. They are to engage in business, to own wealth, to own property. They are to be allowed to excel in academic pursuits. If women are given freedom to excel in academic pursuits, how can we tell them to stay home? What is all this education for? You can't keep her at home to nurse babies. I think all we have to do is to study the treatment of women by prophet Muhammad himself to understand what the World Community of Al-Islam has done.

At one time we had a woman who was plant supervisor. She was head of the *Muhammad Speaks* plant under my own leadership. We have women in key positions in the Masjid. We don't call them Imams, we call them "Instructress." They teach the religion, they propagate just like we do.

CEM: Are members required to use an X as their last name anymore?

WDM: No. Again, that was the play on the power of mystery to contain people. The X was a curiosity; it was a mystery. It made us feel we had something nobody else had. We don't need that anymore.

CEM: The Honorable Elijah Muhammad and his son Emmanuel served time in prison from 1942 to 1946. Was this an asset or liability to the movement? What role did Mrs. Clara Muhammad play during this time?

WDM: The Honorable Elijah Muhammad introduced a new outlook to his temples when he returned in 1946. The early followers were told not to listen to radio. They were told to get all their education in the temple. When the Honorable Elijah Muhammad returned from prison, we started to listen to the radio; soon TV came out. He introduced TV to us. Immediately upon his release, he said we have to become broader in our thinking. We need to establish many more temples and we need to get into business. He came out of prison with a business mind.

During his incarceration, Mrs. Clara Muhammad was the supreme secretary for the whole movement. The orders came from him to her to the minister and captains. Actually, she was like his second while he was in prison. She was executing his decision while he was in prison. I've seen her give instructions to the ministers. I was a child about 9, 10, 11, 12 years old. I saw her give instructions to ministers. They would sometimes be in doubt as to how they should carry them out; she would give them insights. She was a very strong woman and she believed in him. She also believed in his teacher, Master Fard Muhammad. She was the one who served his meals to him most of the time during his stay with the Honorable Elijah Muhammad. She had a personal kind of relationship with W. D. Fard. She had direct faith in him; it wasn't faith introduced by the Honorable Elijah Muhammad. He saw in her someone who wouldn't budge for anything. When I disagreed with my father she would say, "What's wrong with you, boy? You crazy?"

CEM: Why did you rename the mosque in New York City after Malcolm Shabazz?

WDM: Because I felt my own hurt was shared by most of the members in the nation of Islam. I couldn't accept that Minister Malcolm be written off. He established himself. He was the greatest minister the Nation of Islam ever had, except for the Honorable Elijah Muhammad. I can't say he was greater than the Honorable Elijah Muhammad. He was, in my opinion and many other ministers, the most faithful minister to the Honorable Elijah Muhammad in the whole history of the Nation of Islam.

CEM: Was Malcolm Shabazz instrumental in some of the changes taking place now?

WDM: Well, I feel that Minister Malcolm's contribution to the changes that took place in the Nation of Islam was an influence in my life. The thing that distinguished Malcolm X among the ministers was his individuality. Malcolm X was converted in prison. He came right out of prison and became a minister for the Honorable Elijah Muhammad. He didn't take on the thinking and behavior of the old conservative ministerial body. When the Honorable Elijah Malcolm saw his new blood he was excited. He just gave Malcolm free reign to preach his doctrine. The Honorable Elijah Muhammad welcomed this new blood. He told the old ministerial body, "I will never get anywhere with people like you." He said, "All you do is teach the same thing we taught in the thirties." He would say, "Look at this young man"; he would brag on Malcolm. He said, "He's in modern times, he knows how to help me." Malcolm's new thinking, courage, and youth attracted most of the young people into following the Honorable Elijah Muhammad and I was one of them. I used to admire the way he would uncover our own ignorance.

CEM: Who do you think assassinated Malcolm X?

WDM: I don't know; I can't identify people. All I can say is I don't believe the Nation of Islam planned the assassination of Malcolm X. I believe outsiders assassinated Malcolm X and members were used.

CEM: How many members are in the World Community of Al-Islam in the West?

WDM: We haven't really made an effort to count the membership since mid-1976. At that time we estimated a 40 percent increase. That was about a year after I became the chief minister. We estimated 70,000 people who have really declared their faith, but over 1 million live Muslim lives.

CEM: Recently you became the ambassador-at-large for the World Community of Al-Islam in the West. Please explain why you did this and what is your function now?

WDM: I was not satisfied with the response in the ministerial body to my call for us to get out in the broader community and let our contributions be known. We are fighting the same evils that Christians are fighting. We are not fighting our private war. It's a common fight against all evils in society. I didn't really feel the ministers were responding to that. I felt I would serve our community best by getting in the media and doing public speaking engagements. I then took on that role. In fact, I have spoken outside the community more than I have spoken inside.

CEM: Your title is Chief Minister or President?

WDM: No. The title is still Imam, Chief Minister. President—that title is used to preserve my own position of authority in the World Community of Al-Islam in the West. Some people have a habit of trying to give me a purely spiritual role in the community. They do this because they want to control or take over funds. We are aware of this and I think the editors of the *Bilalian News* are aware of that, too. We want the followers to know throughout the country and the world that my leadership is not for prayers only; it covers all the business of the World Community of Al-Islam in the West.

CEM: Are the Fruit of Islam and Muslim Girls in Training still functioning?

WDM: No, not as separate bodies. They are still functioning as Muslim Women in Training. We still have sisters in propagations. They teach Islamic diet, Islamic dress code, . . . Islamic family structure, and women's behavior at home and in public. They teach things they taught us before. In the NOI you were a member of an MGT class and you would have to attend so many meetings a month on Thursday night, take sewing, cooking, and exercise. We don't have that kind of regimentation any more, but the teachings we do have. Anyone who wants to know about Islamic diet is free to go to the Koran. We have women who just spend their time teaching the things the MGT and FOI taught. We have men who do the same thing for a male membership. The Imams take care of that.

CEM: In October of 1975, you met with President Anwar Sadat in the Drake Hotel in Chicago. How long have you had this relationship? Is it still intact?

WDM: That was my first acquaintance with President Sadat and I have since then had one contact with him. That was through the minister of education. I have received good wishes from him and his Muslim holiday greeting. Within the last year, I haven't heard any word from him and I haven't sent him any word.

CEM: What do you think of President Sadat's peace agreement with Israel?

WDM: This is a very sensitive question for me. At the Islamic conference held in Morocco, the 10th Islamic Conference, I spoke to some of the delegations in a private meeting. I told them that I felt the Islamic world leadership had much to gain from the political psychology of President Sadat. I felt a new psychology was needed. What he's doing is inviting his people to come away from an emotional response to the presence of Israel on Muslim land to a more philosophical and rational strategy. To them it may look like Uncle Tomism, but to me it looks like wisdom.

CEM: If you could look into the future, where do you see the World Community of Al-Islam in the West in the year 2000?

WDM: I hope the year 2000 the World Community of Al-Islam in the West will be called American Muslims. I hope Muslims will be so comfortable in America that we won't have to introduce any structure or anything, just be American Muslims.

CEM: Why did you change the University of Islam to the Clara Muhammad School?

WDM: Because those old names were inflated to give us a sense of superiority. There were no real universities. There were grade schools, elementary schools, and high schools. There were never any university levels, except maybe in the way we might interpret some of the theological teachings. No one would get that kind of symbolism in religion except on a college or university level. But as for the general courses taught in the schools, we were never on a university level.

The schools . . . had an aura of mystery. It was creating ab-
normal minds as well as normal minds. We had some people
who thought they were different human beings from others.
They couldn't compete on their level with others in the public
schools but they felt they were superior—they couldn't be penetrated. These cases were very few, not many. We did have this
problem, where so many people were locked up in their own
private world of supreme science. It wasn't anything but elementary knowledge. They couldn't integrate with the general
world's thinking.

CEM: Recently the World Community of Al-Islam in the West received $20 million for food processing. How did that come
about?

WDM: As a result of the World Community of Al-Islam trying to make
practical use and profit from our business holdings. Faced with
management problems, we had to go outside for management
help. I went to the office of minority business enterprises here
in Chicago. Just a thought came to me, "You are now explaining your religion in a way which will gain acceptance in America, so why not go to them for help. I said to myself, "This is
the kind of thinking I have to encourage in our membership." I
told members, "We have people who are taking advantage of
us; they come in and pretend to be professionals and get us in a
lot of mess." I said, "[What] they're doing is claiming to be representatives for us in the outer world." I said, "I am going directly to government agencies. There are officials to aid people
like us, people who have property, ability, some economic
holdings, but don't have the knowledge and experience."

It wasn't any more than a month after I said this, that I actually went. I got the yellow pages and went looking. I said, "We
have holdings, we can do a lot of good. We employ a lot of people, but we ran into economic problems. I think if we can get
some help, some business advice, if we can use your resources,
I think we can make a profit out of some of these holdings and
create more jobs." I explained my business interest was mainly
jobs. I say jobs, because profit and money in the bank mean
nothing unless it is wisely invested to create more opportunities
for people. So I explained this to the Organization of Minority
Business Enterprises, to Mr. Harold Johnson and Mr. Dave Ve-
gan. They seemed to be waiting for us to approach them. They
were happy we came to them. They said, "We think we can give
you a lot of help." They began to make contacts in their organization. We were introduced to Mr. Blackwell, the national
president at that time, and to the members of the Department of

Dr. Abdul Alim Muhammad (right) and author after their September 9 1994, interview.

Commerce in Washington. The work progressed right along and before we knew it, we had a contract with the army.

CEM: Do you have any final comments you would like to make?

WDM: Yes, I do. I am a religious man and a religious leader. I try to represent the religion the way the prophets represented religion. I think that it is being true to the religion. The prophets Moses, Jesus, and Muhammad were all champions of the moral life of the people. You have people losing faith in the future of employment, business opportunities, giving up and accepting crime, welfare, or just idleness. That's a major moral problem. We have to respond as religious leaders, Christians, Jews, Muslims; we have to respond just as the prophets would respond. We, too, can join with government and religious leaders, all people who are trying to preserve the good life for the individual. That means having the opportunity to earn a living with your own individual resources; that is a requirement of life.

Work is sacred. If we can't find a way to give jobs to every able-bodied man and woman who wants to work, we are failing society morally.

CEM: I want to thank you for this interview. One of the prerequisites of a scholar is to be objective. I have tried to be objective and not interject any of my biases. As a young boy growing up in Los Angeles, California, I had the opportunity to witness Muslims in the community working, serving, and propagating the religion. There was always a mystery about the "Black Muslims." Even though we were ignorant of the organization, we all respected them. As I grew older and traveled across the country and observed what the organization was doing in urban areas, I began to respect the individuals. During the time I was doing this study, members of the organization have been warm, kind, sensitive, and understanding. Members have opened their minds and hearts to help me. I want you to know it is an honor and privilege to research the World Community of Al-Islam in the West and have the opportunity to interview you.

WDM: Thank you very much. I am proud of our membership and every time I hear compliments like that it makes me feel very comfortable as a leader in this community.

Appendix B

Interview with Dr. Abdul Alim Muhammad, National Spokesperson for Minister Louis Farrakhan and Minister of Health and Human Resources for the Nation of Islam September 9, 1994—Washington, D.C.

Dr. C.E.M.:	How long have you been a member of the Nation of Islam?
Dr. A. Muhammad:	I accepted the teachings of the Honorable Elijah Muhammad, Labor Day weekend 1968. I think that makes it twenty-six years.
Dr. C.E.M.:	Why did you decide to join the Nation of Islam?
Dr. A. Muhammad:	I joined the Nation of Islam because I felt that what the Honorable Elijah Muhammad's teaching was exactly what we needed as a people. To rise from the condition we have been left in as a result of being enslaved and oppressed for nearly four centuries at that time.
Dr. C.E.M.:	Could you give me some information about your background? Where you were born; where you received your education; your parents?
Dr. A. Muhammad:	I was born and raised in York, Pennsylvania, about ninety miles north of here. Went to public schools there and attended Antioch College in Yellow Springs. I have a bachelor's degree in biology and a medical degree from Case Western Reserve University in Cleveland. I have been a minister in the Nation of Islam since 1973. Currently, I am the national spokesman for Minister Louis Farrakhan and the minister of health and human resources for the Nation of Islam.
Dr. C.E.M.:	In your role of national spokesman for the Nation of Islam and minister of health, what are your functions?
Dr. A. Muhammad:	As national spokesman it's my job to represent the teachings of the Nation of Islam, and to represent specially Minister Farrakhan in many different situations. There are times he has been invited to

speak and cannot attend or does not want to attend for some reason; then I am a stand-in for him. But of course, any large organization such as the Nation of Islam needs someone who can represent our views.

———

There's many people in this country who claim to be members of the Nation of Islam; claim to be spokesmen for the Nation of Islam. And in a hostile environment we always have people in the press; in the media; in academia, who are willing to listen to misrepresentatives. People who are self-styled, as though they somehow represent the authentic voice of the Nation. Minister Farrakhan is the national representative of the Honorable Elijah Muhammad.

———

There's a lot of confusion because people want to pay attention to people who don't speak for the Nation. They take these distorted views as the views. Sometimes it's done honestly and sometimes it's done for the sake of mischief. I certainly appreciate the opportunity to talk to you. I had an opportunity to look through your book. With all due respect your book is full of distortions and misrepresentations of what the Nation of Islam teaches and what we believe!

Dr. C.E.M.:   Can you be more specific in regards to misrepresentations and distortions in the book?

Dr. A. Muhammad: You don't bother in your book to give accurate information about the coming of Master Fard Muhammad. Who he is, what he is, and what he actually taught. The Honorable Elijah Muhammad and what the Honorable Elijah Muhammad taught us concerning Master Fard Muhammad. For example, the history of Yacub and the meaning of all that is not accurately covered in your book. And a person who would read that would come away thinking these persons must be a bunch of fools to believe such nonsense. Because, that's what's represented in the book, nonsense! Not the actual teachings we received from the

	Honorable Elijah Muhammad. It reminded me of the so-called auto-biography of Malcolm X. Where he [Alex Haley] gives a mocking misrepresentation of what he learned from the Honorable Elijah Muhammad. So that if someone takes his [Alex Haley's] mocking misrepresentation, they would have a very dim view of the intellectual capacity and understanding of the Honorable Elijah Muhammad and those that are with him.
Dr. C.E.M.:	What is it about the Honorable Elijah Muhammad and Minister Fard . . .
Dr. A. Muhammad:	Let me stop you there. And I'm trying to be as respectful as possible. When you represent yourself as a scholar and you don't even bother to learn the name of the man who is the founder of the Nation of Islam. When you call him Master Wali Fard Muhammad that's not his name. Where did you get that from? You can't have gotten that from any authentic source within the Nation of Islam. For this kind of misrepresentation, I don't know who Wali Fard Muhammad is.
Dr. C.E.M.:	What is the appropriate title?
Dr. A. Muhammad:	He represented himself as you would find in *the Message to the Blackman*. I don't know if you bothered to read it. But he used different names. But the last name he left us with was Master Wallace Fard Muhammad. But he used W. D. Fard in the early days, sometimes Fard Muhammad, but never Wali Fard Muhammad. That's something we've heard some of our worse enemies, such as Imam Dr. Essa, in the Alsalurah community, making mocking references to the teacher of the Honorable Elijah Muhammad. And I say very frankly we don't appreciate that kind of misrepresentation that is then put into the public as though this is some authentic scholarship; it's not.
Dr. C.E.M.:	Okay, well in regards to Master Wallace Fard Muhammad's theology and ideology, what is it that you would like to clear up that you feel is distorted in the book?
Dr. A. Muhammad:	I don't think I have the time to go point by point, but what I will say is that he gave very clear teachings on the most important subject of all. Which is to say, who is God; what is the nature of God?

It's not just theology; theology refers to a study about God. We are not talking about the knowledge about God. What Master Fard Muhammad taught us was the knowledge of God. The knowledge that belongs to God himself of himself. Not what some scholar or theologian, if you will in some theory about God and the notion of God. The nature of religion, and the relationship between the nature of man and the nature of God. This is not what we teach; we're not teaching theories. We're teaching the actual knowledge of God himself. I would refer you to the transcript of the speech given by the Honorable Elijah Muhammad on February 26, 1969, entitled *The Knowledge of God Himself.* And that would give you a very good basis of it.

I would refer you to the first chapter of *Message to the Blackman,* which gives a detailed knowledge of who and what God actually is. And that's just a base. That's where we start in the Nation of Islam, with the little babies. So to read something from a scholar and you haven't even covered the A, B, C's, well this is actually an insult. And I told Brother Simeon, I said well I want to have a nice time when brother comes you know, but I have to be very frank. That we really in the Nation and I guess in one sense it's our own fault, because well we do write books. The Honorable Elijah himself wrote seven books. Minister Farrakhan has written books.

We have scholars who have written books. But really we get tired of people just looking at the Nation of Islam in some kind of a cheap way. As though we're just some little fly-by-night cult, personality cult, organization that has no substance whatsoever. When in fact, we're in your presence doing things that others can't do. Who claim to have a better understanding of Islam and everything else that we are supposed to have, but yet we do that which they can't do. So I would say

Dr. Abdul Alim Muhammad (left) with Clifton Marsh during their interview.

out of a sense of self-respect. We have to take exception to some of the things that appeared in your books and other books. So-called books on the Nation.

I don't know if Professor Marsh is really an honest scholar. To write a book like that makes me wonder whether or not he's actually intending to tell the truth about the Nation of Islam. Maybe he's a partisan. Maybe he's not interested in an objective examination of the facts. Maybe he's trying to promote a one side of what seems to be a dispute over the other side. To launch into questions. That's okay I guess, but I wanted to have the opportunity to say these things. Because, if you are not an honest scholar and honest man seeking to portray the truth, then I am not interested in talking to you. But if you are interested in the truth, I would employ you to do your homework.

Don't just come talk to me, Minister Farrakhan or anybody if you haven't read *Message to the*

Blackman. If you haven't read that and studied that, and mastered that, you aren't even qualified to ask a question. Cause your asking questions way down here where in fact we are prepared to answer you up here (he made a gesture with his hands, signifying the level of understanding in the Honorable Elijah Muhammad's teachings). If you are not prepared to receive an answer up here, what you will write will be a distortion of what you heard, because you failed to understand the point.

We are not some little lightweight cheap people that people can build their academic careers on. You know people like to make movies about us; documentaries about us. Well the hell with that! We are not interested in your documentary or your research project. We are trying to save our people. That's what we're interested in. We're interested in any scholarship that will help us accomplish that objective. But to build somebody's personal reputation. We got C. Eric Lincoln. He's famous all over the world. Why, because he wrote a book about the Black Muslims in America. He doesn't even bother to check with us to see, did you ever call yourselves Black Muslims? You repeat the same mistake, "From Black Muslims to Muslims." Who ever called us Black Muslims? You probably don't even know. That was a term invented by Mike Wallace. He's the one that called us Black Muslims. We never called ourselves Black Muslims. The Holy Quran doesn't teach people to call themselves by their color. So he called us the Black Muslims in a T.V. program in 1957, "The Hate That Hate Produced." It was a derogatory piece. Then the media picked up that term as though somehow or another we are the Black Muslims. The Honorable Elijah Muhammad answered him, well if you want to call us Black, we don't deny that we're Black, and certainly we are Muslims by faith. So if you want to put the two together and call us Black Muslims, okay. But that's your name. That's not the name we call ourselves. We are formally called the

	Lost-Found Nation of Islam. That's our formal name. But if you wanted to know what is our title, our title is Muslims period. I'm not trying to go off on you.
Dr. C.E.M.:	I understand.
Dr. A. Muhammad:	I want to put things on the right level. I don't want you to have a misunderstanding that somehow I'm flattered just because you want to interview me or talk to me about this book. Because I'll just say for the record, if you plan to do another book like this book just leave me out of it. Don't even mention me, don't mention the Nation of Islam. Don't even mention Minister Farrakhan. Just say this is the opinionated views of someone, and it don't have any bearing on the reality of what the Nation of Islam means in this society. You're sitting in the reality of the Nation of Islam. You came in here and nobody shot you. Nobody tried to sell you drugs. You come in here and there's green grass, trees, and children are playing and it's peaceful and quiet and you see the recent renovations of a housing project. That's the Nation of Islam! This is the original place where the "dope busters" as they called us, got started. This place here, Paradise Manor, was considered one of the ten worst drug markets in America. And we came in by the grace of Allah and cleaned it up. So we can set up a clinic and take care of the health needs of our people. That's the Nation of Islam!
Dr. C.E.M.:	How did you clean it [Paradise Manor] up?
Dr. A. Muhammad:	By the Grace of Allah, who came in the person of Master Fard Muhammad. He's our senior, he is our redeemer, he is the Messiah. He is the Mahdi. He is God. That's what we believe. And it's the power of Master Fard Muhammad as represented to us by the Honorable Elijah Muhammad and Minister Farrakhan that gives us the power to come into a place like this that is being overrun by thieves and robbers, and killers, dope dealers, all kinds of evil going on here, and it is our faith in Master Fard Muhammad that allows us to clean it up, with no violence whatsoever. Because the moral force and power that is generated by the teachings of the Honorable Elijah Muhammad and

his training, and discipline given to us according
to the instructions of Master Fard Muhammad
gives us power in the world to reform our people;
to take people that would ordinarily to control
them you would have to beat them; lock them up
or shoot them or whatever. We can with just a
word control them and reform them. We would
have a total success in that, if we were not opposed
so vehemently by outside forces who still control
the life in the ghetto.

Dr. C.E.M.:   What type of services are provided in the Abundant Life Clinic?

Dr. A. Muhammad: We seek to provide a wide range of medical services. We see patients of all sorts. We treat acute
illness, but what we like to do more than anything
else is get involved in preventive care. We are
probably best known outside this community for
our work in the treatment of AIDS. Three years
ago Minister Farrakhan sent me to Kenya to meet
that man there (pointing to a picture on the wall),
Davey Koege, who had done some fundamental
research in the treatment of AIDS using a substance called alpha enterpheran. We pioneered
this. We've got an improved product formerly
called immunex, now called Lopheron, that we
have been using now for three years in the treatment of AIDS.

We have done some research that shows about
an 82% success rate in reversing the signs and
symptoms of AIDS at whatever stage. We took
this research to NIH in October of 1992. It was a
long day. At the end of the day the officials from
NIH had to admit that this was good work, that we
were presenting them with; that they could not ig-
nore it and dismiss it as bogus research; that it was
scientifically valid; and as such it had to be followed up with a clinical trial. The only question
that Dr. Killen, who at that time was deputy director for the Division of AIDS, had for me at the
end of the day: He said, "Dr. Muhammad, I want
to ask you just one thing. How did you finance
this?" I was very pleased to be able to say we

financed it ourselves. Our own people believed in it. They believed in us. They supported us. They got on the radio; they raised money; they had dinners; they had concerts and raised money so that we could go independently of you and do some work for the benefit of our own people. And we bring that to you, not begging you, but compelling you by the validity of what we've done to go and do further or else be shown up as a fraud and an enemy to the interest of the people.

Dr. C.E.M.:   Could you tell me the type of economic development programs the Nation of Islam is presently operating?

Dr. A. Muhammad: Our number one project now as it was when the Honorable Elijah Muhammad was with us is the *Final Call* newspaper. The *Final Call* was the original name of the newspaper back in the thirties. Then later in the sixties the name was changed to *Muhammad Speaks*. So Minister Farrakhan, when he rebuilt the Nation of Islam, as he began the rebuilding effort of the Nation of Islam having been destroyed under an FBI counterintelligence program through an FBI agent named Imam Wallace D. Muhammad, he [Farrakhan] did not think that the earlier editions of the *Final Call* newspaper were up to the standards of *Muhammad Speaks*. That's why he used that earlier name *Final Call*. When we get the *Final Call* back to the standard *Muhammad Speaks* had achieved in the sixties and seventies, then the name will once again be *Muhammad Speaks,* but it's not quite worthy at this point. We're getting it there. We are at a circulation now of about a half a million every two weeks. That's a million copies per month. That is a large economic venture that brings resources to the Nation. We're using those resources to fund certain projects. We have a brochure there you can have that indicates the building of a bakery complex in Chicago, a restaurant complex. We are purchasing farmland throughout the South. We have several thousand acres of land. All these were things that Wallace D. Muhammad in his wicked opposition to his father sold off. He sold off the million dollar printing press at that time. He sold off the trucks; he sold off the trucks and planes. He sold off all the economic enterprises that his father had built up. So Minister Farrakhan who is not his physical son, but Minister Farrakhan who is the spiritual son, has decided along with those who are with him, that we are going to reclaim for our people in the name of God those things that the Honorable Elijah Muhammad had led us to achieve, and then extend it beyond that to the fullness of the vision of the Honorable Elijah Muhammad.

Dr. C.E.M.:

You mentioned the rebuilding of the Nation of Islam by Minister Farrakhan. In the rebuilding, how is it similar or different from the organization that the Honorable Elijah Muhammad had prior to his passing?

Dr. A. Muhammad:

Well, the Honorable Elijah Muhammad said to Minister Farrakhan before his departure, he said, "Brother I have got to go away to receive the new teachings. While I'm gone don't you change the teachings. If you are faithful then through you I will reveal the new teachings." The Honorable Elijah Muhammad said on another occasion before his departure, he said, "I am going away; the world will say and believe I am dead. But I will not be dead. I am going away to receive the new teachings." He said in 1972, when he stood Minister Farrakhan up before the congregation in the Mosque Maryam in Chicago, "When you see Minister Farrakhan look at him when he speaks, listen to him. What he does, you do it. What he forbids you to do, don't do it. He will get you safely across the river on his back. When he does it, he won't say look what I have done. He will say look what Allah has done. For he is a very humble brother."

So in answer to that question, I would say Minister Farrakhan has been faithful to his leader, teacher, and guide, the Honorable Elijah Muhammad, who is not dead; and he [Farrakhan] has not changed anything. He has kept it [Nation of Islam] exactly the way it was. It is untrue what some

	people say. They say that those teachings were good for that time, but they're no good for this time. We disagree. The teachings of the Honorable Elijah Muhammad were good for that time, they are good for this time, and they will continue to be good until they are superseded by what is considered to be the teachings of the new world that is coming in by the power of the Mahdi, by God in person, who is present; but we won't receive those new teachings right now. We're almost there, but not quite.
Dr. C.E.M.:	How many mosques do you have throughout the country and the world?
Dr. A. Muhammad:	I don't know, but what I will say is this: everywhere you go you find the followers of the Honorable Elijah Muhammad. You find the followers of Minister Louis Farrakhan everywhere. You do an accurate poll among the students, faculty, and the people. You will find most of them in one way or the other are followers of and influenced by the teachings of the Nation of Islam. Recent polls done by *Time* magazine shows that 70% of black people in America consider Minister Farrakhan to be the most influential black leader. I can't remember the exact percent, 69% or something like that felt his views represented their views about certain issues.

As you know we're on our way to Ghana. We're being hosted by the government of Ghana. We are holding the first International Saviour's Day in Accra, Ghana, to celebrate with our brothers and sisters in Ghana, to celebrate the coming of the Mahdi, in the person of Master Fard Muhammad. And the raising up of the Honorable Elijah Muhammad, because he's not just a leader for black people in America or for black people period. The Honorable Elijah Muhammad and Minister Farrakhan are universal leaders for all men and women of goodwill whether they consider themselves to be Muslims, Christians, or Jews. Whether they are black, white, red, brown, or yellow. If they would but listen to what God has

	blessed these men to teach, then all would be lifted up into a better condition.

Dr. C.E.M.: Could you explain the organizational structure of the Nation of Islam?

Dr. A. Muhammad: Well, I have used that word, but the point of fact is the Nation of Islam is not an organization. And as such it does not have what you would recognize as an organizational structure. The head of the Nation of Islam is God himself and we are just his servants and slaves. So, that's basically all that I can say about that. It's not an organization like the NAACP, the World Council of Churches, the Vatican. The Honorable Elijah Muhammad told us very clearly that there never was such a thing as some organized systems of religion to establish a relationship between God and his worshippers. But religion is the nature, this is quoting the Quran, the nature made by Allah in which he created us. So, that when we are given the knowledge of self and kind, that when we are in submission to the nature of ourselves then you find us displaying characteristics of discipline and order and organization. But you won't find that kind of structure you are referring to. It doesn't have to be.

Dr. C.E.M.: In regards to voting, running for political office, serving in the military, do members of the Nation of Islam participate in these activities?

Dr. A. Muhammad: Well you're looking at a man who ran for Congress in Prince Georges County four years ago, because we were sick and tired of the black population of Prince Georges County, which is the majority and the most prosperous black population in the country, sitting around and letting white folks run everything. So, we entered the race to kick down the door and wake everybody up and say, look what in the hell are you doing. Why don't you stand up and run your own affairs. I'm not a politician, but we got involved to show them what could be done. So, the Nation of Islam has always been involved in politics. If you look at the meaning of our name, Nation is a political word. Islam is a spiritual word. So, we are a perfect combination of balanced blending of politics

They are not really separate things. You know the
Bible says it this way: The kingdoms of this world
have become the kingdom of God. That's what
our work is. To make the kingdom of this world
responsive to the laws of God.

———

The Honorable Elijah Muhammad said that we
should put the Muslim program to Congress and be
supported. For example Julian Bond got his first
political endorsement from the Honorable Elijah
Muhammad way back when nobody else would
support him. Adam Clayton Powell; the congressman from Chicago at that time, the Olympic star,
Ralph Metcalf. They were all backed by the Honorable Elijah Muhammad and the Nation of Islam.
So somebody circulated false information all these
years that the Nation of Islam doesn't participate in
politics. That's false, it's always been false. What
the Honorable Elijah Muhammad said is that the
white man's politics is not going to give us our salvation. But he said, where we are dominant in
numbers, we should rule. And he told us a Muslim
always seeks to take over and to run things. Because if God blesses you with knowledge, wisdom,
and understanding, it's not just for you. It's for all
of the people and so you have a responsibility if
you are blessed with knowledge to go forward,
take a leadership position, try to make life better for
everybody, even people who disagree with you.
You should try to make a life better.

———

The question about the military; all the members of the Nation of Islam are organized into military units. The brothers are in a military or army
called the Fruit of Islam. The sisters are in a military unit that is called the Muslim Girls Training
and General Civilization Class. Every member of
the Nation of Islam is a soldier. But we are fighting for Islam. We are fighting to establish universal peace. We are fighting for freedom, justice,
and equality for our people here, and our people
all over the world. We don't think we should join

the army of the enemy. We don't think that we should put on the uniform of those who enslaved us; who oppressed us. We don't think we should uphold a nation or government that is contrary to the order of God. We don't think we should do that.

We don't think that as Muslims we should fight in unjust wars against oppressed people around the world. We don't think we should do that, because we believe that the law of God is very clear. We shouldn't be killing people. There are exceptions in the law of God that say that under certain circumstances, matters of self-defense, you are permitted to take a life. There are certain other exceptions when a human life may be taken. But we don't think that because Uncle Sam calls and says I have an enemy somewhere and won't you go to kill somebody. We are not obligated to obey such an unlawful, immoral, wicked order. We should tell Uncle Sam you kill who you want to kill. But be warned that the day is coming that brings in the judgement of God. Maybe God will kill you, just as you have delighted in killing others.

Dr. C.E.M.:   Could you tell me something about the status of women in the Nation of Islam?

Dr. A. Muhammad: The provisional constitution of the 'Nation of Islam holds that no woman should be prevented from rising as high as her talent would permit. This is something you should study very carefully (giving me a videotape from his bookcase) that's available at the Tape Connection. This was a speech given just recently by Minister Farrakhan. A nation can rise no higher than its women. So, we believe that the status of women is central if you had to say what is the single most important aspect of what has to be done. We have got to love, respect, protect, elevate, nurture the black woman. Because she is the mother of our children. The Honorable Elijah Muhammad once said that when you teach a man, you teach an individual. When you teach a woman, you teach the nation. So, we are very, very concerned about the status of our

women. We have to go to war against any society
that degrades women. And you cannot think of
a society anywhere in the history of the world
that degrades women like this one does. Where
women are merchandised, commercialized upon
like they are just a piece of meat. They are divine
functions given by God to nurture and bring in the
new creation; the new generation is being taken
from them. They are just looked at as economic
commodities to be employed by corporations, factories, and government agencies. The vital role of
mother is ridiculed and laughed at and women are
made to feel something is wrong with them if they
are mothers and homemakers. That is the number
one reason you see this civilization crumbling and
falling apart. Because, the woman is taken out of
the home. If she's not there raising children, cal-
culating values, teaching them the difference between right and wrong. Showing them the beauti-
ful side of life and the rightness of certain actions
and the incorrectness of other actions. Because
this society has taken the mother out of the home
and made it impossible for her to do her duty as
God would have it done. We feel that we can't really make progress unless we bring about reform
in the status of women.

Dr. C.E.M.: What impact would you say Malcolm X had on
the Nation of Islam?

Dr. A. Muhammad: Malcolm was a good brother when he came into
the nation. He was very submissive and he learned
all that he could of the teachings of the Honorable
Elijah Muhammad. Then Malcolm succumbed to
wicked impulses within himself that were further
expanded by wicked impulses outside of himself.
His major flaw was that he became envious and
jealous of his leader and teacher, and at a certain
point he thought that he should have the leadership. Then he used his knowledge of the domestic
life of the Honorable Elijah Muhammad—the
Honorable Elijah Muhammad had wives. He used
that in a malicious, wicked way to undermine the
credibility of his leader and teacher. To slander
him in public, hoping that he could capture the fellowship that was enjoyed by the Honorable Elijah

Muhammad. Then of course we must note that he was encouraged, guided in this line of activity by the Honorable Elijah Muhammad's son Wallace D. Muhammad. So this was Malcolm's mistake. He unfortunately, the last few days of his life, he had written to the Honorable Elijah Muhammad. He wanted to know whether or not he could be forgiven for the things he had done and said. The Honorable Elijah Muhammad answered him and said, "Brother there is nothing unforgivable in Islam." So Malcolm was planning to attend the Saviour's Day in 1965. He was unfortunately assassinated a few days before he would be able to reconnect with his base. He clearly recognized that he had made a horrible miscalculation. He had found out that he was not the leader he imagined himself to be. He found that he had taken the organizational platform for granted. He thought it would be easy to go and do that over again and he was a miserable failure. He reorganized his mistake and wanted to come home. The enemy saw to it that he never made it.

Now Wallace D. Muhammad on the other hand did make it back to the Saviour's Day. He did apologize. His father told him you could be accepted back into the Nation of Islam if they, the believers, will accept you back. So, he forced his own son to go before the believers. This is two or three days after Malcolm's assassination. Wallace D. Muhammad begged the believers in the Nation of Islam to forgive him for the slander that he had made against his father and all the evil things he had done to undermine his father. He said and I quote, "I had no right to judge my father. I am not qualified to judge my father." He begged to be accepted back. In fact, the believers voted to accept Wallace D. Muhammad back into the ranks. It is my belief that if Malcolm had lived, he would have been on that platform with W. D. Muhammad. And he too would have been accepted back by the believers in the Nation of Islam. Who knows what great accomplishments he would have made

	if that had happened. Unfortunately, the enemy got to him before that could happen.
Dr. C.E.M.:	I have three more questions. What do you think are the three or four most significant developments in the Nation of Islam since 1977.
Dr. A. Muhammad:	I'll just say what Minister Farrakhan said just a few days ago. His call, I'm not quoting him, I am paraphrasing him. His call for the Black Summit back in February of 1994, and the acceptance of that call by Ben Chavis, the NAACP and nearly all other black organizations including the Congressional Black Caucus. That is going to prove itself to be the single most important thing he's done. The Honorable Elijah Muhammad called for a National Black Front I believe in 1964. He said all of the organizations whether they are Muslims, Christians, civil rights, human rights, whether they are labor oriented, education oriented; whatever they are; they should all come together under a united banner to fight for the freedom of our people.

The leaders were afraid to embrace the Honorable Elijah Muhammad in the sixties. But now we see a different kind of leadership. Even though there's turmoil in the NAACP, and there's things going on, yet the principle of unity has been accepted by all. So this idea of black unity, black summits, United Black Front, that's going to grow and grow and grow. Then next October, Minister Farrakhan is going to be at the head of a march on Washington. We want to bring one million black men to Washington, D.C. This is a fulfillment of what the Honorable Elijah Muhammad called for in 1963, when he watched the March on Washington on television. He said of that march, "Well that's okay, but you wait until I organize a march on Washington and it won't be a picnic." So, we're coming next year; one million strong; It's okay if whites join in. But we are not counting them in our one million. It will be one million black men plus maybe some white people, Native Americans, Mexicans, some other folks who want

	to tag along. There are going to be one million black men and we are coming to bring a final solution to this problem between black and white. We are coming for justice and we won't depart the city of Washington, D.C. until we get it.
Dr. C.E.M.:	If you look at the historical contributions of Martin Delaney, Wilmont Blyden, Marcus Garvey, Noble Drew Ali. I've often said the Honorable Elijah Muhammad doesn't get enough credit for his contributions. Would you say that he has exceeded and passed those contributions of those who preceded him.
Dr. A. Muhammad:	The Honorable Elijah Muhammad said that the Devil will never give you credit for your righteousness. So, we are not surprised that we see the Honorable Elijah Muhammad written out of history, ignored, and denied his just due. But Allah will never deny you your just due. So, the reward the Honorable Elijah Muhammad and Minister Farrakhan and all of us is with Allah. I think it would be the wrong direction to draw comparisons between leaders. We believe in the work of Martin Delaney, Marcus Garvey, and Noble Drew Ali. All of them were great, great leaders who did the best that they could do at the time that they lived.

We thank Allah for all of them. The conditions were not then what they are now. The consciousness of our people was not then what it is now. We don't see any difference in the correct principles of Martin Delaney, Marcus Garvey, Noble Drew Ali, and the correct principles of the Honorable Elijah Muhammad and Minister Farrakhan and others. They're all the same correct principles, just different personalities that have appeared at different times. If there is a crucial difference between the Honorable Elijah Muhammad and the others that we could mention, it is the fact that none of the others were taught by God in person, face to face. None of the others had the actual backing of God and his power against the enemies of us all.

Let us just face facts. They would have killed the Honorable Elijah Muhammad a long time ago if they could. If they could, but they couldn't as J. Edgar Hoover admitted in his notes. That they tried 2,000 dirty tricks against the Honorable Elijah Muhammad and none of them worked. Let's face facts, they would kill Minister Farrakhan today if they could but they can't. The reason that they can't is not because Minister Farrakhan has some weapon in his hand, but he's backed by God and God won't permit them to do it. If they think they can do it, come and try it. Try it again, I'll say. They've already tried and tried and they can't do it. They would kill those who are with him if they could, but they can't. Because we enjoy the divine protection of God. We have even arrived at the point when we go out on the battlefield, and we mock them. Come against us with everything you have, but when you do our God will kill you. See this is right out of the prophetic history of Moses and Aaron. Pharaoh wanted to kill Moses and Aaron and those with them, but he couldn't. But God always intended to kill Pharaoh and he would never let Pharaoh get out of it. No matter how hard Pharoh tried. You know at a certain point Pharaoh softened his heart. Then he saw God hardened his heart. He didn't want Pharaoh to play some cheap political trick that would get him off the hook from God. So from the very beginning God always intended to kill the slavemaster.

So, we say in this presence too, God intends to destroy America for her wickedness. It makes no difference who is singing God Bless America, or Save America, we love America, we're going to join in the Army of America, we put the flag of Islam in the army, we're going to pray in front of the Senate. The hell with that! God intends to kill his enemies and when he kills them, they will know why they are being killed. It is not because they are white. It is because of their wickedness against the righteousness of God. They will not get away with what they have done to you and to me. When they kidnapped our mothers and our fathers and brought them to the shores of this country and reduced them down to beasts of burden, and tortured them, tormenting them, day and night, and forcing them to work against their will. Even going into the deep recesses of their minds and planting the images of themselves as the image of God. They condemn themselves to death and now that day has come, and they will not escape the doom.

Dr. C.E.M.:   Could you deal with the issue of separatism and the separate state?

Dr. A. Muhammad: Separatism is like divorce. When two people who are married can't get along and all measures to reconcile their differences have failed, then the law of God doesn't encourage, but in fact does permit, a divorce to take place. So it is in the relationship between a slavemaster and a slave. If all efforts to reconcile their differences, to arrive at a just resolution, and solution to the problems that exist between them, social problems, economic problems, political problems, spiritual problems, the whole gamut, if all efforts to solve those problems fail, then separation is the answer.

God created us to be his servants. He did not create us to serve white people or any other people.

God created us to enjoy the blessings of freedom, justice, and equality. So if the government and people of America say, we're never going to let you Negros enjoy freedom, justice, and equality. We are always going to deny your God-given human rights, then we say we reserve as one of our rights the option to separate ourselves from you. Giving ourselves freedom, justice, and equality, and we believe that God is with us. He does not desire for us to sit at your feet in poverty, in squalor, in ignorance, waiting on you to have a change of heart or mind. Suppose America changes? Suppose they look at the Constitution and say we realize we have been shortchanging you all for the entire history of the republic? You all don't own any land, and we're going to see to it that you get a just portion of the country. We're going to see to it that you get ownership of some of the industrial capacity, agricultural capacity. We gonna admit that their black parents have a right to educate your own children. We're gonna give you the spiritual freedom to worship as seems fitting and proper to you. We're going to stop murdering your leaders and allow you to choose leadership that can act independently of us and act in the best interest of yourselves. We are going to now permit that to happen. Then there wouldn't be any need for us to separate. Then we can say, under those circumstances we really do enjoy our human rights. Then we don't have any argument with you anymore. We have a just settlement we could be happy with. But how likely is that coming from the wicked hearts of the sons and daughters of the slavemasters?

Dr. C.E.M.: Originally, you had mentioned the misinterpretation of the Yacub Theory. Could you discuss that?

Dr. A. Muhammad: The Honorable Elijah Muhammad said it took about six hours to explain Yacub history properly. It's very complex; certainly in the few minutes we have I can't do it. I can refer you to the second chapter in the *Message to the Blackman*, entitled "The Devil," which would give you a comprehensive understanding of Yacub's history. Let me be brief, because somebody else is waiting for me.

The whole issue has to do with the nature of human beings. There is no difference in the nature of God and the nature of man, because they are interchangeable. All the attributes of God are the attributes of human beings. We talk about God the beneficent; the only way to understand beneficence or see beneficence is a beneficent person who exhibits it to a particular degree. When we find a human being who can exhibit all of those attributes perfectly, then we're looking at a supreme being among man. But he is not something other than a man, he is a man. Now we know that we have not had anyone among us, even the prophets, who have been able to exhibit the divine attributes of God perfectly. We might see a high expression of divine attributes, but we don't see a perfect expression of it. Why is that? What is it that is in us, no matter how much we love truth, no matter how much we love justice, no matter how we worship the divine qualities and characteristics. Somehow or another, despite our best efforts we seem to fall short of the glory that is God.

But Yacub answered that question. He said that alongside of your divine nature is another nature that's in opposition to the first one. The one is of God, and if let run unopposed and allowed to develop it would. You would achieve perfection with God and you would be God. But there's something in you that's a drag, holding you back, causing you to deviate from your firm resolution to do right.

He [Yacub] was a great scientist. He separated that secondary nature out, into a separate biological form that we identify as Caucasian. We say that is the Devil, but that's just a manifestation of the Devil that's in you. But it's separated out so it could act independently of anything that would tend to modulate it. So, that it could be studied and studied for the purpose of being destroyed. So, the Devil was made to be destroyed not just what we identify as Caucasian people who are a result of Yacub's work. Who's just been on this planet for 6,000 years. Those who submit to that wicked nature, they deserve to be destroyed in God's judgement along with all other wicked people. But the whole purpose of that is in the nature of humanity that has prevented us from achieving perfection. And if we can isolate that and destroy that within people, then what is left can be nurtured under the tutelage of God. Until each one of us doesn't just reach some of our potential, but we will max out on our total of potential. When you see a nation and a generation coming up like that, that is the hereafter, that is paradise, that is heaven on earth. The opposition that has prevented us from doing that since the beginning of time. Since the self-creation of God in the beginning, going back trillions of years. We have never had the opportunity to achieve that.

———————

The Mahdi, Master Fard Muhammad, is present having mastered the two natures that are in people. One he mastered to destroy it. The other he masters to nurture it into perfection. That's what the Nation of Islam is. That's where Yacub's history falls into it. It's not trying. It's not to be smart aleck and call white people a bad name. Although some childish people have misrepresented like that. Malcolm was a big one, you look at Khallid today. They are very childish. Calling people names, that's so far beneath the dignity of what the Honorable Elijah Muhammad taught us. That's so childish, immature, but we are an immature people. Even though I point that out I quickly have to come to the defense of Malcolm to the defense of Khallid. We understand these are immature people who just got a hold of something yesterday. They don't really know the full purpose of something and like children they sort of mess it up. But give them time and they will grow and mature, and ultimately become the master of it, and use it in a proper way. That bestows freedom, justice, and equality on all people.

Dr. C.E.M.:   Is there anything else you would like to add?

Dr. A. Muhammad: All that I can add is what I said before. Just to re-
                     iterate, this book when the brother gave it to me
                     was a big disappointment. I was angry when I read
                     it. Because of gross misrepresentations of what
                     we believe. If we really believed what's repre-
                     sented, we would be a big fool. But I think what
                     the Honorable Elijah Muhammad taught us is
                     pretty powerful stuff. Not lightweight stuff. It's
                     about time that scholars and intellectuals get off
                     his high horse of arrogance and say that even
                     though the Honorable Elijah Muhammad didn't
                     go to college like me; even though he could barely
                     read and write according to the education he re-
                     ceived from white people, even if you're skeptical
                     and say I don't believe Master Fard Muhammad
                     is God; but whoever Master Fard Muhammad is,
                     when he picked up that little man and taught him,
                     he taught him something that confounds scholars
                     like you.

                     ———————

                     We've taken his teachings all over the world.
                     They wanted to know about Master Fard Muham-
                     mad in Mecca. What're we afraid of Mecca? Min-
                     ister Farrakhan goes to Mecca. Okay, what is it
                     you want to know about Master Fard Muham-
                     mad? What questions do you have? You say this
                     is not Islam? This is not the teaching of the Holy
                     Quran? What part of it do you want to question me
                     on? They ask their questions and he answered
                     them and they shut their mouths. They had a death
                     decree on Farrakhan. So, we go right up in your
                     capital. Okay, so what you want to kill me over?
                     What do you have to say to me? You've heard
                     people talk about me, but what do you have to say
                     to me! They found out they weren't dealing with
                     some lightweight ignorant people who don't
                     know Islam. A matter of fact before this is over,
                     those so-called scholars of Islam in the East,
                     they're going to sit at our feet. They don't know
                     the first thing about Islam. They have given Islam
                     a bad name in the world through their misrepre-
                     sentation and mishandling of Islam. We are the

originators of Islam. They have had it in their hands for about fourteen centuries and messed it up. It's new to them, but it's not new to us. So, we have to put it in proper order and when we do the whole world will benefit from it.

————————

So, I just hope that something that has been said here today will inspire you to do better work than this. I'm sure you are capable. Don't be lazy. Go do your homework. If the Honorable Elijah Muhammad wrote seven books, you are obligated to study them and pore over them. Ask questions; he wrote hundreds of articles, just created so much of a library for our benefit and study. So you are certainly obligated to go through all of it. Then after you go through all of it, if you have your criticism then fine. That's an honest disagreement; we can live with that. But to give a cursory treatment, to treat us like we're just some niggers in an alley, like we're just ignorant and we need to be reformed by the real Muslims over in Mecca, that's so insulting. We understand and we forgive you. We're going to read the next book that comes out and to see if you do a better job. If you didn't then we will have to talk to you again.

Appendix C

Directory of Masjids in the United States and Abroad, the World Community of Al-Islam in the West, 1979

ALABAMA

Anniston 36202
AMM Center
600 West 15th St.
P.O. Box 81

Birmingham 35207
Birmingham Masjid
3424 26th St. N.

Dothan 36303
AMM Center
616 West Powell St.

Huntsville 35810
AMM Center
4903 Roebuck Rd., N.W.

Mobile 36605
AMM Center
159 Duval St.

Montgomery 36104
AMM Center
937 S. Hull St.

Opelika 36801
AMM Center
1323 Auburn St.

Tuscaloosa 35401
AMM Center
7th St. 22 Ave.

ARIZONA

Phoenix 85001
Masjid Jauharatul Islam
102 West South Mountain Ave.
P.O. Box 1230

Tucson 85712
AMM Center
1830 S. Park Ave.

ARKANSAS

Ft. Smith 72903
AMM Center
1725 Midland Blvd.

Little Rock 72203
AMM Center
1717 Wright Ave.

CALIFORNIA

Altadena/Pasadena 91001
AMM Center
3184 North Olive Ave.

Bakersfield 93304
AMM Center
1001 8th St.

Comptom 90221
AMM Center
1300 East Palmer Ave.

Long Beach 90806
AMM Center
2104 Orange Ave.

Los Angeles 90011
Masjid Felix Bilal
4016 S. Central Ave.

Los Angeles 90043
AMM Center
5450 Crenshaw Blvd.

Mountain View 94941
AMM Center
779 East Evelyn St.

Oakland 94601
Masjid Muhammad
1652 47th Ave.

Riverside 92517
AMM Center
P.O. Box 5708

Sacramento 95817
Oak Park Community Center
3425 Sacramento Blvd.

San Diego 92102
AMM Center
2575 Imperial Ave.

San Francisco 94117
AMM Center
850 Da Visaderro St.

San Jose 95116
AMM Center
1220 East San Antonio

San Luis Obispo 93401
AMM Center
283 Buchon St.

Stockton 95207
AMM Center
8063 N. Eldorado Suite No. 1

COLORADO

Denver 80207
AMM Center
4438 Sherman St.

CONNECTICUT

Bridgeport 06607
AMM Center
P.O. Box 4297
24 Yar Mich Drive

Hartford 06120
Masjid Muhammad
3284 Main St.

New Haven 06511
Masjid Muhammad
64 Carmel St.

South Norwalk 06856
AMM Center
P.O. Box 41

Stamford 06902
AMM Center
109 Tresser Blvd. 3D

DELAWARE

Wilmington 19801
AMM Center
301 West Sixth St.

DISTRICT OF COLUMBIA

Washington 20001
Washington Masjid
1519 Fourth St., N.W.

FLORIDA

Daytona Beach 32014
AMM Center
P.O.Box 6273

Ft. Lauderdale 33311
Masjid Nykhettah Muhammad
278 S.W. 27th Ave.
P.O. Box 9473

Gainesville 32601
AMM Center
302 N.W. 4th Ave.

Jacksonville 32209
AMM Center
2242 Commonwealth Ave.

Miami 33127
Masjid Al Ansar
5245 N.W. 7th Ave.

Pensacola 32501
AMM Center
1513 W. Garden St.

St. Petersburg 33701
AMM Center
922 Ninth St. South

Tallahassee 32304
AMM Center
115 Bragg Drive

Tampa 33675
AMM Center
6013 N. 40th St.

GEORGIA

Albany 31707
AMM Center
511 Lincoln Ave.

Athens 30601
AMM Center
2685 Danielville Road

Atlanta 30316
Atlanta Masjid
735 Fayetteville Rd., S.E.

Augusta 30901
AMM Center
612 Beaufort Ave.

Brunswick 31520
AMM Center
302 Franklin Ave.

Columbus 30501
AMM Center
1261 Spring St.

Griffin 30223
AMM Center
315 N. 3rd St.
P.O. Box 1042

La Grange 30240
AMM Center
208 Hamilton St.

Macon 31204
AMM Center
2031 East Napier Ave.

Milledgeville 31061
AMM Center
151 W. McIntosh

Newman 30263
AMM Center
12-F Highland Apts.

Savannah 31401
AMM Center
117 E. 34th St.

ILLINOIS

Carbondale 62901
AMM Center
321 S. Cedarview

Champaign 61820
AMM Center
P.O. Box 1746

Chicago 60649
Masjid, Hon. Elijah
Muhammad
7351 S. Stony Island Ave.

Chicago 60627
Roseland AMM Center
11356 S. Wentworth

Danville 61832
AMM Center
P.O. Box 244

Decatur 62521
AMM Center
255 E. Orchard

Evanston 60201
AMM Center
1609 Emerson

Lockport 60441
AMM Center
523 Oak Ave.

North Chicago 60064
AMM Center
11226 Sheridan Rd.

Peoria 61604
AMM Center
2312 North Ellis

Rockford 61101
AMM Center
210 Morgan St.

INDIANA

Ft. Wayne 46806
AMM Center
1024 Oxford St.

Gary 46807
Masjid Muhammad
1473 W. 15th Ave.

Indianapolis 46205
Masjid Muhammad
2931 Central Ave.

Michican City 46360
AMM Center
P.O.Box 629

Mt. Vernon 47620
AMM Center
513 W. 4th St.

IOWA

Des Moines 50314
AMM Center
P.O. Box 1432

KANSAS

Kansas City 66014
AMM Center
1902 Quindard

Wichita 67214
AMM Center
1508 New York

KENTUCKY

Lexington 40508
AMM Center
572 Georgetown St.

Louisville 40211
AMM Center
1142 St. 42 Street

LOUISIANA

Baton Rouge 70805
AMM Center
P.O. Box 53205

New Orleans 70113
Masjid of Al-Islam
2626 Magnolia St.

Shreveport 71109
AMM Center
2401 Milam St.

Slidell 70458
AMM Center
Rt. 5 Box 135 E.

MARYLAND

Baltimore 21217
Masjid Baltimore
514 Wilson Ave.

MASSACHUSETTS

Dorchester 20120
Masjid Muhammad
35 Intervale St.

Springfield 01109
Masjid Muhammad
495 Union St.
P.O.Box 398
Highland Station

MICHIGAN

Benton Harbor 49022
AMM Center
241 E. Main St.

Detroit 48206
Masjid Wali Muhammad
11529 Linwood Ave.

Flint 48505
Masjid Muhammad
402 E. Gillespie

Grand Rapids 49507
AMM Center
1229 Madison

Inkster 48141
AMM Center
27311 Phipps

Kalamazoo 49007
AMM Center
1009 North Westnedge

Lansing 48915
AMM Center
235 Lahoma St.

Muskegon Heights 49444
AMM Center
2444 Park St.

Saginaw 48601
Masjid Abeedur-Rahman
114 North 4th St.

MINNESOTA

Minneapolis 55409
Masjid Mujaddad
3759 4th Ave. South

St. Paul 55104
AMM Center
324 N. St. Albans Ave.

MISSISSIPPI

Biloxi 39530
AMM Center
501-1/2 Keller Ave.

Hattiesburg 39401
AMM Center
903 Elizabeth Ave.

Jackson 39204
AMM Center
1208 Jones Ave.

Jackson 39204
AMM Center
1208 Jones Ave.

MISSOURI

Kansas City 64130
Masjid Omar
2715 Swope Pkwy.

St. Louis 63106
Masjid Muhammad
1434 N. Grand Blvd.

NEBRASKA

Lincoln 28503
AMM Center
P.O. Box 82054

Omaha 68111
AMM Center
2914 Parker

NEVADA

Las Vegas 89106
AMM Center
820 W. Lakemead

NEW JERSEY

Asbury Park 07712
Masjid As-siddig
733 Cookman Ave.

Atlantic City 08404
Masjid Muhammad
107 N. Centre
P.O. Box 782

Camden 08103
AMM Center
910 Broadway

East Orange 07018
Islamic Center of
East Orange
239 Central Ave.

Elizabeth 07207
Masjid Muhammad
P.O. Box 59

Jersey City 07305
Masjid Muhammad
297 Martin Luther King Dr.
P.O. Box 26

New Brunswick 08903
AMM New Brunswick
P.O.Box 1688

Newark 07103
Masjid Muhammad
257 S. Orange Ave.

Plainfield 07060
Masjid Muhammad
321 Grant Ave.

Somerset 08873
AMM Center
382-C Hamilton St.

Trenton 08607
AMM Center
1001 E. State St.
P.O.Box 2454

NEW YORK

Albany 12210
AMM Center
P.O.Box 907

Bronx 10452
Masjid Muhammad
936 Woody Crest Ave.

Brooklyn 14203
Masjid Muhammad
615 Michigan St.

Jamaica 11468
AMM Center
Queens/Corona/Jamaica
10501 Northern Blvd.

Middletown 10940
AMM Center
P.O. Box 364

New York 10026
Masjid Malcolm Shabazz
102 W. 116th St.

Poughkeepsie 12607
AMM Center/Masjid
Muhammad
P.O.Box 21

Rochester 14605
Masjid Muhammad
370 North St.

NORTH CAROLINA

Asheville 28807
AMM Center
P.O. Box 7371

Charlotte 28216
Masjid Charlotte
1230 Beattiesford Rd.

Durham 27701
Masjid Durham
1009 W. Chapell Hills St.

Fayetteville 28301
AMM Center
430 Gillespie St.

Greensboro 27401
AMM Center
1930 E. Market St.
P.O. Box 6201

Raleigh 27610
AMM Center
420 Hill St.

Statesville 28677
AMM Center
525 S. Center St.

Wilmington 28401
AMM Center
719-1/2 Castle St.

Winston-Salem 27105
AMM Center
1500 English St.

OHIO

Akron 44320
AMM Center
875 Garth Ave.

Cincinnati 45207
Masjid Muhammad
Clarion and Trimble Ave.

Cleveland 44104
Masjid Willie Muhammad
2813 E. 92nd St.

Columbus 43205
AMM Center
1677 Oak St.
P.O. Box 7048

Dayton 45401
AMM Center
P.O. Box 244

Lima 45805
AMM Center
435 S. Collette St.

Marion 43302
AMM Center
431 Evan Rd.

Sandusky 44870
AMM Center
P.O. Box 2381

OKLAHOMA

Lawton 73520
AMM Center
P.O.Box 2134

Oklahoma City 73111
AMM Center
1322 N.E. 23rd St.

Tulsa 74106
Al Baaqi Ar-Rashid Center
538 E. Oklahoma St.

OREGON

Portland 97211
AMM Center
5640 N.E. Union Ave.

PENNSYLVANIA

Chester 19013
AMM Center
19 W. Third St.

Harrisburg 17103
AMM Center
1725 Market St.

Philadelphia 19122
Masjid Philadelphia
1319 W. Susquehanna Ave.

Philadelphia 19150
Masjid Elijah
7511 Stenton Ave.

Pittsburgh 15208
AMM Center
7222 Kelly St.

RHODE ISLAND

Providence 02905
Masjid Muhammad
234 Pavillion Ave.

SOUTH CAROLINA

Anderson 29621
AMM Center
1998 Hugo Ave.

Columbia 29203
Columbia Masjid
5119 Monticello Rd.

Florence 29501
AMM Center
410 N. Coit St.

Moncks Corner 29461
AMM Center
Rt. 3 Box 43-B

Orangeburg 29115
AMM Center
P.O.Box 314

Rock Hill 29730
AMM Center
431 Gettys St.

TENNESSEE

Chattanooga 37404
AMM Center
504 Kilmer St.

Knoxville 37921
AMM Center
709 College St.

Memphis 38109
Memphis Masjid
4412 S. 3rd St.

Nashville 37209
AMM Center
3317 Torbett St.

TEXAS

Austin 78744
AMM Center
P.O. Box 18812

Beaumont 77704
AMM Center
P.O.Box 2008

Dallas 75215
Masjid of Al-Islam
2604 S. Hardwood

El Paso 79904
AMM Center
9000 Marks-Apt. 31

Ft. Worth 76104
Hassan Center
1201 E. Allen Ave.

Houston 77087
Masjid of Al-Islam
6641 Bellfort Ave.

Lubbock 79401
AMM Center
P.O.Box 5842

VIRGINIA

Martinsville 24112
AMM Center
1011 W. Fayette St.

Newport News 23607
AMM Center
1145 Hampton Ave.

Norfolk 24016
AMM Center
1106-08 E. 26th St.

Petersburg 23805
AMM Center
1103 W. Washington St.

Richmond 23223
AMM Center
400 Chimborazo Blvd.
P.O. Box 8064

Roanoke 24016
AMM Center
822 Campbell Ave. S.W.

WASHINGTON

Seattle 98118
P.O.Box 18375
Mt. Baker Community Hall
2811 Mt. Ranier Dr., South

Tacoma 98405
AMM Center
2523 S. Ainsworth

WEST VIRGINIA

Charleston 23525
AMM Center
P.O. Box 1124

WISCONSIN

Milwaukee 53212
Masjid Sultan Muhammad
2507 N. 3rd St.

Racine 53404
Masjid Muhammad
815 Silver St.

Outside the United States

Nassau, Bahamas
Masjid Muhammad Nassau
P.O. Box N3232

Belize City, Belize
Masjid Muhammad Belize
10 Race Course St.

Hamilton, Bermuda 5
Masjid Muhammad—Bermuda
Cedar Ave. P.O.Box 1508

Montreal, Quebec, Canada
Fatima Mosque
2012 St. Dominique

Georgetown, Guyana
Masjid Muhammad Guyana
47 Robb St. Borda
P.O.Box 24 G.P.O.

Bridgetown, Barbados
Masjids Muhammad Barbados
c/o Husbands of Barbados
Spry St.

Downsvien, Ontario N3N2TI
Canada
Masjid Muhammad
P.O. Box 2243 Toronto Station C

Kingston, Jamaica
Masjid Muhammad Jamaica
Central Sorting Office
P.O.Box 8045

St. Mary, Jamaica
Masjid Muhammad
9 Kirk St.
Port Maria

Charlotte Amalie
Masjid Muhammad
St. Thoms, U.S.V.I.
P.O.Box 2548

Republic of Trinidad and Tobago
Masjid Muhammad
Trinidad
44-48 Park Street

Bibliography

Books

Ali, Drew N. *The Holy Koran of the Moorish Holy Temple of Science*. Chicago: Moorish Science Temple, 1914.

Apter, David E., ed. *Ideology and Discontent*. New York: Markham, 1972.

Ash-Garner, Roberta. *Social Change*. Chicago: Rand-McNally, 1977.

Ash-Garner, Roberta. *Social Movements in America*. Chicago: Rand-McNally, 1977.

Barbeau, Arthur E., and Henry Florette. *The Unknown Soldiers*. Philadelphia: Temple University Press, 1974.

Bennett, Lerone. *Pioneers of Protest*. Chicago: Johnson, 1968.

Bishai, Wilson B. *Humanities in the Arab-Islamic World*. New York: Wm. C. Brown, 1973.

Blyden, Edward W. *Pan-negro Patriot*. London: Oxford University Press, 1967.

Bontemps, Arna. *Anyplace but Here*. New York: Hill and Wang, 1966.

Bontemps, Arna, and Jack Conroy. *They Seek a City*. New York: Doubleday, 1945.

Boskin, Joseph. *Urban Racial Violence in the Twentieth Century*. Beverly Hills, Calif.: Glencoe Press, 1969.

Bracey, John H., and August Meier. *Black Nationalism in America*. New York: Bobbs-Merrill, 1970.

Brown, Michael, and Amy Golden. *Collective Behavior*. Pacific Palisades, Calif.: Goodyear, 1973.

Carmichael, Stokely, and Charles V. Hamilton. *Black Power*. New York: Vintage Books, 1967.

Clarke, John H., ed. *Marcus Garvey and the Vision of Africa*. New York: Vintage Books, 1974.

Cleage, Albert B. *Black Christian Nationalism*. New York: William Morrow, 1972.

Cox, Oliver. *Caste, Class, and Race*. New York: Doubleday, 1948.

Cronon, Edmond D. *Black Moses*. Madison: University of Wisconsin Press, 1966.

Cruse, Harold. *The Crisis of the Negro Intellectual*. New York: William Morrow, 1967.

Cushmeer, Bernard. *This Is the One*. Phoenix, Ariz.: Truth Publications, 1970.

Dalfiume, Richard M. *Desegregation of the U.S. Armed Forces*. Columbia: University of Missouri Press, 1969.

David, Fay, and Elaine Crane. *The Black Soldiers*. New York: William Morrow, 1971.

Delaney, Martin. *The Condition, Elevation, Emigration and Destiny of the Colored People of the United States, Politically Considered*. New York: Arno Press, 1968.

Draper, Theodore. *The Rediscovery of Black Nationalism*. New York: Viking Press, 1969.

Drotning, Phillip T. *Black Heroes in Our Nation's History*. New York: Cowles Books, 1969.

Du Bois, W.E.B. *Black Folk: Then and Now*. New York: Octagon Book, 1939.

Du Bois, W.E.B. *Dark Princess*. New York: Harcourt, Brace, 1928.

Du Bois, W.E.B. *Souls of Black Folk,* Greenwich, Conn.: Fawcett, Premier Book, 1961.

Du Bois, W.E.B. *The World and Africa*. New York: Viking Press, 1947.

Essien-Udom, E. U. *Black Nationalism: A Search for an Identity in America*. Chicago: University of Chicago Press, 1962.

Eure, Joseph D., Jerome, Richard M., ed., *Back Where We Belong, Selected Speeches by Minister Louis Farrakhan*. Philadelphia: International Press, 1989, p. 126.

Factor, Robert L. *The Black Response to America*. Reading, Mass.: Addison-Wesley, 1970.

Farrakhan, Louis. *A Torchlight for America*. Chicago: FCN Publishing Co., 1993, p. 35.

Fauset, Arthur F. *Black Gods of the Metropolis*. Philadelphia: University of Pennsylvania Press, 1944.

Fax, Elson C. *Garvey, The Story of a Pioneer Black Nationalist*. New York: Dodd, Mead, 1972.

Feuer, Lewis S., ed. *Marx and Engels*. Garden City, N.Y.: Anchor Books, 1969.

Foner, Jack D. *Blacks and the Military in American History*. New York: Praeger, 1974.

Franklin, John H. *From Slavery to Freedom*. New York: Random House, 1969.

Garvey, Amy J., ed. *Philosophy and Opinions of Marcus Garvey*. New York: Athenaeum Press, 1969.

Gerth, H., and C. Wright Mills, eds. *From Max Weber Essays in Sociology*. New York: Oxford University Press, 1968.

Grant, Joanne, ed. *Black Protest History, Documents and Analysis 1619 to the Present*. Greenwich, Conn.: Fawcett, 1968.

Greene, Robert E. *Black Defenders of America 1775–1973*. Chicago: Johnson, 1974.

Grimshaw, Allen, ed. *Racial Violence in the United States*. Chicago: Aldine, 1969.

Groh, George W. *The Black Migration.* New York: Weybright and Talley, 1972.

Gusfield Joseph H. *Protest, Reform and Revolt.* New York: John Wiley and Sons, 1970.

Haley, Alex. *Roots.* New York: Doubleday, 1976.

Hall, Ray, ed. *Black Separatism and Social Reality.* New York: Pergamon Press, 1977.

Heberle, Rudolph. *Social Movements.* New York: Appleton-Century-Crofts, 1951.

Henri, Florette. *Black Migration Movement North, 1900–1920.* New York: Anchor Press, 1975.

Heywood, Chester D. *Negro Combat Troops in the World War.* New York: Negro Universities Press, 1928.

Killian, Lewis M., and Ralph H. Turner. *Collective Behavior.* Englewood Cliffs, N.J.: Prentice-Hall, 1957.

Krauss, Irving. *Stratification Class and Conflict.* New York: The Free Press, 1976.

Lang, Kurt, and Gladys E. Lang. *Collective Dynamics.* New York: Thomas Y. Crowell, 1961.

Lebon, Gustav. *The Crowd.* New York: Ballantine Books, 1969.

Lincoln, Eric C. *The Black Muslims in America.* Canada: Saunders of Toronto, 1961.

Lynch, Hollis. *Edward Wilmont Blyden.* London: Oxford University Press, 1967.

McCartney, John T. *Black Power Ideologies, An Essay in African American Political Thought.* Philadelphia, Temple University Press, 1992.

Malcolm X, and Alex Haley. *Autobiography of Malcolm X.* New York: Grove Press, Inc., 1964; New York: Ballantine Books, 1973, 1977.

Marx, Karl. *A Contribution to the Critique of Political Economy.* Chicago: Charles Hikerr, 1904.

Marx, Karl. *The Economic and Philosophic Manuscript of 1844.* New York: International, 1972.

Miller, Donald L. *Black Americans in the Armed Forces.* New York: Franklin Watts, 1969.

Mills, C. Wright. *Power, Politics and People.* New York: Ballantine Books, 1963.

Mitchell, Paul, ed. *Race Riots in Black and White.* Englewood Cliffs, N.J.: Prentice-Hall, 1970.

Muhammad, Elijah. *How to Eat to Live.* Chicago: Muhammad Mosque No. 2, 1972.

Muhammad, Elijah. *Message to the Blackman in America.* Chicago: Muhammad Mosque No. 2, 1965.

Muhammad, Elijah. *The Supreme Wisdom: Solution to the So-Called Negro's Problem.* Chicago: University of Islam, 1957.

Myrdal, Gunnar. *An American Dilemma.* New York: Harper and Brothers, 1944.

Oberschall, Anthony. *Social Conflict and Social Movements.* Englewood Cliffs, N.J.: Prentice-Hall, 1973.

Parkin, Frank. *Class Inequality and Political Order.* New York: Praeger Press, 1972.

Perlo, Victor. *Economics of Racism U.S.A.* New York: International, 1975.

Plaft, Anthony. *The Politics of Riot Commission, 1917–1970.* New York: Macmillan, 1971.

Raper, Arthur G. *Preface to Peasantry.* Chapel Hill: University of North Carolina Press, 1936.

Rashad, Adib. *The History of Islam and Black Nationalism in the America's.* Beltsville, Md.: Writers Inc., 1991.

Redkey, Edwin S. *Black Exodus, Black Nationalism and Back to Africa Movements 1890–1910.* New Haven, Conn.: Yale University Press, 1969.

Roberts, Ron E., and Robert Kloss. *Social Movements Between the Balcony and the Barricade.* Saint Louis, Mo.: C. V. Mosby, 1974.

Rudwick, Elliott M. *Race Riot in East St. Louis, 1917.* Carbondale: Southern Illinois University Press, 1964.

Schoenfeld, Seymour J. *The Negro in the Armed Forces.* Washington, D.C.: The Associated Publishers, 1945.

Scott, Emmett J. *Scott's Official History of the American Negro in the World War.* Chicago: L. W. Walters, 1919.

Simpson, George E., and Milton J. Yinger. *Racial and Cultural Minorities.* New York: Harper and Row, 1965.

Smelser, Neil J. *Theory of Collective Behavior.* New York: The Free Press, 1962.

Sternsher, Bernard. *The Negro in Depression and War.* Chicago: Quadrangle Books, 1969.

Sweeney, Allison W. *History of the American Negro in the Great World War.* New York: Johnson Reprint Corporation, 1970.

Terraine, John. *The Great War 1914–1918.* New York: Macmillan, 1965.

Turner, Ralph H. and Lewis M. Killian, *Collective Behavior.* Englewood Cliffs, N.J.: Prentice-Hall, 1972.

Vincent, Theodore G. *Black Power and the Garvey Movement.* Berkeley, Calif.: Ramparts Press, 1972.

Wagstaff, Thomas, ed. *Black Power, the Radical Response to White America.* Beverly Hills, Calif.: The Glencoe Press, 1969.

Wakin, Edward. *Black Fighting Men in U.S. History.* New York: Lothrop, Lee, and Shepard, 1971.

Waskow, Arthur I. *From Race Riot to Sit In, 1919 and the 1960's*. Garden City, N.Y.: Doubleday, 1966.

Weber, Max. *The Theory of Social and Economic Organization*. New York: Oxford University Press, 1977.

Wilson, Christy J. *Introducing Islam*. New York: Friendship Press, 1975.

Woofter, Thomas J. *Negro Migration*. New York: Negro Universities Press, 1969.

Government Documents

Bureau of the Census. *Changing Characteristics of the Negro Population*. Washington, D.C.: Government Printing Office, 1969.

Bureau of the Census. *Negro Population in the United States 1790–1915*. Washington, D.C.: Government Printing Office, 1918.

Bureau of the Census. *Negroes in the United States, 1920–1932*. Washington, D.C.: Government Printing Office, 1935.

Bureau of Education. *Negro Education in the United States*. Washington, D.C.: Government Printing Office, 1917.

Chief of the Statistics Branch of the General Staff. *The War with Germany*. Washington, D.C.: Government Printing Office, 1919.

Committee on Classification of Personnel in the United States Army. *History of the Personnel System*. 2 vols. Washington, D.C.: Government Printing Office, 1919.

Department of Interior. *The Urban Negro Worker in the United States 1925–1936*. Washington, D.C.: Office of the Secretary, 1934.

Department of Labor. *Negro Migration in 1916–1917*. Washington, D.C.: Government Printing Office, 1919.

Federal Bureau of Investigation. *The Black Muslim Movement*. Washington, D.C.: U.S. Department of Justice, 1973.

Federal Bureau of Investigation. *The Nation of Islam*. Washington, D.C.: U.S. Department of Justice, 1960.

Federal Bureau of Investigation. *Nation of Islam, Cult of the Black Muslims*. Washington, D.C.: U.S. Department of Justice, 1965.

Historical Section, Army War College. *Order of Battle of the United States Land Forces in the World War*. Washington, D.C.: Historical Section, Army War College, Government Printing Office, 1931.

Lee, Ulysses. *The Employment of Negro Troops, U.S. Army in the World War II*. Washington, D.C.: Office of the Chief of Military History, United States Army, 1966.

Second Report, Provost Marshal General to the Secretary of War. *On the Operations of the Selective Service System to December 20, 1918*. Washington, D.C.: Government Printing Office, 1919.

Journals

Adelasa, Kala, Sources in African Political Thought Part I. *Presence Africaine,* 70 2nd Quarter 1969.

Aubrey, H.L., Ph.D., ASA, Abdul Alim Muhammad, M.D., Barbara Justice, M.D., "The Efficacy of Multiple Sub-Type Low-Dose Orally Absorbed Alpha-Interferon Therapy in Patients with HIV Infection: A Clinical Retrospective Analysis" (abstract) October 26, 1992.

Beynon, Erdmann D., "The Negro Cult among Negro Migrants in Detroit." *American Journal of Sociology,* 6 (May 1938): 894–907.

Curry, George, "Farrakhan, Jesse, and the Jews," *Emerge,* July/August 1994.

Du Bois, W.E.B., "An Essay toward a History of the Black Man in the Great War." *The Crisis,* 18 (May–October 1919).

Emerge, September 1994.

Farrakhan, Louis, "BBB interview Minister Abdul Farrakhan." *Black Books Bulletin,* 1978.

The First World, "First World Interviews Minister Farrakhan," Spring, 1978.

Hatchett, John F., "The Muslim Influence Among American Negroes." *Journal of Human Relations.* 10 (Summer 1962): 375.

Karenga, Ron M., "Afro-American Nationalism, Beyond Mystification and Misconception." *Black Books Bulletin,* vol. 6. no. 1 (Spring 1979).

Karenga, Ron M. "Strategy for Struggle: Turning Weakness into Strength." *The Black Scholar,* 5 (November 1975): 15–19.

Mamiya, Lawrence, H., "From Black Muslim to Bilalian." *Journal for the Scientific Study of Religion,* June 1982.

Scott, Emmett J., "The Participation of Negroes in World War I." *Journal of Negro Education,* XIII (Summer 1943).

Turner, James, "Blyden, Black Nationalism and Emigration Schemes." *Black Books Bulletin,* vol. 6. no. 1 (Spring 1979).

Phonograph Records

Farrakhan, Louis, "Black Family Day," New York: Nation of Islam Recording, P.O. Box 2231, May 27, 1974.

Muhammad, Elijah, "Muslim Wants and Beliefs." Chicago: Produced by Muhammad's Mosque of Islam No. 2, (no date).

Muhammad, Elijah, "Speaking of Judgement." Chicago: Produced by Muhammad's Mosque of Islam No. 2, (no date).

Muhammad, Elijah, "The Time and What Must Be Done." Chicago: Produced by Muhammad's Mosque of Islam No. 2, (no date).

Newspapers

American Muslim Journal, Tony Brown, Editorial, May 3, 1985, p. 6.

Baltimore Afro-American, July 2, 1994.

Baltimore Sun, April 11, 1994.

Baltimore Sun, June 13, 1994.

Baltimore Sun, August 22, 1994.

Bilalian News, "Year of Progress for W.C.I.W. Under Imam Muhammad's Leadership," Chicago, January 20, 1978, p. 4.

Bilalian News, "Imam Wallace D. Muhammad's Appeal to Minister Farrakhan," Chicago, April 28, 1978.

Bilalian News, October 24, 1976.

Bilalian News, November 21, 1975.

Chicago Sun Times, "Farrakhan Plays for Harmony," August 8, 1991.

Final Call, February 16, 1994.

Final Call, March 16, 1994.

Final Call, April 3, 1994.

Final Call, April 27, 1994.

Final Call, June 8, 1994.

Final Call, Anthony 2X, "Arsenio Hall Standing Up as a Black Man in Hollywood," July 6, 1994.

Final Call, July 20, 1994.

Final Call, Louis Farrakhan, "Are Black Leaders and Organizations Really Ours," September 14, 1994.

Final Call, Minister Louis Farrakhan, "Fulfilling the Vision," September 28, 1994.

Final Call, November 2, 1994.

Final Call, The Honorable Elijah Muhammad, "A Program for Self-Development," September 14, 1994, p. 19.

Los Angeles Sentinel, "N.A.A.C.P., Nation of Islam Unite for Black Survival: Could Impact Nation," Thursday, September 20, 1979.

Los Angeles Sentinel, "Muslims Emerge as Community Force, October 2, 1980.

Los Angeles Sentinel, October 2, 1980.

Los Angeles Times, February 31, 1994.

Los Angeles Times, Charisse Jones, "Gang Youth Get Farrakhan Peace Message," October 9, 1989.

Muhammad Speaks, Special Issue, April 1972.

New York Amsterdam News, "Split Muslims Seeking Peace," vol. 69, no. 2, Saturday, January 14, 1978.

New York Amsterdam News, vol. 69, no. 2, Saturday, January 14, 1978.

New York Amsterdam News, "Malcolm X Killer Talks; Names 4," vol. 69, no. 17, April 29, 1978.

New York Daily News, "Muslims Ask Return of Separatism." October, 1982.

Newsday, "Muslims Reveal Debt," New York: March 12, 1976.

Newsday, "Farrakhan to Get Bush on Arsenio Hall Show," February 8, 1994.

New York Post. February 23, 1965.

New York Post. February 28, 1965.

New York Post, Roy Wilkins, "The Muslims," June 28, 1975.

New York Times, "Black Muslims' Harlem Temple Renamed in Honor of Malcolm X," February 2, 1976.

New York Times, "Transfer of Funds to Muslims Voided," February 18, 1982.

New York Times, "An Heir's Error," February 21, 1982.

The New York Times, Nathaniel Sheppard, Jr., "Nationalist Faction of Black Muslim Movement Gains Strength," March 8, 1982.

New York Times, "Black Muslims Will End Long-time Ban on Whites," June 17, 1975.

New York Times, "Muslims to Sell Holdings: Losses and Taxes Cited," August 8, 1976.

New York Times, "Interracial Fete Symbolizes Changes in Black Muslims," September 1, 1975.

The New York Times, Lena Williams, "Move to Heal Black Muslim Rift Appears to be Underway amid Pressures," November 19, 1986.

New York Village Voice, Nat Hentoff, "How Minister Farrakhan Became a Part of My Life," April 30, 1991.

Pittsburgh Courier, January 18, 1958.

Pittsburgh Courier, March 6, 1965.

Washington Post, January 29, 1994.

Washington Post, Sara Horwitz and Michael Abramowitz, "Muslims in Mayfair Mansions Drug Patrols," April 21, 1988.

Washington Post, "Armed in Faith, Muslims Wage War in Brooklyn," April 26, 1988.

Washington Post, William K. Stevens, "Muslims Keep Lid on Drugs in Capital," April 26, 1988.

Washington Post, Majory Hyer, May 9, 1985.

Washington Post, Nathan McCall, "Vote Calls, D. C. Council into Conflict," December 11, 1989.

The Washington Post, Dorothy Gilliam, "Winds of Change for Muslims." (month unknown) 1985.

Unpublished Material

Hall, Raymond. "Black Separatist Movements." Ph.D. dissertation, Syracuse University, 1972.

Nation of Islam. *The Muhammad Appreciation Day Journal.* Pamphlet. Chicago: Nation of Islam Publication, June 1975.
Nation of Islam. *The Nation of Islam in Action.* Pamphlet. Chicago: Nation of Islam Publication, 1976.

Public Address

Dr. Abdul Alim Muhammad, "The Nation of Islam," Morgan State University, April 13, 1994.
Louis Farrakhan, "The Nation of Islam," Virginia Union University Student Assembly, Richmond, Virginia, February 4, 1976.
Wallace Muhammad, "Public Address." Richmond, Virginia: Temple No. 24, April 1, 1977.

Interviews

Dr. Abdul Alim Muhammad, Abundant Life Clinic, Washington, D.C., September 9, 1994.
Alif Muhammad, member of the Nation of Islam, Washington, D.C., June 6, 1976.
Benjamin 4X Jackson, member of the Nation of Islam, Richmond, Virginia, April 1, 1977.
Bill El, member of Moorish Science Temple, Richmond, Virginia, August 4, 1976.
Charles 4X Jackson, member of the Nation of Islam, Los Angeles, California, April 4, 1971.
Fatima El, member of Moorish Science Temple, Richmond, Virginia, August 4, 1976.
Frank, Bey, member of Moorish Science Temple, Richmond, Virginia, August 10, 1976.
George Bey, minister of Moorish Science Temple No. 6, Richmond, Virginia, August 4, 1976.
Imam Warith Deen Muhammad, Chicago, Illinois, 1979.
James 2X Jones, member of the Nation of Islam, Richmond, Virginia, July 5, 1976.
Karen El, member of Moorish Science Temple, Richmond, Virginia, August 4, 1976.
Kareem Muhammad, member of World Community of Al-Islam in the West, New York City, December 22, 1975.
Muhammad Akbar, Muslim Official World Community of Al-Islam in the West, telephone interview, April 21, 1977.
Sam Bey, member of Moorish Science Temple, Richmond, Virginia, November 12, 1975.

Sharon Shabazz, curator of Master Elijah Muhammad Library, New York City, December 16, 1975.

Wallace Muhammad, chief minister of World Community of Al-Islam in the West, Chicago, Illinois, July 25, 1979.

Television Programs

The Arsenio Hall Television Show, February 25, 1994.

20/20, Barbara Walters, Interviews Minister Louis Farrakhan, 1994.

Phil Donahue, Interviews Minister Khallid Muhammad, 1994.

Ed Gordon, Interviews Minister Louis Farrakhan, Black Entertainment Television (B.E.T.), April 1994.

20 Contemporary Citations

Battle, V.D.W. "The Influence of Al-Islam in America on the Black Community." *The Black Scholar,* 33-41. California: Black Scholar Press, 1988.

Clark, S. *Malcolm X Speaks to Young People.* New York: Pathfinder, 1991.

Cone, James H., *Martin and Malcolm and America, A Dream or a Nightmare,* London: Fount Paperbacks, 1993.

Curtis, R.M. Mukhtar, "Urban Muslims: The Formation of the Dar Ul-Islam Movement," *Muslim Communities in North America,* Haddad, Y.Y. & J. Smith, eds., New York: State University of New York Press, 1994.

Dyson, Michael E., *Reflecting Black African American Cultural Criticism,* Minneapolis: University of Minnesota Press, 1993.

El-Amin, Mustafa, *The Religion of Islam and The Nation of Islam: What is the difference?* Newark, New Jersey: El-Amin Productions, 1991.

Evanier, David and Alan M. Schwartz. "Louis Farrakhan: The Campaign to Manipulate Public Opinion." *ADL Research Report.* New York: Anti-Defamation League of the B'Nai Brith, 1990.

Hadad, Yvonne Y., Ed., *The Muslims of America,* New York: Oxford University Press, 1991.

Halasa, M. *Elijah Muhammad: Religious Leader,* New York: Chelsea House, 1990.

Hauser, Thomas, *Muhammad Ali. His Life and Times,* London: Robson Books, 1991.

Johnson, Steven A., "Political Activity of Muslims in America," *The Muslims of America,* Haddad, Y.Y. Ed. New York: Oxford University Press, 1991.

Lee, Martha F. *The Nation of Islam: An American Millenarian Movement.* The United Kingdom: Melen House, 1988.

Lee, Martha, and Thomas Flanaga. "The Black Muslims and the Fall of America: An Interpretation Based on the Failure of Prophecy." *Journal of Religious Studies* 16 (1990): 140–56.

Lee, Spike. *By Any Means Necessary. The Trials and Tribulations of the Making of Malcolm X.* New York: Hyperion, 1992.

Leigh, David J. "Malcolm X and The Black Muslims Search for Ultimate Reality." *Ultimate Reality and Meaning: Interdisciplinary Studies in the Philosophy of Understanding* 13 [March 1990]: 33–49.

Lincoln, C. Eric, "The Muslim Mission in the Context of American Social History." *African American Religious Studies,* Wilmore G.S., ed., Durham and London: Duke University Press, 1989.

Lincoln, C. Eric and Lawrence H. Mamiya, *The Black Church in the African American Experience,* Duke, NC: Duke University Press, 1990.

Malcolm X [Malik-Shabazz]. *Malcolm X on Afro-American History.* New York: Pathfinder, 1990.

Perry, Bruce. *Malcolm: The Life of a Man Who Changed Black America.* New York: Station Hill Press, 1991.

Waugh, Earle H., Baha Abu-Laban and Regula B. Quere Shi, eds. *The Muslim Community in North America,* Edmonton: The University of Alberta Press, 1993.

Million Man March Citations

The Million Man March, Day of Absence. Mission Statement. Washington, D.C., Chicago, Illinois: Final Call, 1995.

Video Tape

The Million Man March, October 16, 1995. The Honorable Louis Farrakhan Speaks. A Day of Atonement and the Proclamation of Exodus. Washington, D.C., C Span, 1995.

Video

Minister Louis Farrakhan delivers the Historic Address at The Million Man March, Chicago, Ill: Final Call, 1995.

Index

About the Author

Clifton E. Marsh [B.A., M.A., California State University, Long Beach; Ph.D., Syracuse University] is the Interim Dean of Arts and Letters at Morris Brown College, Atlanta, Georgia. He is the author of four books, including *The Emancipation of 1848 and the Labor Revolt of 1878 in the Danish Virgin Islands, From Black Muslims to Muslims: The Transition from Separatism to Islam, 1930–1980 (First Edition),* and *From Black Muslims to Muslims: The Resurrection, Transformation, and Change of the Lost-Found Nation of Islam in America, 1930–1995 (Second Edition). Harford County, Maryland, Homeless and Shelter Survey: Housing and Shelter in a Community in Transition, 1993.* Some of Dr. Marsh's research articles have been published in *Phylon,* the *Western Journal of Black Studies,* and the *Journal of African Civilization.*

Dr. Marsh's research interests include African American social history, domestic violence/sexual assault, homelessness and collective behavior/social movement. Dr. Marsh has received several awards and honors, Minority Faculty Development Fellowship; Outstanding Young Men of America, National Endowment Humanities Fellowship and is included in the Bio-Bibliographical Dictionary of Black Writers of the United States.